UGC NET : REVISED FORMAT

Library and Information Science

UGC NET : REVISED FORMAT

Library and Information Science

Volume III

ANALYTICO/EVALUATIVE QUESTIONS AND ESSAY WRITING

C.K. Sharma
Akhil Kumar Singh
Rakesh Kumar

ATLANTIC
PUBLISHERS & DISTRIBUTORS (P) LTD

Published by

ATLANTIC

PUBLISHERS & DISTRIBUTORS (P) LTD

7/22, Ansari Road, Darya Ganj, New Delhi-110002
Phones : +91-11-40775252, 40775214, 23273880, 23275880
Fax: +91-11-23285873
Web: www.atlanticbooks.com
E-mail: orders@atlanticbooks.com

Printed & bound in India by Atlantic Print Services

Preface

The University Grants Commission has revised its syllabus of National Eligibility Test (NET) for social and humanity disciplines. This book Library & Information Science in 3 volumes is based on the revised format of UGC NET.

Volume I contains the multiple choice questions (MCQs) of the following type:

(a) Multiple choice—tick the correct option.

(b) Matching type.

(c) True/False.

(d) Assertion-Reason type.

There will be 50 multiple choice questions. Each question will be of 2 marks (Total 100 marks).

Volume II covers Sections I and II of Paper III—which will have 4 sections.

Section I requires a candidate to write a critique of a given passage from a known thinker/writer or of a stanza from some poem of an established poet. There will be five questions asked from a given passage requiring an answer based on the contents and inferences of the passage. This Section shall carry 5 × 5 = 25 marks.

Section II requires a candidate to answer 15 questions asked across the syllabus for Paper III (Part A). The questions will be definitional or seeking particular information and are to be answered in about 30 words each. The questions in this Section shall be numbered from 6 to 20, and each question shall carry 5 marks, making a total of 5 × 15 = 75 marks.

Volume III caters to the evaluative and essay type questions asked respectively under Section III and IV of Paper III of UGC-NET revised format. Structured in two sections, the book contains both brief and detailed explanation of terms related to library and information science in an alphabetical order.

In the combined form, all the three Volumes constitute an ideal book on library and information science for the aspirants of NET. It will not only enhance their knowledge of the subject but will also help them revise the known facts in a quick manner. I wish all my readers a great success in National Eligibility Test (NET).

I am very much thankful to Dr. K.R. Gupta, Chairman of Atlantic Publishers and Distributors (P) Ltd., New Delhi who found this book worth publishing.

C.K. SHARMA

Contents

VOLUME I

	Preface	*v*
	Acronyms	*ix*
1.	Print & Non-Print Media	1
2.	Information Technology	3
3.	General Questions	31
4.	Classification	38
	Appendices	203

VOLUME II

Preface .... *v*

Section-I

Critique 1

Section-II

Definitional Questions 29

VOLUME III

Preface .... *v*

Part-I

Analytical/Evaluative Questions 1

Part-II

Essay Writing 231

Part-I

Analytical/Evaluative Questions

A

Accelerated Graphics Port: Accelerated Graphics Port (AGP) is an interface specification that enables 3-D graphics to display quickly on ordinary personal computers. AGP is designed to convey 3-D image (for example, from websites or CD-ROMs) much more quickly and smoothly than is possible today on any computer other than an expensive graphics workstation. It is especially useful in conjunction with games, three-dimensional (3D) video, and sophisticated scientific/engineering graphics programmes.

The interface uses the computer's random access memory (RAM) to refresh the monitor image and to support the texture mapping, z-buffering, and alpha blending required for 3-D image display. AGP offers high-speed data transfer to and from RAM, optimizing the use of memory and minimizing the amount of memory necessary for high-performance graphics. The AGP main memory use is dynamic, meaning that when not being used for accelerated graphics, main memory is restored for use by the operating system or by other applications. AGP runs at several times the bus-speed of conventional Peripheral Component Interconnect (PCI). Because of this, the data transfer rate using AGP is significantly greater than with PCI video cards. AGP employs eight sideband address lines, so that multiple data transfers can take place concurrently.

Access Method: (1) In computing, an access method is a programme or a hardware mechanism that moves data between the computer and an outlying device such as a hard disk (or other form of storage) or a display terminal. The term is sometimes used to refer to the mechanics of placing or locating specific data at a particular place on a storage medium and then writing the data or reading it. It is also used to describe the way that data is located within a larger unit of data such as a data set or file. (2) An access method is also an application programme interface (API) that a programmer uses to create or access data sets or to read from or write to a display terminal or other output device. Examples are the Virtual Sequential Access Method (VSAM) and the Virtual Telecommunication Access Method (VTAM).

Access Provider: An access provider is any organization that arranges for an individual or an organization to have access to the Internet. Access providers are generally divided into two classes: Internet access/service providers (ISPs) and online service providers (OSPs). ISPs can be local businesses that pay for a high-speed connection to one of the companies (such as AT & T, Sprint, or MCI in the US) that are part of the Internet. They can also be national or international companies that have their own networks (such as AT & T's WorldNet or IBM's Global Services). OSPs, sometimes just called "online services", also have their own networks but provide additional information services not available to non-subscribers. America Online is the most successful example of an OSP.

Access Time: Access time is the time from the start of one storage device access to the time when the next access can be started. Access time consists of latency (the overhead of getting to the right place on the device and preparing to access it) and transfer time.

The term is applied to both random access memory (RAM) and to hard disk and CD-ROM access. For RAM access, IBM prefers the term cycle time. However, the use of access time for RAM is common. Access time to RAM is usually measured in nanoseconds. Access time to a hard disk or CD-ROM is usually measured in millisecond.

Adaptation: A book which has been rewritten or remodelled, usually to fit it for some special purpose or for a class of reader different from that for which the author originally wrote, e.g. Eleanor Farjeon's *Tales from Chaucer* (A rewritten version of Chaucer's *Canterbury Tales* for children). An adaptation is normally to be entered in a catalogue under the name of the original author as main entry heading (A.-A.: 17; Cutter: 17), and added entry made under the name of the adapter, where the adaptation has been so freely made as to bear little relation to the original work, or if the adaptation has become a classic in its own right, A.L.A. 2nd ed., 223, allows the main entry to be made under the adapter.

Added Class Entry: An added entry in the classified catalogue necessitated by a book dealing with two or more distinct subjects. The book itself may be filed at only one place on the shelves and normally the classification number for such books is in accordance with:

(a) the subject dealt with most fully, or

(b) that which comprises the largest portion of the book, or

(c) where each is treated equally, the one which occurs first, or

(d) that which is most important to the particular library.

The main entry for such a book is filed at the shelf classification numbers representing those subject.

Added Entry: A secondary catalogue entry, i.e. any other than the main entry. Added entries may be made for editors, translators, titles, series, subjects, etc., and usually display less information than the main entry, sub-title, annotation and all or part of the imprint or collation being omitted. Where unit cards are used, an added entry is a duplicate of the main entry but with the addition of a special heading for editor, translator, etc. to be distinguished from a reference entries.

Ad-hoc Network: An ad-hoc (or "spontaneous") network is a local area network or other small network, especially one with wireless or temporary plug-in connections, in which some of the network devices are part of the network only for the duration of a communications session, or in the case of mobile or portable devices, while in some close proximity to the rest of the network. In Latin, ad hoc literally means "for this", further meaning "for this purpose only", and thus usually temporary. The term has been applied to future office or home networks in which new devices can be quickly added, using, for example, the proposed Bluetooth technology in which devices communicate with the computer and perhaps other devices using wireless transmission.

Alternative Location: Term used in classification for the practice of allowing more than one possible place in a scheme for the location of a class or subject.

It is employed when there is no generally accepted agreement on the correct place of a class or subject, in the arrangement of knowledge. A classifier may then decide on the best location for his purpose. Having done so he must continue to use his chosen alternative for all books on the subject.

Ambiguous Title: A title, the terms of which are so imprecise that various meanings may be ascribed to, or so vague that it may even convey a wrong impression of the book's subject, e.g., File and filling. To be distinguished from a fanciful title, such is often chosen for purely literary work.

In a catalogue it is usual to amplify an ambiguous title, either in brackets immediately following the title, or in a note at the foot of the entry.

Analog-to-digital Conversion: Analog-to-digital conversion is an electronic process in which a continuously variable (analog) signal is changed, without altering its essential content into a multi-level (digital) signal.

The input to an analog-to-digital converter (ADC) consists of a voltage that varies among a theoretically infinite number of values. Examples are sine waves, the waveforms representing human speech, and the signals from a conventional television camera. The output of the ADC, in contrast, has defined levels or states. The number of states is almost always a power of two, that is 2, 4, 8, 16, etc. The simplest digital signals have only two states, and are called binary. All whole numbers can be represented in binary form as strings of ones and zeros.

Analytical Bibliography: A kind of bibliography which determines facts and data concerning a publication by examining the signatures, catchwords, conceits and watermarks and making record in an approved form of the results. Also called critical or historical bibliography. It involves investigation of the physical nature of the book which can be sufficiently exhaustive to enable all the circumstances of the books manufacture and history to be revealed. This bibliography deals with a physical description of the book. In case a book does not give the required facts on its face, then much research will have to be carried out to establish satisfactorily, information about the authorship, edition, date, place of printing and perfaction of copy.

Analytical Entry: The entry in a catalogue for an individual part of a work, or of some article contained in a collection (a volume of essays, serial publication, etc.) including a reference to the publication which contain the article of work entered, e.g. SHARMA, KRIPA *The Rising Sun* (In Verma, K.A., *Lighting Day*. Five new one-act plays 1961).

The kind of entry is most often made for a distinct part of a work written by a person who is not the author of the whole work, but may be made for chapter or article on a subject which is not treated by any single book in the library. The value of the analytical cataloging of periodicals in accordance with this letter instance is thus easily seen, for usually the most recent developments in any field of knowledge are the subject of articles in periodicals before appearing as the subject of a complete book. In special and technical libraries analytical entries may be made for a single significant paragraph of a table, as single statement of a figure.

Andhra Pradesh Public Library Service: Andhra Pradesh introduced library legislation in 1955. It is under separate Minister for Public Libraries who is also a Chairman of

State Library Committee. At the district level Zila Granthalaya Sansthan have been constituted for 23 districts. There are one 1 Central Library and 5 Regional Libraries, 1 Research Library, 1 City Central Library, 21 district Central Libraries, 795 Branch Libraries, 200 Village Libraries, 620 Book Deposit Library Centres and 2,350 Panchayat and added libraries.

Anglo-American Cataloguing Rules, 1967: H.A. Sharp (1961) and Saymour Lubetzky (1956) proposed new code of cataloguing rules. American, British and Canadian committee jointly engaged on the formulation of new rules. Lubetzky provided a preliminary review of AACR in 1964. The separate texts, British and American, had to be produced with difference of some rules for corporate bodies, serials, court rules, treaties and inter-government agreements. Basic rules of entries—chapter 1 falls in three main groups: General rules (1-19); Special rules (rules 20-32), Added entries (rule 37), Chapter 2 falls in two sections: General rules (rules 40-51) and Special rules (rules 52-53); Chapter 3 forms two main section: General rules (rules 60-68), Basic rules (rule 60); Rule for choice and form of name (rule 6), conventional names (rule 63), Chapter 5, Reference rules (rules 120-126); Chapter 6 monographs; (rules 130-156) Chapter 7, Serials (rule 63); Chapter 8, Incunabula (rules 184-185); Chapter 9, Photographic and other reproduction (rules 190-191).

A.A.C.R. was revised in 1978 with special rules of ISBD (maps) (S) (G) and for other non-book material. A.A.C.R.2 (1978) does not have artificial distinction between society and institution.

Anonymous: A work is said to be anonymous in the strict sense, if the author's name does not appear anywhere in the work. In this strict sense the term is used by cataloguers, although it is usual for the layman to regard works as being anonymous if the author has been definitely tracted from any reputable source.

Strictly anonymous works are usually catalogued under their titles, or as also works the authorship of which is indicated by initials, typographical devices or a descriptive or generic work or phrase, e.g., 'by a student of the law'.

Application: (1) In information technology, an application is the use of a technology, system or product. (2) The term application is a shorter form of application programme. An application programme is a programme designed to perform a specific function directly for the user or, in some cases, for another application programme. Examples of applications include word processors, database programmes, Web browsers, development tools, drawing, paint, image editing programmes, and communication programmes. Applications use the services of the computer's operating system and other supporting applications. The formal requests and means of communicating with other programmes that an application programme uses is called the application programme interface (API).

Architecture National Library: In the first half of the 19th century the increase in the number of books and in the number of readers gave rise to new ideas in library planning. The problem of storage began to be a real one, and it became necessary to separate the storage space from the reading room space. At the same time every volume was to be quickly accessible. This is still the main planning problem of large libraries. In Europe upto 1850 it had been a matter of adapting old palatial and monumental buildings to accomodating an ever-increasing number of books and readers.

But when the rotary press came into general use about mid-19th century, such measures as adding galleries to one-hall baroque library buildings were no longer adequate. Libraries needed thence forward specially planned buildings.

The earliest attempt at a major solution of the problem was the building of the British Museum Library in 1854-57, conceived by the librarian Panizzi, and designed by the architects R & S Smirke. It consisted of the well-known circular reading room for 450 readers, surrounded by bookstacks. Daylight from the dome above was more essential than now, in the absence of electric lighting. The dome is largely supported by the surrounding stacks. The stacks were constructed of cast iron, which was the great new material of the period used in great contemporary buildings.

Bibliotheque Nationale, Paris—In 1720 the Royal Library of France had moved into buildings on its present site, known as the Hotel de Nevers; the Galarie Mazarine was not used for the library purpose until the 1820. Visconti, who became architect to the Bibliotheque in 1825, has already proposed the construction of a new building, and in 1854, Henri Labrouste succeeded him and carried out the restoration, adaptation and rebuilding.

The problem of relating bookstack to readers was in this case solved by a four-storey stack adjoining the reading room with an alcove in between to accommodate the librarians who supervise the room and are intermediaries between the books and the readers. These two departments of the Library are placed end to end, which unfortunately created long distances for the staff to 'run' in the 1930. Much was added to the existing building to adapt it to present-day needs. In 1937 the extension to the original building was completed and the Sale Ovale was adapted for use as newspaper and periodicals reading room for 300 readers. It is a reinforced concrete 8 floor storage library, with glass bricks built into the walls to admit light. Another similar block was built in 1953. The Prints Department was built in 1946 and extension made in 1971.

Library of Congress, Washington—The Library of Congress, Washington followed the British Museum plan with a central, but octagonal, reading room and the bookstacks further away. The design suffered from monumentality, and unfortunately later the spacious courtyard round the reading room has to be filled in with bookstacks, thus spoiling the natural lighting. This was a less successful variant of the British Museum plan.

From the foundation of the library in Washington in 1802, it was housed in the Capital, where it remained until the new building was completed in 1897, designed to hold 5 million volumes and in Italian Renaissance style. In its interior decoration, including many printings and sculptures, it is an echo of the monumental Baroque Library, and in plan an echo of the British Museum. But it is of course also a modern storage library, with mechanical book conveyors and pneumatic tubes for conveying book requisitions. The reading room was designed for over 300 readers, while the same number again is accomodated in carrels in the bookstacks and in Study Rooms, and in specialized reading rooms. From 1929-33 a Rare Book Room, a Union Catalogue Room and study room were added, but without basically solving the space problem.

This necessitated the building of the great Annex on an adjoining site on the east of the main building and next to the Folger Shakespeare Library. The fifth floor is entirely reading space. The main building shelves about 5 million volumes, but the Annex, although smaller, shelves about 12 million.

Archives: Archives are those records, irrespective of their physical form, which are generally preserved on account of their enduring value by an organization or an individual responsible for its creation. It forms the integral part of every organization. They preserve the records essential not just for self-knowledge but also for the protection of the rights of the individual and the state.

Mostly archives are government managed organization. In many countries archives are framed under Archival legislation. Archiver are now entrusted to identify in a systematic manner from the great mass of records only those possessing permanent value for official and research purposes and for safeguarding the legal and other rights of the individual citizens.

The Archives are required to watch over the handling of records with the creating agencies when these are still required for the day-to-day transactions by the department to watch over the custody of the records in their semi-current stage in economical intermediate record centres. Generally, Archive institutions follow the thirty-five years date limit on access to documentary sources in the custody of archives. Mostly regional archives are controlled by State Archives under State Government except few controlled by National Archives. There is no centralization of Archives network. National Archives has formulated archival policy of providing training facilities and guidance to all archival agencies.

In India there is a National Archives in Delhi. State Archives are controlled by State Government with three Regional Archives. There are private archives functioning under the guidance of National and State Archives.

ARCNET: ARCNET is a widely-installed local area network (LAN) technology that uses a token-bus scheme for managing line sharing among the workstations and other devices connected on the LAN. The LAN server continuously circulates empty message frames on a bus (a line in which every message goes through every device on the line and a device uses only those with its address). When a device wants to send a message, it inserts a "token" (this can be as simple as setting a token bit to 1) in an empty frame in which it also inserts the message. When the destination device or LAN server reads the message, it resets the token to 0 so that the frame can be reused by any other device. The scheme is very efficient when traffic increases since all devices are afforded the same opportunity to use the shared network.

Authority File: A list of the headings selected for use in a catalogue, compiled as an official work of reference by the cataloguers for use in the cataloguing department. The file registers are approved form of each heading to eliminate further search if the same heading be required again for the cataloguing of later books.

Name of persons, places, corporate bodies, conventional titles of anonymous works, series titles used as headings for series entries, and names of subjects may all be entered in the authority file. Subject headings, however, are more often entered in a separate file.

The file is usually compiled on cards or slips, vertically filed, a slip being made for each heading newly established. The form authorized for use as heading is shown exactly as regards fullness, punctuation, capitalization, italicization, and for personal names, any additional designations, degrees, etc. including in the heading (e.g. editor, translator, compiler etc.) is not shown, since one person may act in different capacities with respect to different books.

Automatic language translation: Automatic language translation is the use of a computer programme to translate input text from one national language to another while maintaining the original document format. Yahoo and some other sites offer what is sometimes called instant translation using such a tool. Since language is heavily dependent on context and connoted as well as denoted meaning, a programme needs to have access to such context as well as the ability to use it. Since providing enough context is difficult, automatic language translation thus far seems to be successful only in limited and well-understood situations and as a first time-saving step toward translation (or "post-editing") by a human being.

B

Bar Code: A set of parallel lines of varied thicknesses and space on products sold in supermarkets. The lines represent alphanumerical characters which can be recognized and interpreted by an optical scanner. The code represented by bars is known as Universal Product Code.

It is specially designed label consisting of closely spaced lines of varying widths which is used to encode a numeric identifier. A typical barcode label measures 1.5 to 2 inches in width and 0.6 to 0.75 inches in height.

On the other hand, State University, New York Upstate Medical Centre adopted this system that counted of identification card, plastic book card, and IBM Transmission Card, employing addressograph class 9500 optical code reader, IBM 1440 computer and IBM collator. The system uses one borrower card with different colours for students, faculty and staff. Four lines of data are recorded on each card. A ten-digit number is empossed on the top of the card in numeric and bar code form, which is machine readable, by optical character reader identifying the borrower by category, school, year of graduation or department.

Most of the barcodes formats employ a 14 to 16 digit number. Barcode labels which may be affixed to documents or other objects are read by specially designed scanners that interpret the number they represent and transmit them to a computer. Barcode scanner is an optical device used to decode the information present on any document or object.

Bibliography: Bibliography is a systematic description and history of books, their authorship, publication, editions (Oxford English Dictionary). It is a list of books of a particular author, printer or country, or those dealing with any particular theme, i.e. the literature of a subject. Bibliography is the study of books as material objects, irrespective of their contents. A bibliography may include a detailed description of the books themselves and in this sense the bibliographer requires a knowledge not only of the history of typography but also of book-binding and paper making. A bibliography may be an author bibliography, descriptive bibliography, textual bibliography, analytical bibliography, critical bibliography and bibliography of bibliographies.

A bibliography covers title pages, including ornaments and borders, imprints, colophons implicits and explicits, binding and casting preliminaries, imprimaturs, advertisements, texts and collation, prefaces, dedications, etc.

Collation paragraph has full standard description, short, medium and full standard descriptions are accepted as the normal types of entry.

Bibliographies further cover maps, illustrations, songs and gramophone records and thematic catalogue.

Bibliographical Control: It means the adequate listing of records of knowledge in all forms, including published as well as unpublished documents. There should be an effective access to information about documents in the subject by providing systematic bibliographies. Bibliographical control deals with the whole range of bibliographies consisting of comprehensive, elective, current and retrospective ones. These different bibliographies should complement each other so that they are able to satisfy different points of views and approaches. The objective should be that a set of bibliographies in a given subject taken together are able to achieve bibliographical control on each major branch of knowledge.

In October 1961 the International Conference on cataloguing principles was held in Paris. This is known as "Paris Principles". The principles apply to choice and form of headings only.

There are various factors which control the knowledge through bibliographies or by listing the knowledge to present before the readers, i.e. Dictionary catalogue, Classified catalogue, Union catalogue, Library catalogue, Book catalogue, Card catalogue, Computer-output microform catalogue, On-line catalogue, Shelf-lists subject catalogue, Mechanical catalogue, (Mark format), Index abstracts, Cumulative indexes.

Bookamatic: An addressograph-multigraph book charging system which uses embossed plastic bookcards and readers cards. These are inserted in an imprinter which records the details on the pre-numbered transaction slip which is produced in triplicate by means of carbons. One slip is inserted in the book pocket and a joined pair is filed in numerical order. When books are returned the slips are removed and later stored into numerical order to reveal missing numbers which represent books still on loan. The library's slip corresponding to these overdues are removed from file and the remainder discarded. One of each retained pair is kept as the continuing loan record and the other copy which was preprinted with appropriate wording, is sent as an overdue remainder.

Bookbinding: It is the art of attaching stout covers by means of tapes or cords to the books for their protection and convenience of handling. This practice originated when the codex form displaced the rolled manuscript. These boards or cover, which may be of wood, millboard, straboard, parchment or similar durable material, are usually made attractive by coverings which in turn may receive ornamentation of various kinds. The coverings of the boards have been traditionally of leather of goat, sheep, calf, pig, or deer skin, and textiles, such as velvet or coarsely woven material like buckram. Ornamentation like metal work, carved ivory, were in use. Gold tooling (Italy), Pointille of Morocco leather, Dentelle (lace borders around a plain centre panel) were also used. In 1830 the craft binding was introduced. In modern times, plastic binding, spiral binding, surface binding are in use.

Borrowers Register: A record of those persons who have been issued membership cards or tickets, entitling them to borrow books from a library. In libraries using a book issue record which identifies readers by a number, the alphabetical and numerical files are needed. If readers numbers are not used in charging, a simple alphabetical file is found to be sufficient.

Borrower register is also used for issuing books. It is also called as Ledger register. In small libraries having a small number of borrowers, the page number is allotted to a group of borrowers or the individual borrower and all transactions of loan (issue and return) of books is made on this register. In fact it is a record of the borrowings. In case of large libraries this register is maintained by faculty in college libraries and authorities in public libraries.

Borrower register is prepared of good quality of ledger paper and are hardbound. It has many columns:

1. Date
2. Author of book
3. Title of book
4. Class number
5. Accession number
6. Signature of the borrowers.

Some libraries also incorporate the following columns:

1. Date
2. Accession number
3. Signature of the borrower.

Bound with Works: A term used by cataloguers to denote works originally published independently but subsequently bound together.

Such volumes may be catalogued in two ways:

1. Where the Volume has a collective title-page, the main entry may be out of this, while for a collection or a composite work, the contents being listed in a contents note, the analytical entries are made for the individual items.

2. Where the Volume has a separate title-page for each work, separate tables of contents and separate pagination, each work is given its own catalogue entry which includes a note stating the other works with which it is bound. These being only one volume, the call number for all such entries is identical.

Braille: Finger-reading for the sightless, it is an obviously expedient idea of embossed printing for blind readers. Most of the early notations used consisted of little more than embossed alphabets and of those only 'moon' (devised by Dr. William Moon (1818-94) of Brighton). Alternatives were Pitman's shorthand, and Dot-system of Louis Brille (1809-52), blind son of a harness maker of Coupvray, near Paris.

The Braille system of 1825 was based on dot-system devised by Charles Barbier. Using four embossed dots Braille devised basic symbols which represented the letters A-Z. Letters K-T were obtained by adding a uniform fifth dot to each of the original term symbols, the addition of a uniform sixth dot completed the alphabet and made provision for accented letters. Since the dots forming the domino 6 have 64 permutation, an adequate number of combinations remained for the signs of punctuation and for abbreviations.

British Council Libraries India: BCLI services were developed over 30 years in India to offer special libraries and information services to those involved in research and professional practice. The libraries support British studies, development studies, and information services. The first Council Library was established in 1950 which eventually developed to 30 libraries in India with a stock of 7 lakh books in 1995 and membership above 1 lakh. There are nine regional libraries in India: Madras (1950), Calcutta (1950), Bombay (1953), Delhi (1956), Bangalore (1960), Patna (1960), Pune (1960), Lucknow (1961), Ranchi (1962), Trivendrum (1964), Bhopal (1965), Ahmedabad (1979) and Hyderabad (1979). Each regional library offers a current awareness or SDI services of some kind. Lending services started in 1984-85. It has contacts with UK libraries through Standing Conference of National and University Libraries

(SCONOL), Council of Polytechnic Libraries and Standing Conference of Cooperative Library and Information Services. It has increased BLAISE-LINK search services. The British Library and the University of Bradform Library have worked in collaboration on a project DOCM-ATCH.

British National Bibliography: This is the official catalogue of British publishing established in 1950. It is issued in parts weekly which are cumulated quarterly and annually. There is also a cumulated index covering the first five annual volumes. The part of the bibliography published weekly is both a subject list arranged by the Dewey Decimal Classification system and an alphabetical author/title list. In the last issue for each month the author/title list contains the entries for the whole month and in addition, an alphabetical subject index.

The lists are compiled from books and pamphlets received under the provisions of the copyright act at the British Museum. The compilation of the bibliography is done by a team of bibliographers working in the British Museum and great effort is made to ensure accuracy. The bibliography has a worldwide circulation among libraries of all kinds and important bookshops. It is tool for cataloguer providing him with a definitive catalogue providing entry framed according to the Anglo-American Code and a Dewey Decimal Classification number. It plays an important part in inter-library cooperation.

The British National Bibliography is quite unsubsidized and is controlled by a body of representatives of the principal organizations in the country concerned with books, publishing and libraries. The controlling body is the Council of the British National Bibliography Ltd., with its headquarters at the British Museum. The Council was set up in 1949 and the first issue of British National Bibliography appeared in January, 1950.

C

Card Catalogue: A catalogue on cards of a uniform size, each card bearing a single entry or reference, filed vertically in special drawers housed in a cabinet. Early form of card catalogue consisted of handwritten slips filed in shallow trays, and as yet known the earliest use of such was made by the Abbe Rosier who in 1775 described the method in his preface to the general index of the publications of the Paris Academy of Science. Unlike catalogues in book form, the card catalogue has the supreme virtue of allowing the withdrawal of out of date entries and the insertion of new one easily, without disturbing its structure or sequence. Thus, it may be kept current at all times. In addition, physical damage is rather slower than any other physical form of catalogue, due to the protection afforded by the surrounding cabinet, and the fact is that normally only the edges of the cards are touched during use.

Catalogue: A list of books, as distinguished from a bibliography, it is confined to the contents of a particular library or collection, arranged in a recognized order. The entries which it contains are formulated in accordance with specified rules, providing bibliographic information and often further elucidations and appraisal.

The term catalogue has been formed from Greek phase 'KATA', meaning 'According to' and 'LOGUS' meaning 'order of reason'. Logos also denotes logical concept which is based on the reasoning.

The purpose of a catalogue is to act as a key to the library's stock. The arrangement and display of the materials comprising the stock of a library are conditioned by the physical form of that stock, which leads to linear filing of the material by only one characteristic, usually author's name, or subject plus aspect or form. The catalogue, therefore, is an instrument designed to enable the enquirer to find a particular book of which some or all the details are known, to convey the entire bookstock or sections of it, or to select the books which will best serve his purpose.

A book may be sought in the catalogue by author, title, subject, series, literary or physical form or by some other factor. The basic kinds of entries are author entry, title entry, series entry, subject entry, form entry and analytical entry. The Dictionary Catalogue is the only type of catalogue which includes all these kinds of entry in one sequence. Other types have different features, and those serving more limited purposes are the Classified, Alphabetico-classed, Alphabetical subject, Author and Name catalogue. Until 19th century catalogues were handwritten or printed in book or guard book form. With the advent of sheaf and card catalogues, the twin virtues of hospitality and flexibility were introduced, each of these forms allowing entries to be inserted into their correct place or withdrawn, with the utmost ease whilst preserving the catalogue structure and sequence and enabling the catalogues to be kept up to date despite changing book stocks. In modern times a computerized catalogue system is being used in big and university libraries including technical libraries.

CD-ROM: It is growing and advanced technology and holds great promise for libraries as an alternative for both online database and printed sources. CD-ROM is an upcoming technology in the library world. CD-ROM has been built on the success of CD. CD Phillips and Soni are the companies which first exhibited CD-ROM players at COMPEX, the computer dealer exposition in Nov. 1984. Later Microsoft proclaimed the importance of CD-ROM produced by Library Corporation that contained MARC (Machine Readable Catalogue) record. CD-ROM stands for Compact Disc-Read Only Memory. Both disc and drive are based on the computer audio consumer product. The disc is 120 mm in diameter, single sides and holds upto 660 megabytes of data. One CD-ROM is equivalent to 10 computer magnetic tapes, hundreds of pages of microfitche or millions of pages of CD-ROM which challenges current practices of publishing and intimating information in a fundamental way. Its highest storage capacity (20,0000 pages of coded tect) is major advantage. CD-ROM being based on CD-Audio discs, are rugged, portable media and they are capable of being transported via postal services. It is good for database in libraries particularly in Library of Congress.

Circulation Statistics: It is necessary to review the development of library services every year. Circulation statistics included the number of borrowers, readers in reference section and other sections. Necessary records are maintained in each department and development charts and tables are prepared for comparison.

Traditional issue methods involve either written records of two groups of facts—the one concerning the book, the other the borrower which may be set down once for all by the library, or copied afresh by the reader each time the book is taken, or they use code forms of these, such as books and reader number. These records may be kept in order of issue, thus saving sorting and filing or re-arranging into an artificial order, by author, classification or accession, so as to facilitate searching for any particular title.

Librarian must know what material are on loan and when they are to be returned back. To keep all information up-to-date, the following statistics is maintained in circulation department.

Daily Statistical Register—Circulation

Sl.No.	Subject	Date 1, 2, 3, 4,....31	Total

Librarian Signature | Section Incharge Signature

Daily Statistical Register—Reader-wise

Sl.No.	Type of Readers	Date 1, 2, 3, 4,....31	Total

Book jackets are designed in many forms:

1. Book jackets which are pasted or fixed with the upper binding cover.
2. Book jackets which are kept loose and work as wrappers and can be removed at any time.
3. Book jackets do not highlight the actual title of the book.

Book jackets are required:

(a) to protect the book

(b) to decorate the book

(c) to highlight the title and author of the book.

Treatment: Book jackets are treated in many ways in a library which are purchased or received.

1. Book jackets are removed from the book.
2. Book jackets are pasted on the book.
3. Book jackets remain with the books.

Circuits-Switched Network: When a very large number of devices wish to communicate with each other, circuit switched networks are more appropriate than LANs. In this type of network, each device is connected to a switching centre, which handles all message routing.

Classification Schemes: It is a systematic arrangement, be it of ideas, scientific specimens, books or documents. It is vital if one is to obtain the best use of one's collection. Classification is an act of classifying or arranging in classes according to common characteristics or affinities. Books are written expression of man's ideas and these ideas are complicated. Several subjects may be discussed in one book, or one subject may be discussed in one book. One subject may be discussed from several aspects. However, both factors may appear together.

Classification schemes which attempt to list all parts of knowledge so that a librarian may pigeon-hole his book neatly are called enumerative. Sub-classes are formed from a more general class deductively. To divide a class of books into smaller groups a characteristic is chosen which should be used consistently at any one step in the division. A characteristic is a quality which is common to all divisions but appears with a difference to each, e.g. history may be divided by time and within each division the time will be different.

In other terms, each subject may be divided into a series of more specific subjects in chain. It is also necessary in libraries to arrange the similar subjects such so that it may be considered side by side in array, e.g. physics, chemistry and mathematics belong to the same class science; arithmetic, algebra and geometry are co-equal divisions of the class mathematics.

Classification schemes must allow new subjects to be inserted at the suitable point without dislocation of the rest of the scheme. The most famous schemes are:

Decimal Classification of Melvil Dewey

Expansive Classification of C.A. Cutter

Subject Classification of J.D. Brown

Bibliographic Classification of H.E. Bliss

Colon Classification of S.R. Ranganathan

Universal Decimal Classification

Library of Congress Classification

Rider International Classification

Book classification schemes require certain parts and features to make them workable, viz: (a) schedules, (b) notation, (c) index, (d) class or classes for general works, (e) class or classes for books in which the presentation is more important than the subject matter, (f) facilities for making special collection of books, and (g) auxiliary schedules and tables, used within the notation for indicating aspects that occur constantly in several different subject.

Classified Catalogue: A catalogue of subject entries arranged in systematic order according to a scheme of classification. Unlike other subject catalogues the entry headings are not verbal statements of subject but consist of notation symbols which represent subjects forms and aspects, and also convey the order of the schedules of the classification scheme adopted. Therefore, a classification scheme which groups related subjects and aspects together and also displays a logical hierarchy of subjects will achieve these results when its notation is used for the arrangement of classified catalogue. Consequently, the chief value of this catalogue lies precisely in its systematic arrangement, enabling the enquirer methodically to survey the library's resources within a subject class with ease, and aiding the single subject enquirer by filing the entries for works on allied and related subjects in proximity.

In classified catalogue indexes are usually provided to act as keys to the arrangement and allow approach through the factors of subject name, series, author, editor, and other name. These indexes are arranged in alphabetical order and refer the reader by means of the classification number to the relevant point in the catalogue sequence (ENCY LIBNSHP).

Communication: It stands for a process of imparting ideas and making oneself understood by others. Communication is the sum of all the things one person does when he wants to create understanding in the minds of another. It is a bridge of meaning. It involves a systematic and continuous process of telling, listening and understanding. Communication can be upward, downward and horizontal communication; formal and informal communication; and oral, written and audio-visual communication.

Man has used various means for communicating his ideas, his benefits, his faith, and his sorrows. He communicates by gestures, facial expressions, grunts and cries which can very effectively communicate emotions. Man also communicates by touch, by visual signs and symbols, by music and dance and above all, by words—spoken and written. The spoken word as the unit of language has been the most laudable achievement of *homo sapiens* in developing complex societies. Only now we have started realizing how deeply relevant communication is to the progress of man. The next important means of communication is the invention of writing. There was no longer any barrier to communication among living men or between the past and present. Yet another media is printing by means of which what has written could be reproduced and distributed in quantity. The latest and also a significant media is electronic systems of communication—the telegraph and telephone, radio, television, and satellites.

Hence, communication means to talk, confer, discourse, and consult with others. By communication man share knowledge, information and experience, and, thus, understands, persuades, convert, or control his fellows.

Computer Aided Instructions (CAI Software): It is a powerful tool for instructing students. CAI can be classified as one of the audio-visual materials in education in addition to computer application. It could be used by libraries and information centre in orienting the library users. A CAI (Tutorial) is conducted between computer programme and student and the responses derived from the programme are highly responsive to the questions, answers and directives given by the student. CAI material can be used for drills, skills practice, programmed tutorials, dialogue tutorials, simulation, gaining information, retrieval process, computation and problem solving.

Computer Assisted Instruction (CAI): Computer assisted instruction is one in which computers are used as tools of instruction rather than objects of instruction. CAI is defined as the use of computer to provide course constant instruction. This is known in USA as CBI, i.e. Computer based instruction or computer based education.

It is necessary to establish effective educational programmes. Librarian and teachers must extend the goals of end-user training beyond system. They should develop technique to embrace information literacy. Information literacy has been an important challenge before the libraries. Recently few programmes have been introduced after thorough discussion on national and international platforms. These programmes were to review the individuals' ability to recognize the need of information and its motivation to satisfy the needs, and develop a strategy to find the needed information and organize the use of information in effective way.

Instructions are given by the librarian upto the level of his ability and capacity. But it is seen more on higher education level. In schools this service is neglected which has affected the professional image. More emphasis is needed at school level. Instruction is a vast concept and a difficult task. Since there is no systematic effort at standardizing the instruction practice, there are many ways, even at local stage, in which libraries are performing through:

1. Classroom instructions/guidance
2. Off-hand instructions
3. Under-planned and structural programme
4. By library orientation
5. Lectures
6. Printed handouts
7. Audio-visual programmes
8. Training programmes
9. Computer assisted instructions.

CAI is a modern method. This method is applied to variety of services and facilities, i.e. catalogue mechanism, indexing, thesaurus, online access, database, information service, special materials and information retrieval techniques. In addition to all these factors, the most vital aspect that require special attention is information seeking behaviour. It may be in two ways:

1. Library instructions are given for a group of uniform set of people, equally good in comprehension, retrieval and reciprocation. It need not to give weightage to behaviour and information seeking.
2. Library instructions to human being viewing their specific needs as complex. World has made even information seeking a complex subject of study and research. Users are thus of different levels.

Library instructions should be exhaustive and pinpointed which require effective and related training of librarians specially at school level. Library instructor is supposed to remove barrier between themselves and the users through language comprehension and other medias to satisfy the user. Professionals should learn new methodologies and learn more to provide more effective instructions.

Computer Based SDI Services: INSDOC and I.I.T. Bombay has been offering computerized SDI services since Jan. 1976. The IBM 370/155 computer system is being used as UNESCO that provided initial support as a Pilot project, with the CA CCNDEN STATES database. The services has been extended with the INSPEC-A&B database. These programmes are operated in the format phases—conversion of data into the MARCII, compilation of profiles, search, fonting and printing. The computerized data system has record of current information of books, journals, reports, patents and conference proceedings from Chemical Abstract CONDEN STATES tapes. The weekly SDI bulletin is served to scientists. Department of science and technology (DST) provides SDI services under the name ALERT services. DESIDOC provides computer based SDI.

Computer Maintenance Corporation (CMC, INDIA): It was established in 1975 and provides every service that a computer user might require in hardware, software, application and development. CMC has developed a general purpose add-on semi-conductor memory for integrating with the existing systems. It has installed DEC 10 system at I.I.T. Kanpur, Bangalore, DEC 20 at Regional computer centre, Chandigarh, Roorkee University, and CH_HB 64 consultancy services to many organizations.

Computer Network in Indian Libraries: Resources sharing using the modern technology of computers and communication has given rise to library network. The document that used to be delivered by mail, and inter-library loan are being transferred through 'Electronic Mail'. A network usually consists of formal institutional arrangements, whereby material, information and services are provided by variety of libraries. Library can provide many network facilities like monitoring or vital social economic projects on line, retrieval and update of information, optimum utilization of costly computer resources, sharing latest software tools, dissemination of information, exchange of messages and emergency communication system. There are four characteristics of retrieval network—data, retrieval, access and users. Computer network has five national network—INFLIBNET, NICNET, INDONET, ERNET, and INFNET; three regional network—CALIBNET, DELNET, MALIBNET and two local network—LIBSYS, (Dialog database) and LIBRATOR.

Cooperative Cataloguing: The production of catalogue entries or printed book catalogues through the joint action of several independent libraries so that each library, and usually other non-cooperating libraries as well, may share the benefits of such cataloguing. It has as its twin objects the avoidance of duplication of effort in the co-operating libraries by sharing of work and coverage of wide field of publications of such cataloguing. Cooperative cataloguing may operate on local level as between two or more adjacent library systems at regional level, as in the compilation of regional union catalogues; or at national level where national cooperative cataloguing is often combined with national centralized cataloguing so that the widest possible coverage of publications is represented by catalogue entries available to any library.

Coordinate Indexing: Coordinate indexing, a system invented by Dr. Mortimer Taube and his associates in Documentation incorporated, is based on the conception of the uniterm. The theory is that each book or periodical title, each periodical article, etc., can be reduced for indexing purposes to a number of basic ideas capable of being represented mostly by single terms. In the uniterm system each book, document, or other item is numbered as it is received and, if a record is kept of the number registered each day or week, it is possible to gain an approximate idea of such receipts each day or week. It is also possible to gain an approximate idea of the date of any currently published item from its serial number. The title, salient contents, etc., of the document to be indexed are then analysed into fundamental terms usually of one word each. These constitute the uniterms and a separate card entry is made for each uniterm. Each card allows for sufficient space in the vertically ruled ten columns representing the numbers 0 to 9. The serial numbers of relevant documents are entered in the column of appropriate uniterm cards according to the last digit—the purpose of the columns being merely to break up the numbers on the cards into roughly ten equal groups, which not only makes the utmost use of available space but also helps to accelerate the finding of document.

Thus, a title called *Uniformity in Groups* could be indexed under the uniterms mechanisms, pressures, uniformity and groups. Serial numbers common to two or more cards indicate documents relevant to the subject and scrutiny of the document themselves will finally identify the one required. Thus, if four salient terms are remembered correctly, it is probable that the exact document will be discovered immediately, no matter in what order those terms are recalled.

D

Database Design: The database concept is an advancement over the nation of an integrated set of files. The design of database will provide table of description of interrelationship (structure) separate from the data (content), mechanisms for accessing the data elements and sets directly and indirectly via indexes, pointers, conversions, or computation, a capability for movement of individual data items or group from the associations in which they are stored to the associations, in which it is processed and send back to the storages, protection of integrity and security of data items or groups of data items, management control of usage, content structure and optimization data that represent the activity of the enterprise.

A necessary criterion in the creation of a database is that creators must agree on a common set of definitions for all information in the database, which is not always practicable because of problems of synonymous, alternative definitions and two different names used to describe different pieces of data with definitions. Hence, database designer should develop the complete dictionary of definitions. Data structure has a bearing in the determination of processing the data and the access procedures. There are two different approaches to accessing the data. These are sequential access organization and direct access. In sequential organization, records are located in sequence. Direct access permits the location of individual record without searching, but is less efficient for maintaining a file with high activity. The store media must be selected on the speed with which access to data is to be provided.

DESIDOC (Defence Scientific Information and Documentation Centre): Defence service organization formed in 1948 was confirmed to the indexing of current literature and building of Defence Science Library. In 1958 Scientific Information Bureau was set up, which later became Defence Scientific Information Documentation Centre. It was put under Defence Science Laboratory, now called Defence Science Centre. In July 1970 DESIDOC was declared independent unit under the Defence R & D Organisation. Its objectives are to function as scientific information and documentation centre, to collect, collate and disseminate scientific and technical information, to act as depository for all technical and research reports connected to Defence Science, to maintain close liasion with INSDOC and to transfer literature and reports from foreign languages. DESIDOC has been organized in a number of divisions like Library, Documentation, Publication, Computer-based information network, translation, training, union catalogue project; and also supporting services of drawing and design, reprography, printing etc. DESIDOC is publishing *DESIDOC List of Current Scientific Literature* (bi-monthly), SDI Bulletin (Ad hoc), and *Patents Information Alert* (bi-monthly), *Defence Reports Abstracts*, *Defence Science Journal* (Quarterly), *R & D Digest* (bi-monthly), *R & D Bulletin* (quarterly), *Popular Science and Technology* (half yearly), and *DESIDOC Bulletin* (monthly). DESIDOC has subscribed NTIS, INSPEC, CAS, COMPENDEX to achieve wider coverage of the information sources.

Direct Positive Papers: In documentary reproduction, sensitized silver halide papers on exposure to light and developing become white—the exact opposite being the case with ordinary silver halide papers. A positive copy of a line original may thus be made by either reflex or transmission copying, the print laying the same tones as the original document. Its translucency enables it to be used as a master for making diazo copies. It can also be used to obtain at one exposure a positive 'right-reading' copy of a double-sided or opaque original by reflex copying. To obtain a satisfactory result the original, in this case, must be a document with sharp contrast between the printing and the background. 'Inverpos', 'Directpos', and 'Auto-positive' are three direct positive papers made by different manufacturers.

Document Categories: Documents can be divided on the basis of their physical forms, nature of presentation, publication characteristics, purpose, information content, level of treatment, etc. Generally documents are divided into two categories—Primary and Secondary publications. Ranganathan has categorized documents in four categories: (1) Conventional: Books, publication, map, atlas etc., (2) Neo-conventional: Standard, specification, patent, data, (3) Non-conventional: Microcopy, audio, visual, audio-visual, (4) Meta Document: Direct record unmediated by human mind. C.W. Houson has divided documents into two categories: (1) Primary—books, journals, reports, patents, trade literature, theses; (2) Secondary—indexing and abstracting series, reviews of progress reference books (encyclopedia, dictionaries, handbooks, tables, formularies, treaties, monographs, textbooks, etc. (3) Tertiary—yearbook and directories, bibliographies, guide to the literature, list of researches in progress guide to libraries and source of information guide to organizations etc.

Documentation Activities: It would be worthwhile to analyse and see what exactly are done for the analysis of literature, what tools are created as a result of such analysis so that easy access is available when required and also the different phases of literature searching. Activities are Active Documentation—abstracting services, indexing services, subject bibliographies, reviews, state-of-the-art publications, translations, current awareness services, SDI services, and union catalogue; Passive Documentation—literature service and preparation for reading lists, location of documents, document procurement, location of translations, preparation of copies of documents, and reprographic services.

Documentation Research and Training Centre: DRTC was established in January, 1962, in Bangalore as unit of the Indian Statistical Institute. It started functioning in

April, 1962. It was established in the perspective of the recommendation of the International Congress of Libraries and Documentation Centres held in Brussels in 1955. Dr. S.R. Ranganathan was appointed as first Chairman of DRTC project committee. In 1949 Dr. S.S. Bhatnagar of CSIR took interest in the proposal. He authorized Dr. K.S. Krishan, Director of National Physical Laboratory and Dr. S.R. Ranganathan to negotiate with UNESCO for aid to establish DRTC. The result was DRTC came into existence in September, 1951, as a unit of Indian Statistical Institute. The vast amount of information service activities in the ISI libraries would provide a great opportunity for developing and testing tools and techniques of information science including the considerable research in scientific foundation of services and he introduced the term 'Libramentry' which later became 'Bibliometric' to denote such type of studies. Regular full-time course started in city university (UK), Georgia Institute of Technology (USA) in 1964 and in DRTC in 1962. DRTC started the courses 'Documentation and Information Science'.

DRTC has been established to contribute to develop information science, to help development of information centres, to disseminate result of research, information analysis to develop manpower with appropriate professional skill and to ensure the development of the man-power. DRTC organized many programmes, viz. Research programme, Advisory Service programme, Extention programme, Publication programme, Training programme, Employment Information programmes, Continuous Education programme, and Faculty Development programme.

Documentation Services: It is a process of reproducing any available material and making it available to readers. It includes documentation list, reprographic services, translation services, Union catalogue and reference service.

Due to large production of books and a large number of authors as well as large number of Academic Research Institutions, team research and lastly the development of libraries have caused the introduction of documentation service. Documentation has its origin in itself. Dr. Ranganathan used document as recorded thoughts, embodied thoughts, expressed thoughts and formed as Conventional documents, Micro-documents, New-conventional documents and Meta-documents.

Documentation service is a process of reproducing any available material and making it available to readers. Documentation service includes the document lists, reprographical service which means reproduction of reading material on demand in the form of micro-film, micro-card, microfitche and microprints, translation services in various languages, adhoc bibliographies, Union catalogue service, and reference service.

Documentation Work: It is the technique of collecting, cataloguing, classifying and abstracting of both published and unpublished material. It includes acquisition, selection, indexing, classifying, arranging and compilation of list.

"Documentation work is a technique of micro-bibliography". Ranganathan referred it as the old-bibliography building with emphasis on micro-literature. Documentation work is a technique of collecting, cataloguing, classifying and abstracting of both published or unpublished material. It includes: (1) acquisition of periodicals and other forms of micro-thoughts like serials, monographs, translations, patents, standards, specifications, reports and current research dissertations, (2) selecting and working of items of documentation lists, (3) indexing of select items, (4) classification, (5) arrangement, and (6) compiling the list with suitable subject headings, author, title etc. It may also include annotations.

Ranganathan has categorised documentation work as: (1) scanning the contents of current periodicals, (2) classifying each article and cataloguing with all the necessary cross references or subject analytical and alphabetical indexes, (3) listing the entries of all nascent micro-documents with feature headings, (4) feeding every researcher pinpointedly, exhaustively and timely, and (5) providing information to each research worker about new micro-thoughts relevant to him.

E

Entry: A single record of a book in a catalogue, bibliography, etc., to be distinguished from a reference. *Specific Entry*: A record having as its primary objective to specify a document along with its address. *Reference Entry:* A record having as its primary objective to draw attention from one item of information to another, or from one form of an item of information into its another form.

According to *CCC*, entry is an ultimate unit-record in a catalogue or a documentation list. According to *AACR*, entry is a resisting of a book and record of library holdings. In other words, entry is a recorded elimination of the unit record. It is to enter a thing or information of a documents in a catalogue and arrange in a systematic way. Entries are source of representing documents in a particular sequence and in a particular form. Tauber says, "Entries may bear the description of the volumes entered in a library." Entries are of many types like entries of classified catalogue (classified part and dictionary part) and entries of dictionary catalogue.

F

Facet: A particular aspect of a subject or train of characteristics. E.g., in literature there may be four facets: language, form, author, and work. The term is used chiefly by Ranganathan in the colon classification and explained in detail by B.I. Palmer in his book *The Fundamentals of Library Science*. Ranganathan defined it as the totality of the sub-classes of a basic class derived by the use of single train of characteristics. So, factors are division of a main class through which all the entries of a class are first grouped under each possible category and then individualized. The facet of class are determined with the help of a certain train of characteristics which are applied to the subject for its division. There are many trains of characteristics each of which divides a subject. A certain number of trains of characteristics will yield an equal number of facets of a class.

It is a concept of 20th century for knowledge classification. It is universally accepted. The credit goes to Ranganathan. All modern researches in documentation, coding, and classification have been influenced by the concept of the facet analysis. Metcalf is not clear in his thoughts as he says, "Facet Analysis seems to mean either what has been called subject analysis of particular documents as a step to their synthetic representation by so-called class or code numbers, or it means the analysis of subject field to discover a basis for its classification, whether enumerative or analytico-synthetic."

Wildback considered the facets as a synonym of "point of view" according to which subject is divided.

Facsimile: Facsimile or fax was developed at the turn of the century to transmit images such as newspapers and photographs by telephone line. A fax machine contains a photoelectric cell which scans the image and converts the blacks, grays and whites into electric signals and modulates the telephone carrier wave.

Mackeean says, 'Facsimile is the only non-surface mail document delivery method which can handle graphics as an integral part of the text, which transmit non-roman alphabets with ease, and which can convey signatures, handwritten drafts and sketches etc. It is an image, it cannot be said to be character-oriented.

Facsimile system is used to deliver message or document to remote locations electronically which is known as telex machine. Communicating word processors alongwith display system and computer terminology with printing facilities it can form an 'electronic mail network' where messages can be obtained on display screen, in the form of paper document, computer output microforms, or machine readable data form or recorded in magnetic storage unit.

There were other facsimile systems introduced like Xerox Magnavox telecopier (1969) used in State Library of Columbia, Xerox telecopier and Fax telecopier produced by Xerox Corporation in April 1966, LDX (Long Distance Xerox) system provided 135 lines per inch and electrostatic printing on paper, INTREX conducted by MIT called as 'Information Transfer Experiment'. It consists of three parts: (1) a flying spot scanner, (2) a receiver, and (3) a video transmission channel. Bell system 'Tiplak A', teletype was installed in 1950 in USA. Telex (UK) needed no attendant.

Facsimile system is also known as electronic mail and message systems. The latest technology is E-mail system extensively used across WAN. There are different types of E-mail options—telex-based E-mail (teleprinter exchange), Teletex-based E-mail (super telex), facsimile based E-mail (fax), and computer-based E-mail. India has made a significant contribution in developing indigenous software at par with international standards. There are Doot, a computer software package developed by NCST, and X-400 communication software provided by ERNET group of the Dept. of Electronics.

Farmington Plan: A voluntary agreement under which some sixty research libraries in the United States, as a means of increasing nation's total resources, have accepted special responsibility for collecting. In practice, the plan has not attempted to cover the publications of other countries, and has confined itself to current books and pamphlets, excluding serial and other such category of material as juvenile literature, textbooks and translations. Ideally, it would make sure that at least one copy of each new foreign publications, and that might reasonably be expected to interest a research worker in the United States, would be acquired by American library, promptly listed in the National Union Catalogue and made available to scholars through inter-library loan or photographic reproduction. The plan was first discussed in 1942 and the Carnegie Corporation of New York provided grant in 1958 to the Council of Library Resources. The following countries were covered—Australia (1951), Belgium (1949), Luxemburg (1954), Mexico (1949), The Netherlands (1949), Portugal (1951), Spain (1951), Sweden (1948), Switzerland (1948) and South Africa (1954). Each of these countries obtain a copy of each new publication and fell under the plan to send it to the library and has accepted the responsibility for the subject it treats. Total receipt of the books from the countries amounted to 3000 to 400,000 volumes per year.

A distinctly different procedure have been followed for countries having languages that few American Libraries are prepared to handle and for such objective single library has taken the responsibility. Other procedures for acquisition and distribution have been framed.

FID: It is known as International Federation of Documentation/ Federation International-de Documentation. It is situated in Hague. It was founded by Paul Outlet and Henri La Fountain in Brussels in 1895. In 1924 statutes were revised and in 1938 named as FID under the sponsorship of UNESCO with its General Secretary F. Donkar Knyvis. A conference at Brussells was organized in 1955 to formulate the FID. It has 21 members states (16 Europeans, 3 Asians, 1 African and 1 American). Membership increased up to 85 in 1989. It is managed by an Active Council, Executive Committee and nine Study Committees. Membership is for individuals, document organizations, research councils and one national member from one country. The important publications are International *Forum on Information and Documentation* (quarterly), *R & D Projects in Documentation and Librarianship* (bi-monthly), and *FID News Bulletin* (monthly).

Fines: Although it is customary to include in Public Library Regulations, the penalty of a 'fine' for non-observance of the regulation relating to the return of books within a specified period, there is no statutory authority for such a practice. Regulations made under the Public Libraries Acts cannot be enforced by judicial process. So-called 'fine' have been recovered from time to time by action in the court but such actions usually go by defaults. If, however, a defaulting borrower did challenge the library authority to establish its power to impose such a penalty, the authority could not do so and the action would fail; that part of the action seeking to recover the book itself could normally, of course, be successful.

Some countries have overcome the problem by means of a Local Act of Parliament under which power is given to impose fines on failure to return books. Again, a similar provision is now being made in by-laws which can be enforced by legal process.

Floppy Disk: A circular magnetic disk made of flexible plastic sheet coated with magnetic material.

Microcomputer based on microprocessor technology possesses floppy disks serving as standard media for additional secondary storage of data. It records for fewer tracks per inch, but a single surface still holds upto two and a half million characters. Data are recorded on the floppy disk on tracks in the form of concentric circles as in case of hard disks. A standard floppy disk will have 77 such concentric tracks, 8 inch in diameter, divided into 26 sectors. Its storage capacity for diskette begins at about 90,000 bytes or characters for a "single sided" 5¼ inches drive, and expands with "double density" recording of 180,000 bytes on a 5¼ inches drive and 25,000 characters on an 8 inch drive, and total recording of data on both sides of the diskettes will be 360,000 characters for a 5¼ inch diskette and 500,000 characters for an 8 inch diskettes. Some microcomputer system will allow attachment for up to four such double density, dual-sided disks, giving them a total capacity of 2 million characters in storage.

Freely Faceted Classification: A freely faceted classification is a scheme for classification guided by explicitly stated postulates, canons and principles for the three planes of work and involves the analysis of the subject into its facets in the idea plane, their transformation into kernal terms in the verbal planes using current standard technology, and these translation to kernal numbers in the national plane according to a scheme of classification and the synthesis of kernal numbers into a class number. This methodology is based on postulates about the structure and development of the universe of subjects, and theoretically admits the addition of the large number of the characteristics one after another in a large number of facets to be added one after another in the classification of the universe of subjects.

Freely faceted classification involves the following:

(1) Analysing and synthesizing the subject,

(2) Exploration of subject adjusting newly assigned subjects in a tolerably helpful sequence,

(3) Structure of Banyan tree analogy,

(4) Concept of Meccaro analogy, and

(5) Anatomy to classifier.

Full Cataloguing: That kind of cataloguing whose object is to provide, for each work catalogued, sufficient information for the work and its author to be identified positively, to specify its special bibliographic features and to give an indication of its contents by tabulation, by summary or by appraisal.

Personal names are given in full in headings, including designation, degrees and distinctions. The standard description for each work includes a complete transcript of the writers of forewords, etc., imprint and detailed collation. The appropriate entries include additional notes regarding the book's series in physical description, its literary form, authorship, bibliographic history, relationship with these books, its internal arrangement and contents. Annotation, descriptive or critical, is also frequently given.

G

Geographical Filing Method: The arrangement of material or of entries in a list, catalogue, bibliography, etc. according to place. The term includes both alphabetical arrangement by place-names, and filing by a geographic classification scheme, and also sub-arrangement by place within a given filing system. Gesner, Knorad Von (1516-65) invented a scheme that is often considered the first serious book on classification. While a professor at Zurich University, he published the *Bibliotheca Universities* (1545) and a supplement. It is a systematic arrangement of books according to subject employed. Sayers argues that a "Hierarchy of knowledge of an 'ideal kin' result...it is the great medieval attempt to relate the arrangement of books to the educational and scientific consensus of the day."

Gistnic: The general information service terminal—National Informatics Centre—is designed with an objective to make available general information to public about India, important national and international information, infrastructural and recreational and international information, infrastructural and recreational facilities and other static and near static information through a query system. Its range is farmers, tourists-students, researchers, government officials and foreigners. The information requirements of individual can be of varying nature cutting across a host of activities. The information can be derived from a number of large databases being created and maintained upon NICNET using computer system at NECS-1000 at the headquarters and the regional centres, NES-50 systems, equivalent at the state centres and the super PC-AT at the district centres of NIC.

Guard Book Catalogue: A catalogue in book form (bound or loose-leaf), the entries being written or typed or made on slips and pasted on blank pages. The entries are spaced widely to allow for the insertion of additions and when a page becomes full or correct, interfiling is no longer possible; they are cut out and distributed over two pages. This form of catalogue seeks to retain the simplicity and ease of consultation common to book catalogues, securing also a degree of the flexibility common to card and the sheaf catalogues. It is successful where alternations, additions and deletions are relatively infrequent but where these are common the labour and expense of its upkeep often prove uneconomic.

H

Half Title: (1) A brief title usually without author's name or imprint on a full page in front of the title-page, but not the series title. Called also fix the bastard title and false title. (2) A brief title printed on a separate leaf or page, preceding the text or introducing the sections of a work. Although the brief title printed at the beginning of the first page of text is sometimes called the half-title, the term caption title is to be preferred. The half-title introduces a section title. (3) By extension, the page or leaf bearing the half-title; although strictly these should be called half-title page and half-title leaf.

According to *CCC*, it is a title usually given in short on the page of a printed book, and generally found before the page containing the full title of the work contained in the book.

According to *AACR-II*, half-title is a brief title of a publication appearing on a leaf preceding the title page.

It is also a chief source of information for printed monographs. If there is no title page, half-title page may be used as source of information. For example, the book *Classified Catalogue Code* by S.R. Ranganathan.

Heading: The word, words or phrase at the beginning of a catalogue entry, by which the place of that entry in the catalogue is determined. The heading forms the first of the five parts of a standard catalogue entry and is chosen by the cataloguer to indicate some special aspects of the work catalogued (authorship, series, title, subject, literary form, etc.) or to place an entry at a point in the catalogue where an enquirer may reasonably look. Generally, headings will consist of the name of an author, editor, compiler, etc.

(whether individual or corporate), or the name of subject or literary form or the leading word of a title, or the name of a series. Both the choice of headings and the form in which each is to appear, are usually decided by reference to a code of cataloguing rules.

In AACR-II heading is rendered on leading line on main entry from the first indention. A heading may be of a person or corporate body. While in CCC the heading section is the second section. It is rendered on the first line after the leading line and second in sequence after it is put in title section. In CCC the heading is given as call number on heading line.

Hypertext: Text is an assembly of words which is formed out of letters organized according to the set of principles. In Hypertext, instead of continuous flow, information breaks into units or fragments of information which are linked in a non-sequential manner. In Hypertext, information is represented in discrete units known as nodes or cards, and users are allowed to access information without much regard to where the location of information is. Hypertext has no limit for pages and is multifaceted with many points to add or delete the information as per the user needs.

The fundamental functions of digital library are to create an integrated network of digital knowledge that facilitates universal access to compound electronic documents which include text, video, audio, images, graphics and animations. The complexity of information format of the document change the character of retrieval tools. The Hypertext technology has brought a revolutionary change in the organization of knowledge in the digital format. Vennevar Bush, the scientific advisor to the U.S. President, had introduced the concept of Hypertext in 1945 and developed a system. It was known as MEMEX which was based on indexing and used to retrieve information in non-linear manner. Theodor Nelxon developed a more advanced system in 1960 called MANADO which facilitated non-sequential reading and writing but it was a Hypermedia which linked text alongwith graphics, video, audio and aminations etc.

The major components of Hypertext are 'Nodes' or fragments of information and links or cross references, which link the information associatively. A self-learning tool for CDS/ISIS was created by using a software called 'Hyperwood'. This software were in DOS platform. Hypertext documents can be created by writing programmes in an application software such as FoxPro. A teaching aid for colon classification was designed by using FoxPro in DOS environment. In Internet hypertext environment is usually created by using HTML (Hypertext Mark-up Language). A Tamil script Bamini was copied in microsoft word and the hypertext document was created.

Hence the Hypertext is an effective tool for knowledge organization for various purposes. The success of the system depends on the links created. A user might get lost in hyper-space while navigating in a huge database. This can be prevented by creating a number of appropriate links which would guide a user to jump to the desired node from any point of the database. This requires a systematic mapping of the links before creating them.

Human Interface: There are four elements playing important role in information systems. These are seen in Shemon communication system model applied in library and information centres. Shamon model includes:

1. Source
2. Transmitter
3. Channel
4. Receiver
5. Destination.

- The part of a source is taken by authors.
- The transmission is taken by publishers and other document producing organisations.
- The channel connects production function with consumption function, which are means of document distribution on the outside as well as

acquisition, cataloguing, and storage functions carried out inside the library.

- The receiver in library consists of equipment, procedures and people comprising the retrieval capability, since there are messages and documents to get them to destination.
- The destination is the reader or the user.

Every information has a communication purpose. It correlates two concepts:

(1) Complexity of information system

(2) When the information system is applied.

Complexity in all human contributions are summarized under the three headings:

- Beginning—The people who originate information in the beginning.
- Middle—People who use it between performing system.
- End—People who use it at the end.

There are other two groups who contribute to the information transmittal process, but not directly related:

(1) System designers.

(2) Developers.

Information systems are created for people. They consists largely of people. They are also put together by people.

The last group, though large in size, inside, outside and all-round, are considered. The environment of a system consists not only of things and what things to do, but also of people—all the people.

I

Illustration: (1) Matter supplementary to the printed text which is either elucidatory or ornamental. Should be distinguished especially in manuscripts from **Illumination** which uses precious metals and from **Type Flowers** or **Borders**. Illustrations may be produced by many relief, intaglio or planographic processes, in black and white or colour and the method chosen will determine the paper necessary. The type of book also greatly influences the illustrations process. (2) In the narrow sense, it is used in cataloguing pictorial representations occurring within the text, as distinct from photographs, maps, plans, facsimilies, tables and diagrams.

Imprint: Publishers statement: (1) the place of publication of a book, publisher's and/or printer's name, and publication date, ordinarily printed at the foot of the title-page of a modern book. Before the separation of the businesses of printing and publishing, the term applied only to the printer's name and place of business, normally forming part of the colophon. (2) A catalogue entry giving the publication details as follows:

(a) Place of publication
(b) Publisher's name
(c) Publication date.

For example, Delhi: Metropolitan Co., 1973.

Indentation: The individual distances from the left edge of a catalogue card at which the various lines of headings and description begin. On a standard ruled card the first indentation (outer or author) is at the first vertical line from the left, the second indentation (inner, title or paragraph) is at the second vertical line and the third as far to the right of the second as the second is from the first.

The same proportions are generally preserved on unruled cards, i.e. 9, 13 and 17 typewriter spaces.

The purpose of indentation is to differentiate and emphasize the various groups of information.

In CCC the word 'indentation' is not used. Instead, CCC used leading line or horizontal red line and other 9 black ordinary lines and 2 vertical lines red in colour. Rendering is explained by first vertical, second vertical etc.

In AACR-II the distance between the two vertical lines (red) is called indentation, i.e. first indentation, second indentation.

Indentation is important item and necessary to indicate the rendering positions in main entries and other entires.

Indian Agricultural Research Institute Library: It started as part of Imperial Agricultural Research Institute at Pusa (Bihar) in 1905 which was later shifted to New Delhi in 1936 and after independence redesignated as Indian Agricultural Research Institute (IARI). The library has a collection of more than 4 lakh books, 5000 current serial titles from 90 countries in 40 languages and maintains a comprehensive collection of indexing, a monthly *Bibliography of Indian Agriculture* (since 1944) and monthly press clipping service *Development News in Agriculture* (since 1985). It has links with the databases of the International Nuclear Information System (INIS) and International Information System in Agriculture Sciences and Technology (AGRIS).

Indian Association of Special Libraries and Information Centre (IASLIC): It is a national library association. It came into existence at a General Meeting held on 3 September 1955, at the Indian Museum, Calcutta. It deals and discusses various problems of science, technical and other special libraries of India and survey their activities and make recommendations for their development to cope with the needs of the clientele—IASLIC publishers and IASLIC bulletin. IASLIC is affiliated to the International professional organizations like IFLA and FID.

IASLIC's main objects are to encourage and promote the systematic acquisition, organization and dissemination of knowledge, to improve the quality of library and information services and documentation work, to coordinate the activities of special libraries, to improve the technical efficiency of library workers. IASLIC promotes inter-library cooperation and draft inter-library code, and holds conference, seminars, symposia. It has six divisions—documentation, education, documentary reproduction and translation, publication and publicity, library and information services, and library cooperation and coordination.

Indian National Bibliography (INB): Central Reference library produces the Indian National Bibliography. INB seeks to map out in a scientific manner the reading material published in the country on the basis of legal deposit act known as Delivery of Books Act. Union Government appointed a committee to prepare a framework of INB and laid down the principles, coverage, area, script and classification. The bibliography made its first appearance as a pilot issue in 1958. Till 1963 it was published annually and after that changed to monthly periodicity. Since 1950 there has been no major change in the general format but change was effected by pruning author entry to contain only essential information (1979).

As a current Bibliography it became virually non-existent. Hence, Central Reference Library decided to arrange the regular printing. An Alpha photo typesetting equipment (Alphacamp) was imported from United States in December 1983. It has three units: operation, memory and printer. It can produce master copies of a sheet of 100 feet length in a matter of 25 days (monthly issue), INB coverage is 60% of the publication of the country. CRI prepare bibliography in different languages, but it is irregular.

CRL is being modernized and computerization of information retrieval and INB has been started, which will prove a loan to the users of India and abroad.

Indian Standard in Library and Information Science: The library has become formidable information storage and retrieval centre engaged in transfer and dissemination of information. The enormous resources available in libraries are not exploited fully and there are problems in access to information and publication. It requires financial resources. However, Government of India appointed a sectional committee of Indian Standard Institutions under the chairmanship of Dr. S.R. Ranganathan. The committee recommended the standards of 'Author statement' and also 58 standards in the area of bibliographical references, books and periodicals, indexes and abstracts cataloguing, classification, buildings, furniture and fittings, microfilms etc.

INDONET: INDONET is a commercial distribution computer network to provide access to the considerable computing and software resources of the CMC Ltd. and public sector company in India. INDONET has three IBM moviframes at Chennai, Mumbai and Kolkata and small computers at Delhi and Hyderabad. The network used dedicated lines operating at 2400 to 4806 bhs. The Mumbai node of INDONET is connected to VSNL's GPSS enabling computer-to-computer communications via networks abroad.

Issue (edition, etc.): Specifically, a distinct group of copies of an edition, distinguished from the rest by more or less slight but well-defined variations in the printed matter. Different issues are those in which international changes have been made without resetting the type for the whole work. Such issues may be the result of: (1) The distribution of the sheets of a single impression among two or more publishers, those copies issued by each being distinguished by different imprint or title page and possibly different preliminary matter; (2) The issue of the sheets of an existing impression with a new on changed title-page, preface, notes in a different numbers of volumes, etc., or (3) A new impression for which revisions have been incorporated in the original type or plates, e.g. a 'revised' (or corrected) impression (A.L.A. Gloss).

J

Jacket: A loose wrap-round cover to protect the binding, also called dust cover or wrapper. Currently for library use, it is further protected by an outer protective cover of transparent plastic (polyvinyl chloride or acetate) foil. These covers may either be purchased readymade in a variety of size for the jackets to be inserted or the foil may be obtained in sheet form and cut to size in the library. The first English book jacket was produced in 1832, but dust wrappers did not come into general use in Britain until about 1890. In India it was first used in 1905.

K

KARDEX: Three types of Kardex are used for keeping the record of periodical called ***Three Card System***: Typical visible index, Robot Kardex and Kardex, Typical Visible Index (checking record cabinet) are of metal. Cards are held in paper pockets with a transparent strip at the lower edge, on which the title of the periodicals is usually typed, may be inserted. Robot Kardex is manufactured by Remington Rand Co. It contains sixty slides in two banks of thirty slides each, which move up and down on a renner. Kardex is popular and used for keeping visible record. It is of steel and the cabinet is approx. 10½″ broad, 24″ deep and 20″ high. One unit contains 7 trays containing 504 card holders with sliding dust cover and locking device.

L

Lenin State Library: The Lenin State Library and Book Chamber of the Byelorussian USSR, are one of the important centres for library work and bibliography in the Soviet Union. The library contains 12 lakh books of USSR and other countries. There are 15 reading rooms used by 2,500 readers everyday. It has a membership of 85,000 readers. Different queries are answered by the library annually through its catalogues which contain 15 million cards. Its department of Byelorussian literature and bibliography deals with wide range of works on regional studies. It has a collection of 5 lakh books and periodicals published in Byelorussian since the beginning of 19th century. The library is the centre of extensive network of public libraries. It has contacts with 450 institutions in 39 countries.

Letter by Letter Filing: A method of filing, in alphabetical order, the entries in a list, catalogue or bibliography. The basic principle being followed is that each heading, whether consisting of one or more, is regarded as one unit. Thus, the significance of the individual works is disregarded and the whole heading is considered as a sequence of letter. Often called the 'all through' method, e.g.:

Green acres
Green banks
Green folds
Green Howards
Green shank.

The same entries filed by the alternative word method would appear as follows:

Green Acres
Green Howards

Green banks
Greenfold
Green shank.

Library (Information) System for Serials: (1) **OCLC's SCS:** Online computer library centre has housed the conversion of serials (CONSER) and database. OCLC's SCS provide librarians with local serials control as well as access to OCLC online Union Catalogue which contains over six lakh serials bibliographical records. SC-350 developed for use with the OCLC M-350 workstation, a modified IBM personal computer support, a full range of technical services, including bibliographical record selection and transfer, automatic check-in and claiming routine, binding, financial control, OCLC user, the MARC. SC-350 maintains links to the OCLC online system. (2) Serial control is a major operaton. Computerised system helps handling the operation more easily, quickly and economically. It controls the performance of data entry take, i.e. title of the serial, journal, periodicity, date of issue, individual article and author, locus, abstract and key work etc.; order of new serials, renewal of subscription of title on current subscription list, and cancellation of subscription; recording receipt of issues; sending reminders, output of various lists, budget control, binding control etc.

Library and Society: Library is a centre of learning and knowledge explosion. Library is a social institution and a part of an over-all development, representing specific stage and a specific function in it. Librarian has a super sensitive receptive mind, having an almost intuitive feeling of the finer shadings of the mental needs of the society. Library has two pre-eminent active functions towards the society: to 'entertain' and 'to educate'. The predominant ideals of the modern society are based principally on democratic conventions underlining the ideas of freedom of thought, freedom of circulation of knowledge and freedom of interactions. It is library whose function is to upheld the sanctity of such ideas. The most surprising thing is that, in spite of T.V. providing entertainment round the clock, at a small cost, the use of books from public libraries has continued to rise. Recreational reading is mainly reading for pleasure which gives the reader the entertainment he seeks and the public library is mainly responsible for catering such needs in the society. The public library cater the needs of individuals and groups. It is a matter of fact that those who can read, needs a steady supply of reading material to suit his purpose. Library is the institution which has the ability to serve his purpose.

The public library is very important in this context. The system, with its network of branches and book mobiles, established an active reader contact, building up a potential for functional relationship between demand and supply. The clientele of the public library, which is a cross section of the community, expresses its corporate requirements not only in terms of reading for entertainment or relaxation, but also for information and knowledge, both of which can be a pleasure. Hence, if the goal of libraries, specially public libraries, is to contribute towards the unification of the society by re-directing and re-interpreting group interests in terms of the ultimate interest of a society. The function of the libraries whatever their type—public, academic, special, government or national, in the social context is to serve the social purpose of entertaining, educating and informing the people.

Library Committee: A body consisting of certain responsible persons which work for the proper management of a library. There may be sub-committee for some specific purpose. Library Committee may be executive or advisory. There are many kinds of library committees—self perpetual committee and executive committee, adhoc committee, (nominated), elected committee, and advisory committee. The library committee review the library problems, discuss and make recommendation of library rules and regulations, maintenance of library statistics, annual report, finance, stock verification, staff meetings, library welfare, timings, and development planning.

Its meetings are held after a certain period. Period varies from library to library. Period may be once a year, twice, quarterly or monthly for meeting of library committee.

Library Committee is constituted differently in various libraries, i.e. university, college and school libraries, public libraries, technical and special libraries. It consists of one chairman, and members specialised in academics, science and industries. Librarian becomes the members secretary of the library committee.

The Head or Superior authority of the Institute or Chairman of the Library Committee becomes a member of Executive Committee or an Advisory Committee.

Library Development in Andhra Pradesh: The state of Andhra Pradesh was formed on Nov. 1, 1956. The enactment of an integrated Andhra Pradesh Public Libraries Act, 1960 ushered in the orderly development throughout the state. This was the result of Andhra Pradesh Library Association. Government of India appointed Advisory Committee for libraries in 1958. Public Library system in the state consists of State Central Library in Hydrabad, 6 Regional Libraries, 794 Branch Libraries, and 320 Village Libraries. There are 591 book deposit centres, one mobile library, 400 aided libraries, 1,540 Panchayat libraries and 67 cooperative society libraries. There is State Library Committee headed by the Minister for Libraries. Director for public libraries is the member-secretary of the committee. Under this system there are sufficient provision for reading material, building facilities, trained personnels, and effective library service.

Library Development in West Bengal: Calcutta Public Library was established in 1956. The West Bengal Public Library Act was passed in 1979. There is provision in Act for State Library Council with Minister of Library Science as its Chairman, separate Directorate of Library Science, Local Library Authority, and District Library Officers at the district level. There are 2,421 government, four staff members in every town library and ten staff in every District Library.

Library System in Assam: Assam is a gateway of NE Region in India. The state first established State Central Library in 1954 in Shillong. There are 21 District Libraries. Mobile libraries are controlled by Director of Public Libraries since 1984. State Central Library is functioning as 'Research and Reference Library'. There is separate children library established in 1987 with a rich collection in English, Assamese and Hindi Languages. At present there are one Branch Library, one Children Library, one Reference and Research Library, one Science and Technical Library, 18 District Libraries, 14 Sub-Division Libraries, and 204 Rural Libraries. There are 8 staff members in District Libraries, 4 staff members in Sub-division libraries, 2 staff members in Rural Libraries.

Library System in Himachal Pradesh: Himachal Pradesh get full-fledged statehood on Jan. 25, 1971. This State has 8th position in literacy in India. The first Municipal Library was opened in 1930, Sanatan Dharam Library in 1936, and First District Library (Chamba) in 1952. There are 11 District Libraries, 5 Municipal Libraries, 3 Tehsil Libraries, 9 Block Libraries, 5 Community Centres, 50 Paragana Libraries, 138 Panchayat Libraries, 5 District Libraries (Information centres), and 11 reading rooms. There are 5 mobile libraries vans giving library service to the village centres. It needs more extension as the state has peculiar geographical conditions and scattered population in remote areas, all libraries are administered by Director of Education except Municipal and Panchayat Libraries. There are library committee at the state and district level.

Library System in Karnataka: Karnataka Public Libraries Act was passed in 1965. There are one State Central Reference Library, Bangalore Public Technical Library, 15 City Central Libraries, 20 District Central Libraries, 487 Branch Libraries, 487 Book Delivery Stations, 551 Mandal Libraries and 8 model Libraries. There is a provision of clause in the Act @ 6 paise per rupee on tax on land and buildings. The salary of the staff is paid by the consolidated fund of the state. Few city Central Libraries are equipped with audio-visual aids.

Library System in Manipur: Manipur is a smallest state of India and situated in the North East region. This state emerged in 1971. Manipur Library Association was rejuvenated on 24 May 1987. Public Library Bill was introduced in Manipur Legislation Assembly on July, 1988 and passed on August, 1988, implemented in August, 1993. There is provision of department of Public Library Committee and District Library Authority.

Library Development in Kashmir: Kashmir besides being a tourist centre, has been a seat of learning from very early time. The Chinese traveller Huen Tasang came to Kashmir and appreciated glory of Kashmir. Vasugupta, founder of Shaiva philosophy, wrote *Spanda Karika* in 9th century. Utpaldeva lived in 10th century. A new school of thought emerged with the contacts of Islamic and Hindu cultures, which resulted to many Sanskrit work like *Satikusmunjal* (1350 AD), *Balbodhini* (1975 AD) and *Viganana Bhaisavi* (1950 AD).

It was, however, in the Dogra period (1846-1947) when the state became one of the largest princely states of India and educational development was done by Dogra rulers who donated their revenue in education and free book service. Two major public libraries were established by Maharaja Ranvir Singh and Maharaja Pratap Singh in 1879 and 1898 respectively. By 1972 about 6000 primary schools, 1200 middle schools, 500 high/higher secondary schools, and 27 colleges were started. A separate university and medical college were established for Jammu.

Free book service was extended to the village under the National extension scheme on 19th June, 1966. The library association was formed. A library bill was drafted in 1953 by the Director of Libraries and Archives and submitted before the Prime Minister of the state Shaikh Abdulla. It has a provision for a Central Library in Srinagar and Jammu District libraries and no provision of library cess.

Government has provided District Libraries at each district headquater. The progress in the field of public libraries is not satisfactory.

Library History (India): Since ancient times India has been the home of great scholars and famous centre of learning as Taxila, Nalanda, Udantpuri, Vallabhi with well-stocked libraries. During Muslim period many great libraries were established. The oldest library surviving in India is the Tanzore Saraswati Mahal Library established in 15th century. East India Company had its libraries in its factories in Bombay in 17th century. In 1784 Sir William Jones founded Asiatic Society of Bengal, Calcutta, and other Presidency towns had public libraries like Dalphian Library set up in 1817, Madras Library Society in 1812, Calcutta Library Society in 1818, Bombay General Library in 1930, and Calcutta Public Library in 1855. Madras Public Library was established in 1860 by Jesse Mitcud. In 1896 Cannemera Public Library was established. In 1976 Khuda Buksh Library and in 1891 Imperial Library were opened and Imperial Library became National Library with the merger of Calcutta Public Library in 1948. In 1920 Maharaja Shivaji Rao Gaikwad of Baroda established a Central Library and many other libraries under the guidance of an American, W.A. Borden. In 1951 Government of India started Delhi Public Library and INSDOC. In 1972 Raja Ram Mohan Roy Library Foundation was established. Government passed Press and Registration Book Act 1867 and amended in 1958. Government of India set up Advisory Committee in 1957 who recommended library legislation. So far academic library is concerned, in 1858 three university libraries were established—Calcutta, Bombay and Delhi and now there are 175 university libraries. Public Library was established in 7 states and Central State Libraries in all states.

Library Movement in Gujarat: Gujarat state came into existence in May, 1960. There has been sufficient library development in Gujarat. There are one State Central Library, 17 District libraries, 4 Govt. libraries, 2 women libraries, 2 integrated libraries, and 36 Taluka libraries. There are grant-in-aid libraries in the state, e.g. 21 city libraries, 28 city branch libraries, 330 town libraries, 6,351 village libraries, 49 children libraries, 67 women libraries and 6 special libraries. Government formulated grant-in-aid rules in the state in April 1964 and revised in 1974 and 1989. The total amount paid by state as grant-in-aid is Rs. 200 lakhs. It is paid annually. There is Director of Libraries controlling this network. State has made provision of Rs. 77 lakh for computerization of state libraries of Baroda and Gandhinagar.

Library Science Education in Asia: The first library school was started in Baroda in 1911, by W.A. Borden, an American librarian appointed as the first Director of State Library Department of Baroda. This school started short course and opened to non-graduates. The second library school was started in Lahore in 1915 by A.D. Dickinson, an American librarian appointed in Punjab University. The third library school was started in Madras in 1929 by Ranganathan. It started certificate course of three months for non-graduates. In 1937 it was taken over by Madras University. The education in library science in India consists of two distinct levels: (1) the semi-professional and (2) the professional level. Certificate and Diploma courses are run for semi-professionals and degree and postgraduate courses are run for professional level. Research in Library Science are also conducted in library schools run by universities in India. At present there are more than 100 universities that are running semi-professional courses in more than 200 institutes.

Library Software for Teaching DDC in Library Science: In teaching library science subjects an equal emphasis is being placed in order to simplify teaching, and to adopt to computer aided teaching techniques. In fact many CIA programmes in library education were initially based on genralised packages like PLATO and CICCIT. School of library science, Aberdeen (UK) developed a package named as DC (Several acronyms such a CBE, CBL, CBT, CML, CAMOL, CAL, CAI are used to designate the concept of computerized learning and teaching. The programme is written in BASIC version 1.12 of 1982 (Microsoft BASIC). The package can be used on a PC or PC/XT (IBM compatible) with either single or double drive for floppy disk, as both BASICS-A computer are stored with the package programme on a single floppy disk. The storage is made on a single 5.25" floppy disk DD/DS soft sector, 48 TPI.

LEARN DDC uses PC DOS or MS DOS operating system version. It is interpreted by BASIC and follows mostly INSI stands for BASIC. Both text and data files are written using 'READ' and 'DATA' statement, hence there are no separate files to be accessed by the programmes.

Library System & Creativity: Modern management system has to handle a variety of problems arising from individual and group behaviour, assimilation of technology, changing social values and the need to make the best use of human talent. Creativity is the gift of nature. It is the ability to generate new ideas and perceive things in a unique way. Creativity and intelligence seem to be two distinct forms of mental ability. Creativity in organization needs to scout for ideas and opportunities which leads improvement in methods and policies, creation of new products or modification of existing lines of production, cutting costs, diversification into new areas, merger of units, separation and a host of other means that give them a competition edge.

The problem in libraries is how the creative spirit so obviously alive in librarianship can be fostered, not just in the upper ranges of management, but through library and information science organizations. A few examples are book classification by Melvil Dewey, unit card system and faceted classification by S.R. Ranganathan, computer generating, keyword index by H.P. Luhn, and critation index by Engenegarfied.

Potentiality for creativity exists in most people, albeit in varying degrees. These techniques can be grouped in four categories: (a) Analytic (attribute listing, input-output technique, Grid analysis), (b) Free association techniques (brain storming, synectics, forced relationship techniques, catalogue techniques), listing techniques, focused object techniques), (c) Overdoing creativity, and (d) Delphi technique.

Library System Performance Evaluation: Evaluation is basically a judgement of worth—an appraisal of value. It means assisting the worth value of the unit to the people for whom it is meant. By and large evaluation means testing the service or system for effective efficiency. The basic elements and the steps involved in an evaluation study are identification of the item of programme to be evaluated, defining the objectives of evaluation, selection of criteria by which performance is to be assisted, selection of appropriate measuring techniques/methods, formulation of hypotheses, collection of data, analysis and evaluation of data, and derivation of results.

Library acquire bibliographic material relating to the interest of the particular user population, actual or potential, organize and display these materials in various ways, and make them available to users. Exposure of library users to materials in the library is the use of material by library users and indirect exposure is the use of collection by library staff on behalf of the users.

Library evaluation of library effectiveness reveals the following: (1) library input, (2) the relationship between the objectives of the organization and individuals' demand, library's interaction with users, impact on society in relation to library work and service. Evaluation of information services and system is concerned with the aspects of information retrieval and users study.

Loan Methods: Financial administration of a lending library depends on the method of recording loans. Not only does the process take up much staff time but it affects almost all other tasks. The form of the records governs the facility with which overdue notices, reserves and stocktaking are dealt with and may have an influence on accession methods. Any permanent records kept are of value in book selection, binding and withdrawal.

A written record of each loan may be made in reference and research libraries and also in some university and school libraries. Such records are made in multiple copies to provide upto three files—by date, by book, and by borrower. In public lending libraries, written records are made only for special categories of loans, such as those made through the post; for dealing with thousands of personal borrowers, faster techniques have been evolved.

The intending borrower's right to use the library is usually checked once at the time of registration and thereafter the production of a membership card or reader's ticket is accepted as sufficient proof of identify. Pocket-card charging was adopted in almost all public libraries with open access and it has also proved efficient in many school and college libraries and in at least one university library. It has been less used in America, where the network charging method was most widely favoured.

From the beginning of the 20th century, attempt has been made to mechanise the charging process, the first inexpensive machine being the Dickman Book Charger, which came into use about 1927. The principles of transaction charging effected something of a revolution and made possible photo-charging in 1940 and audio charging in 1948. During 1940-48, punch card charging and the use of IBM machines were developed. In the last few years, the impetus has been maintained with the development of the Photoclerk and Bookamatic systems and also the experimental Brodac.

M

Map Library: Of special interest to librarians is the problem of the storage and conservation of maps. A report setting out both the ideal and the minimum standards was prepared by a committee of the Royal Geographical Society in 1954. Atmospheric conditions are important, if damage by damp or organic growth is to be avoided, and the recommendations are for a steady temperature between 55°F and 60°F, a relative humidity of less than 65%, adequate ventilation and non-exposure to bright light. Ideally, maps should be preserved in their original physical form. If they are to be folded, they should be dissected and mounted on linen, Holland or jaconette. Repairs should be done with handmade repairing paper, parchment or vellum, according to the original, and silk gauze using only pure flour paste. The chief storage method are horizontal or vertical filing or in portfolios. Small and folded maps are usually kept in boxes or on shelves, and wall maps on rollers, hung or in racks.

Mechanized Cataloguing: Basically it is the process of reproducing catalogue entries in quantity by some method of duplication. This is done either by photographic, mechanical or chemical means; in a wider sense it includes the administrative and routine methods attendant upon the introduction of such duplication. Once the standard catalogue entry for a work has been established by the cataloguer and the member of entries required to represent it in all the catalogues has been divided, a duplicating machine will produce identical entries without error, usually improved in quality and cheaper than the copy-typing. The advantages are comparable with those conferred by the purchase of printed cards from a national centralized cataloguing agency. The local mechanization may in fact be cheaper, covering all accessions and enabling local catalogue codes and modified classification schemes to be used direct.

With the exception of the American 'Flexo writer', automatic duplicating typewriter, all methods of duplication rely upon the production of correct master entry upon a printing plate, wax backed stencil, spirit offset stencil, which is used to produce all the entries required. Other factor in the choice of process are simplicity and cleanliness of operation, and the ability to produce all the desired number of copies legibly on the kind and size of paper or card required. In modern times, computerized bibliographical services are taking place.

Medium Cataloguing: That kind of cataloguing in which, as a general policy, entries give only limited information sufficient to identify the book, little bibliographical information rarely include annotations. The chief omissions from 'full' cataloguing to 'medium' entries are:

(1) The names of the author and writers of introductions, prefaces, etc.

(2) The place of publication and publisher's name.

(3) Detailed pagination, statement and specification of the kinds of illustrations (from the collation).

Micro Processor Technology: In early 1970s, a pocket calculator was used for ordinary arithmetic operations. This increased computer power, which further led to the newly emerging micro-processor technology. In this technology, microminiaturigation of circuits has been carried to a point where a single silicon clip, measuring one generator of an inch square, has the computing power and multiple copies of these clips can be automatically produced in incredibly low cost. Micro-comber based on micro-processor technology possesses its own CPU, floppy disks, keyboard, visual display unit (VDU). VDU is in TV screen and printer to check up the retention in hard copy form. It makes it technically feasible now for librarians and information specialists to work as part of large information system. BLAISE (British Library Automated Information Service) has developed a software called CORTEX which meets the need of data entry and record editing system, enhance information retrieval capabilities and in-house activities (ordering and inventory control).

Micro-Recording: Micro-recording, or micro-copying is a form of photocopying in which the copy on film or paper is made at a size reduced so greatly that it cannot be read with the naked eye. It requires enlargement by projection or in a 'reader'. Micro-recording serves the following purposes: for storage of files, books, periodicals; for duplicating materials, a safeguard means of making rare and valuable documents accessible to the public as a medium for publishing material which cannot be published economically by ordinary means, etc. Micro-recording is a fully photographic process. It employs a camera.

Micro-Opaque Card: These cards may be produced photographically from 16mm microfilm and are mechanically printed by the offset process from special microfilm. There are 3″× 5″card on which textural materials has been produced photographically at reduction of 15 to 23 times and in some cases contain in normal size print either an abstract or a catalogue heading. Upto 80 pages of conventional text can be photo printed on one of these cards and 85 cards can be shelved **to every inch**. Alternatively, the two sides laminated microcard can contain 160 pages of text and be shelved at 65 cards **to the inch**. Whilst these micro opaque are produced from roll film, the microlex, which is a limited card 6½″ × 8½″, is produced from sheet negatives and each double-sided card contains 400 pages of original text.

Mnemonics: These are memory-aiding devices used in the notation of classification schemes that enable an enquirer to associate a certain symbol arrangement with a certain subject concept. They may occur by the use of initial letters to indicate certain classes. For example, in the Library of Congress Classification, general works are indicated as A and encyclopedias are AE, newspapers are AN. This type of mnemonic should be used casually without distorting the proper sequence of the scheme to get the mnemonic. Similarly, in the bibliographic classification, B is Physics, C is Chemistry and CB has been used artfully for Physical Chemistry. These are called literal or verbal mnemonics. But the most important mnemonics are those auxiliary tables which in various classification schemes may be applied systematically to the whole or part of the table to denote particular forms or aspects of books. Those denoting one particular aspect are known as constant, while those which may be used to denote different aspects according to the context are variable. The Decimal Classification can use only combinations of number in its auxiliary tables, but they are arranged skillfully so that they are applied properly.

Seminal or unscheduled mnemonics are names sometimes given to the combination of different parts of the notation which are not scheduled to be used together, but which may be made up by the classifier himself to convey a recurrent idea. These can be most useful when new subjects or approaches to subjects are to be classified. Besides, assisting in the codification of scheme and aiding the classifier in 'num building' mnemonics tend to make the schedules smaller, as the same concept need not be repeated constantly.

Multimedia Information System: Multimedia in computer systems means using many input media (text, speech, gestures, direct manipulation) and output media (text, sound, graphics, video) in the same application. Multimedia technology allows all types of information including full motion video, still images, audio, text and graphics to be stored and distributed on an all digited sources. PC can manage all of the information as digital files and deliver it to the computer-user from CD-ROM or hard disk, or sent over between or telephone lines. A CD-ROM disk can store 74 minutes of audio or only 90 seconds of video. It cannot sent a full 30 frame per second of full screen, full motion, video date to the computer. DVI (Digital Video Interactive) uses single storage device and a set of chips to produce live-action video, synthetic video or audio under the central of PC. DVI has facilities to create computer regenerated images in real time—DVI technology has developed two video processor chips, one called pixal processor (microprocessor) that runs at 12.5 million operation per second, while the second is the output display processor which acts as a super CRT controller.

Multimedia system needs multimedia PC-MPC. Multimedia system can be applied to market research, education and training, health care, security and consultancy.

Museum Library: It is special and reference library. It needs special technical staff and special collection. It is equipped with a representative subject collection of standard works dealing with the subjects in the museums collections for the use of its staff and for visitors who may wish to peruse their studies. A museum library can arouse museumological interest amongst intelligentia and develop better understanding and precaution of the museum material.

Museum library not only house the collection of books but also of pictorial materials such as photographs, colour prints, slides and other reproductions. A library is to be used by both the visitors and the staff. They need all books available for consultation at all times in a reference library.

In a specialized museum library, informed selection of books and other materials is of vital importance. Books are selected through bibliographies, publishers catalogue and personal contact with subject specialists.

The library should have spacious premises, specially and aesthetically designed for it. Library building should be well planned. It should be fairly large with provision of stacks, which can be extended, reading room for visitor, cubicles for scholars, a lounge for relaxation and study. There may be vertical galleries in two/three tiers on four sides of hall.

There should be a provision of natural light, linoleum floors and dignified furniture. The reading hall should be air-conditioned.

There should be adequate staff in the library to provide efficient service to visitors/readers.

N

NASSDOC (National Social Science Documentation Centre), New Delhi: ICSSR (Indian Council of Social Science Research) was set up in 1969. The council set up its one unit NASSDOC to create facilities of documentation and bibliographical services for research scholars in the field of social sciences. This centre works for compilation of union catalogue, directory of social science institutions and social scientists, and area study bibliographies.

NASSDOC provides bibliographic services, document, location services, document supply services on loan basis, sale of Government of India publications. It has set up Inter-library Recourses Centre in Collaboration with Jawahar Lal Nehru University. It also provides input data regarding Indian Publications to International Committee for Social Services Information and Documentation (Daris). NASSDOC is represented in IFLA. It holds membership in ILA, IASLIC, AGLIS, FID, IFLA and ISI.

National Archives of India: NAI located in New Delhi came to existence after independence with a new name. It was formerly called Imperial Record Department (1891) located at Calcutta. It was shifted to New Delhi in 1936. The total shelf space is around 36 kms. It has regional responsibilities at Bhopal, Jaipur and Pondicherry. It has holdings of more than 1.5 lakh volumes, 6.5 lakh loose documents, 2000 maps, and authenticated bills passed by various legislatures in the country. It publishes *Indian Archives* (since 1947) and *The Archeion*.

National Bibliography: *Indian National Bibliography* (*INB*) was started in 1958 and published by National Reference Library, located in the campus of National Library,

Calcutta. *INB* is compiled on the basis of material received under delivery of books and newspapers (Public Library) Act 1956. It is published monthly and has annual cirulations. It has DDC classification followed by alphabetical indexes. Colon classification numbers are also given. Central References Library also produces *Index India*, a quarterly index of articles appearing in current periodicals in major Indian languages.

National Science Library (NSL): It was started as part of INSDOC in April 1964 under Council of Scientific and Industrial Research (CSIR). It aims at collecting items in almost all branches of science and technology excluding medicine and agriculture. It receives about 5000 current serials title and 650 Russian journals.

NCSDCT (The National Centre for Software Development and Computering Techniques, India) was established in 1974 at the Tata Institute of Fundamental Research, Bombay. The work is centered around operation of the DEC1077 computer system, education and advance training in computer networking and application, technology development, interactive graphics and computer aided design facility.

Network Charging System: It is the method of recording book loans which is most widely used in America. Each borrower has a ticket or card with spaces for recording loans. Each book is represented by a book card which is normally kept in the book. When a loan is made, the date is stamped three times—on the reader's card, on the book card and on the date label. The borrower's ticket number is mentioned on the book card and, in the full form of the system, the book number is entered on the reader's ticket. Only the book card is filed as a time record, the borrower retaining his ticket after the entries have been made. At the return counter the date of return is stamped on the readers' ticket and, when convenient, the book card is removed from file and replaced in the book.

Simplified versions of the method are also used, including self-charging systems, in which the borrower does the writing, and mechanized versions such as the Dickman system and Gaylord Electric Automatic charging system.

Network Selection Criteria: Having decided to participate in network, an intending library is faced with the question of selecting the most suitable network. The following factors help in making the choice:

(1) Available network operations.

(2) Criteria to be used in deciding the network, method of evaluating, completing network (e.g. OCLC-VS-BALLOTS), ODIALOG-VS-BIT).

(3) Selection of functions of the network to be used.

(4) Reliability of the system.

(5) Quality control standards decided by the network.

(6) Cost.

In India, the commissioning of the communications satellite INSAT-1B has resulted in a number of applications including broadcasting and data communication. There are many data communication networks like NICNET, INDONET, VIKRAM, BTISNET, CALIBNET, DELNET, DESINET (or DESIDOC), CSIRNET, ERNET (Education and Research Network), INFLIBNET, and VIDYANET.

Network Structure and Management: The structure greatly influences information flow, communication, and decision-making on library and information network problems related to selection of configuration, i.e. non-direct or direct, types of transactions, message formats, types of nodes, and traffic requirements. Factors that favour centralization are ability to built large databases, leading to a universal bibliographical index, desire to have information for inter-library lending, need to impose and maintain standards, availability of inexpensive telecommunication facilities and machine readable formats and the possibility of overcoming economic and time pressures through shares.

Network System: A library network consists of six basic components—information resources, uses, intellectual access system to the documents, physical access system, formal organization, and bidirectional communications. The physical access system and the communication system are mainly concerned with those who operate the network and deal with physical channels of communication, equipment, physical interconnection of network models and levels, speed of processing data and file structure.

Network structures consists of:

(a) elements, (b) configuration, (c) level, and (d) topalasy.

Configuration is of many types: (1) monolithic, (2) free unorganized, and (3) free organized. In other words, configuration may be categorized as under:

(1) ***Star***—Totally centralized, central node, control activities and services.

(2) ***Ring***—Access in the sequential order of nodes.

(3) ***Distributed***—Decentralised functioning, direct communication from one node to every other node.

(4) ***Hierarchical***—Nodes arranged in levels. Access hierarchical vertical communications.

(5) ***Bus***—Used in local area networks. Linear nodes attached directly.

NIC (National Informatics Centre): It is under Electronic Department and responsible for establishment and development of the computerized information system for the user Government departments, ministries and autonomous organizations. NIC has built an Intra-city computer network in Delhi by connecting six minicomputer terminals to the host CYBER computer system using lease telephone lines and Radio (VHF) frequencies. It has successfully conducted the Delhi-Ahmedabad satellite. NIC has developed more than 100 softwares.

NICNET: A unique infrastructural networks with a history that goes back to 1978. The National Informatic Centres (NIC) network is called NICNET. It is a satellite-based communication using low cost roof-top micro-earth statics to connect 450 district headquarters and 32 states and Union terriroty capitals with a central hub at Delhi. It uses 500 very small operative terminals (VSATs), each of which is connected to specific outbound and inbound channel on a satellite's transponder. VSATs have been used to connect computers, terminals, telexes and other devices to other computers/devices via the satellite. NICNET is desired primarily to be a government information network. Its objectives are to promote the collection, storage, analysis transmission, and exchange of data at district, state headquarters and central ministries and departments at New Delhi for use in planning, management and monitoring of projects and government sponsored programmes.

NISSAT (National Information System for Science and Technology): UNESCO expert Dr. Peter Lazer visited India in April, 1972 to study infrastructure and draw a plan for developing Information System. Government of India appointed a National Committee for Science and Technology to draw up a science and technology plan and establish National Information System for Science and Technology. First meeting of UNISIST was held at Columbo and second at Delhi (18-20 March, 1976). In India an information group was constituted. NISSAT was established in 1974 and came to effect from 1977 with Dr. V.A. Kamath as read. It has sectoral information centres on leather technology in Central Leather Research Institute, Bangalore and Drug and Pharmaceuticals at Central Drug Research Institute, Lucknow. It has regional centres at INSDOC, New Delhi, IIT Bombay, IIEM, Jadarpur and CIRL, Madras. NISSAT is conducting training programmes at DRTC, Bangalore, IIT, Madras (computer), INSDOC, New Delhi, BARC, IIEM, Calcutta and IIT, Bombay.

Normative Principles of Cataloguing: These have four groups: (1) General Laws, (2) Laws of Library Science, (3) Canons of Cataloguing, and (4) Law of Local Variations. Ranganathan developed the normative principles in his book *Headings and Canons*. These were discussed in ICCP, Paris and AACR adopted these principles. There normative principles are best judged for evaluating the best catalogue code. These principles guide every problem in cataloguing like drafting of a catalogue code, interpreting the rules to meet new situation, guiding for a cataloguing work. CCC has incorporated the fundamental laws and canons of cataloguing in its first parts.

O

OCLC (Online Computer Library Centre): It is a cooperative effort and grew from a regional co-operative network in the state of Ohio, US in 1967 to a National Network and further to the International Network of over 8000 libraries in 26 countries. OCLC maintains the largest computer and telecommunication network of libraries and information center in the world. OCLC online Union Catalogue consists of over 18 million unique record in eight formats: books, serials, sound recording, audio-visual media, scores, maps, archives and manuscripts and machine readable data files, and also 300 million location symbols of libraries are used over 300 languages and represented in this database cataloguing which is a specialized activities of library professionals. Every library engage cataloguers and prepare catalogue entries. Proper entries are possible only when professionals have knowledge of subject and language fully. Each library would hire a large number of cataloguers. It is costly and time consuming if we calculate the cost of cataloguing of 20 countries' libraries. It is however wastage of money. The OCLC online system makes it possible and feasible for libraries worldwide to share the wisdom of cataloguers and burden of cataloguing. As a result, each item needs to be catalogued only once and OCLC users can benefit from the wisdom and expertise of that cataloguer. This system allows modification to master records, 90 per cent titles are catalogued once and rest 10 per cent require original cataloguing by cataloguing libraries. OCLC provide inter-library loan service also.

P

Panizzi Sir Anthony (1797-1879): He was keeper of printed books in the British Museum from 1837 until his appointment as Principal Librarian in 1856, the post which he held for further decade. He is renowned as a librarian for his tenacious enforcement of the copyright act, for the conception which he inspired for the British Museum as the second best library in the world for the literature of major language other than English, for his collaborative formulation of the 91 cataloguing rules to be used in the museum and for the great circular, centrally administered reading room of the Museum designed in detail by Smirke. He returned to his native country, Italy, where he died in 1879.

Papyrus: A writing material used in ancient Egypt, derived from a species of reed plentiful in the Nile delta. As described by policy, the manufacture involved unrolling the stem, and laying the flat sections across each other with the fibres immersed in Nile water, pressed together and dried in the sun, afterwards giving a high polish. Pieces of papyrus were frequently joined into a roll, the extreme length now surviving being the Harish Papyrus (133 × 16¾ ft.). Sheets were also folded once into groups or quires and, then stabbed together with a binding cord known as a Codex. It represents the early form of the modern book. Under the peculiar conditions of Egypts, it is an excellent writing material, and documents survive from the 3rd Millennium BC. Christian literature survive only in papyrus text.

Parchment: (1) A thin strong writing material made from real goat-or sheep-skin. (2) Paper made to simulate the real skin, i.e. vegetable parchment, thin, grease proof sulphate paper.

Various industrial types of parchment are soft vegetable parchment, oiled parchment, and glazed imitation parchment. Parchment substitute, a hand made paper usually with deckle edge used for legal documents, has a characteristic greasy surface and is suitable for steel pen and Indian ink.

Personal Communication Services (PCS): An evolving service that incorporates both the concepts of:

(1) Terminal mobility, which allows subscribers, via their terminals, to originate and receive calls as they travel nationwide.

(2) Personal mobility, which is achieved through the use of intelligent switching networks and common channel signaling, and which allows subscribers to obtain consistent service (e.g., digital voice, voice mail, fax, or paging), and billing information regardless of their physical location in the network.

Personal Management: Personal management is also known as labour management, industrial management and manpower management. Personal management is the planning, organizing, directing and controlling of the performance of those cooperative functions.

It is an integral but distinctive part of the management, concerned with people at work and their relationship within the enterprises, seeking to bring together effective librarian, the man and woman who staff the library and thereby enabling each to make his own contribution to its success both as individual and as a working group.

Phase: The use of a particular method of division in classification, where the method is loosely connected with the subjects divided. When a fresh 'phase' of division is introduced some classification markers use a symbol to denote the change ('o' in Decimal classification). Phase also occurs when two or more subjects are connected in some way in a book and relationship has to be shown (in colon classification).

Planes: Library classification should preferably be made in three distinctive plane—idea plane, verbal plane, and notation plane. Delineating the structure of the universe of subjects, studying the interrelations among subjects, and fixing the preferred sequence of the subjects—past, present and future, are the distinctive functions of the idea plane. Name each subject by the homogeneous free term, single worded or multiple worded, is the distinctive function of the verbal plane. Implementing the findings of the ideas plane is the distinctive function of the notation plane.

Press and Registration of Book Act: This act was passed in 1867 as XXV Act. This act was enacted with the view of controlling the publications of the Indian Press and at the same time to enrich the British Museum and India Office Library collection with Indian publications for the use of European scholars. According to the Act, three copies of every book were required to be delivered to the government offices specified under the Act, out of which two copies were earmarked for the British Museum and India Office Library and third for disposal of the Government.

Pseudonymous Works: A work is said to be pseudonymous when the writer has concealed his identity under a false name which appears in the books as the name of the author. The librarian and cataloguer, who must consider both the convenience of the reading public and desirability, for ease of official reference, assembling of the writings of a single person together on the shelves, need to decide whether pseudonymous works shall be represented under pseudonym or real name.

Public Libraries in India: India is a democratic country with second largest population in the world. Before independence Lord Curzon established National Library in 1902 under the name Imperial Library, now called National Library. There were 8 lakh educational institutions in 1990 with total students of 18 crores. Kothari Commission recommended more extension of education. National Policy of Education was implemented in 1986. Government of India has formulated a literary drive under a programme 'National Library Mission'. The open school and open university are recent developments in extension programme.

The survey of public libraries in India conducted by a working group of the planning commission showed the existence of 13 State Central Libraries, 205 District Libraries, 1,380 block libraries and 28,317 village libraries in A.P., Gujarat, U.P., Delhi, Himachal Pradesh and Tripura. UNESCO recommended that public libraries should be established under the clear mandate of law. Ranganathan suggested a Public Library network and drafted a Model Library Act and presented in 'All Asia Educational Conference' at Varanasi in 1930. In 1948 Madras (Now Tamil Nadu) enacted the Public Library Act while the Public Library Act of Andhra Pradesh was enacted in 1960, Karnataka Public Library Act in 1965, Maharashtra Public Library Act in 1967, West Bengal Public Library Act in 1982, Kerala Public Library Act in 1989, and Manipur Public Library Act was enacted in 1987. There is no Public Library Act in U.P., Bihar, Madhya Pradesh, Delhi, Jammu & Kashmir till yet due to weak and ineffective leadership in the library field and inactive library associations.

R

Registration of Readers: Only a proportion of those entitled to use a library will make use of its facilities. Those intending to borrow books are asked to 'register', usually by completing an application form containing and undertaking to comply with the rules. After the qualifications have been checked, the intending reader is supplied with a membership card or reader's ticket and the application form is filed in a register of borrowers.

Resource Sharing: It is a mode of operation whereby, functions are shared in common by a number of participants having the same objective or goal in mind. Resource sharing means the sharing of information resources available in one library by the clientele of other libraries. Sharing may be in the field of cooperative acquisitioning, cataloguing and classification, training and development of professional workers in public libraries.

Round off: (1) To round, by adjusting the part of the numeral retained by adding 1 to the least significant of its digits and executing any necessary carries, if and only if the most significant of the digits deleted was equal to or greater than half the radix of its digit place; for example, the numerals 12.6375 and 15.0625, when rounded off to two places, become 12.64 and 15.06, respectively. (2) To round, by adjusting the part of the numeral retained by adding one to the least significant of its digits and executing any necessary carries if:

(1) the most significant of the digits deleted was greater than half the radix of that digit place;

(2) the most significant of the digits deleted was equal to half the radix and one or more of the following digits were greater than zero; and

(3) the most significant of the digits deleted was equal to half the radix, all the following digits were equal to zero, and the least significant of the digits retained was odd. For example, the numerals 12.6375 and 15.0625, when rounded off to three places, become 12.638 and 15.062, respectively. In this definition, "even" may be substituted for "odd".

S

S. Basiruddin: He was librarian of Aligarh University. He has unique distinction of being in active library service for over 50 years. Emerging from a humble beginning of lab-boy of the Deptt. of Library Science he became Professor of Library Science of the same university. He is the architect of the present building of the Maulana Azad Library. In 1961 he was appointed Director of Libraries in Jammu and Kashmir. He resigned and joined at Jaipur as University Librarian and Head of the Deptt. and remained there for two years. After the death of Shri S. Das Gupta, Prof. Bashiruddin joined Delhi University as Librarian. He went back to Aligarh Muslim University for two years. In 1971 he again joined Kashmir University as University Librarian.

He started B.Lib.Sc. course in Aligarh Muslim University in 1957 and established the department. He was a member of UGC Committee with S.R. Ranganathan as Chairman. He presided over 11th ILA Conference, held at Calcutta in 1956. He was President of U.P. Library Association in 1972.

Prof. S. Bashiruddin was recipient of 'Padmashri' Award given by the Government of India and was also given State honour on 26 January, 1976.

Satellite Communication in India: Govt. of India set up the space commission in 1972 to promote the development application of space science and technology. The space activities are carried out by ISRO (India Space Research Organisation). India has tested a satellite Aryabhata in 1957, Bhaskara in 1979 & April 1981, orbited INSAT-1A in 1982 and Rohini in 1980. The first National Satellite System was aimed at 3 series telecommunications, metrology and TV Broadcasting.

The INSAT-I was operated by the P & T Department for telecommunication grant segment and utilization. INSAT-1A, the first operational satellite of the INSAT system, was orbited in April 1982 and utilized for network system in India.

School Libraries in India: Ranganathan stressed for better school libraries. A habit starts from tender age and early stage becomes an integral part of life at later stage. New education policy started from 1986 on the principles of distance education open school, operation block, board and model schools, viz. Navodaya Vidyalaya in every district. Higher education cannot be qualitative unless school education is well qualitative. Computer education has been made compulsory from class IV particularly in Central Schools, Navodaya Vidyalaya and Public Schools.

In the present school system there are 5-year primary school and 8-year middle school. Primary education is free and library services are available to every students at class level.

Secondary and senior secondary schools have good libraries managed by professional librarians. Secondary Education Commission (1952-53) stressed for good school libraries. Teachers are usually available for school students but there is non-availability of literature for general reading, particularly in local languages.

Script: (1) A term applied to any type face resembling handwriting. (2) A typescript, specifically, of a play, or film play or the text of the spoken part of a radio programme etc. (ALA Gloss).

Sector Device: Division of an array into sectors.

Sector Notation: Colon classification provides for sector notation, one out of 9 digits in Arabic number is scarified resultantly. Divisions of 9 are not used as sub-divisions of 9. They enjoy a co-ordinate status with the digit 1-9, the first eight digits are said to form first sector and the second 8 digits are said to form second sector and so on.

Sector	1	2	3	4	5
	1	91	991	9991	99991
	2	92	992	9992	99992
	3	93	993	9993	99993
	4	94	994	9994	99994
	5	95	995	9995	99995
	6	96	996	9996	99996
	7	97	997	9997	99997
	8	98	998	9998	99998

See also Reference: A direction in a catalogue with a heading below which entries are listed of another term or name under which additional or allied information may be found. In the alphabetical subject catalogue and the dictionary catalogue, **see also** subject; references are made from general subjects to their subordinate subjects, e.g. Economics **see also** Banks and banking; Capitalism; Factory system, **see also** Economics—Periodicals; they are also made from subjects related to co-ordinate subjects, e.g. Needlework **see also** Embroidery, or Publishing.

Selective Cataloguing: The practice of selecting certain kinds of material in a library for cataloguing in various degrees of fullness, others being left uncatalogued. A measure of economy is achieved by selective cataloguing, the practice being based on the principle that the value of standard reference books, up-to-date textbooks, authoritative works and standard classics merit full cataloguing. The books of secondary importance, little-used works and obsolete editions merit only brief or partial cataloguing, whilst ephemeral items need not be catalogued at all.

The extent to which selective cataloguing may be practiced depends largely on the character of the library and the demands made on it by its readers. The existence of a complete shelf-register in addition to the catalogue is also a primary consideration, particularly with regard to the non-cataloguing of ephemeral items and pamphlet materials. Where the stock is thus recorded in shelf order such a finding list may indeed be all that is required for ephemeral fiction and the like, and a special arrangement of uncatalogued materials on the shelves may be deemed sufficient. For books of subject interest or author interest only, the provision of catalogue entries only under subject or author will effect economy of staff, time and catalogue space whilst retaining their essential representation in the catalogue. Again, where a library purchases all items of a given series or collection or by a given publisher (e.g. Her Majesty's Stationary Officer) it may be deemed unnecessary to catalogue them on the grounds that they are too numerous and are entered in any case in catalogues (e.g. H.M.S.O. daily, mostly and consolidated lists) which can themselves be easily provided.

Sensibly used, selective cataloguing achieves a logical relationship between the value of a work and its treatment in the library, the catalogue revealing adequate information regarding the essential stock with the minimum of cost. Its use tends to decline, however, with the introduction of centralized or co-operative cataloguing ventures, which confer commensurate economics whilst still allowing the compilation of complete catalogues.

Selective Dissemination of Information (SDI): This service is almost similar to that of current awareness service with the difference that it is more extensive in scope and besides including current literature it also includes literature published earlier, i.e. it provides retrospective searching for locating information not necessarily current with the help of computers and other data processing equipment. There are several international data banks where services can be conveniently availed by research workers of the country for quick S.D.I. such as C.A. condensates (chemical Abstract), TIS (D.S. Deptt. of Commerce), COMPENDING (Engineering Index), MEDLARS (US National Library of Medicine), BIOSIS, EXCERPTD MEDICA CAN/SDT (Canada Institute for Science and Technical Information, NRC (Ottawa), TITUS (Textile Information Treatment User's Service), INSPEC (Information Service on Physics, Electro-Technology and Computers and Control), VINITI (Indian National Scientific Documentation Centre) and DST (Ministry of Science and Technology, India).

Small Enterprises National Documentation Centre (SENDOC): was established at the National Institute of Small Industry Extension Training (NISIET), Hyderabad in 1971. It provides Systematic information service to industrial enterprises and entrepreneurs consultants. Since 1973 SENDOC has been offering anticipatory documentation services through its publication *SENDOC Bulletin.*

Serial: (1) A number of separate works, usually related to one another in subject or otherwise, issued successively by a publisher, is a rule in uniform style, with a collective series title which generally appears at the head of the title-page, on the half-title or on the cover. (2) Each of two or more volumes of essays, lectures, articles or other writings, similar in character and issued in sequence. (3) Several successive volumes of a periodical or other serial publication numbered separately in order to distinguish them from preceding or following volumes of the same publication (A.A. Code).

Sheaf Catalogue: A catalogue of paper slips, each bearing a single entry, held in loose-leaf binders which are labelled and shelved in specially designed racks.

Its use in libraries dates from the third quarter of the 19th century, possessing as it did, certain distinct advantages over the then prevalent printed book catalogue. The sheaf catalogue allows insertion and withdrawal of entries with comparative case without destroying its structure or sequence. It is portable, familiar to the user in so far as each sheaf binder resembles a book, and although occupying greater space, the printed book catalogue is in this respect more economical than the card catalogue.

The most usual sizes of sheaf slip are approximately 8″ × 5″ or 7″ × 4″, thus providing ample space for full cataloguing with annotations. The regional bureau, most of which the sheaf form for their Union catalogues, utilize this space for location symbols.

Simplified Cataloguing: That kind of cataloguing in which the forms of entry and headings are curtailed, and inessential entries omitted. Simplified cataloguing is commonly adopted as a measure of economy, eliminating the necessity for time-consuming bibliographic research, clerical or typing work, and requiring less catalogue space. It may also be adopted to suit the catalogue to the character of the library (especially in the case of children's libraries).

In its commonest form the catalogue entries omit essential matter and mention of prefaces, etc., from the title-page, the place of publication and publisher's name from the imprint, most individual specifications of illustrative matter and the size of the book from the collection and annotations. Personal author headings are given with initials instead of full forenames, and distinguishing dates of birth and death are omitted except for the obvious requirements of names such as Smith, Jones, etc. Whilst every book is given a main entry in this simplified form, added entries under editors, illustrators, translators, titles, series or forms may be omitted.

Few libraries catalogue their stocks in the fullness demanded by strict adherence to the Anglo-American Code, but in considering the adoption of a rigorous policy of simplified cataloguing there lies the very real danger that the value of the catalogue as the most efficient key to the stock may be impaired. Indeed, the initial saving of time sometimes proves to be a false economy when in subsequent years re-cataloguing and the expansion of headings may become necessary in order to distinguish the authors and entries sufficiently.

Subject Authority File: A list of subject headings and subject references selected for use in a catalogue, compiled by the cataloguers for use in a cataloguing department as a substitute for, or additional to, a general printed list of subject headings (such as Sears's or the Library of Congress list).

For ease of interfiling and keeping the list current it is usually compiled on cards or slips, vertically filed. For each new heading the slip is established, giving the exact form of heading, together with some or all of the following information:

Scope notes, defining the heading and stating how, when and where it is to be used.

Synonymous terms, opposites, obsolete terms, etc., from which **see references** have been made.

The broader, more comprehensive heading from which **see also references** have been made.

The co-ordinate related headings from which and to which **see also references** have been made.

The subordinate subjects to which **see also references** have been made.

The source of the heading is a citation of the work which occasioned the establishment of new or unorthodox heading.

Syndetic: Applied to an alphabetical subject catalogue or dictionary catalogue which includes cross-references as connecting links between subjects. Such cross-references attempt to mitigate the disadvantages of the separation of many related subjects by the alphabetical filing of their different names, common to these 'specific entry' catalogues. The references are of two kinds:

(1) *Hierarchy references*: These refer from a comprehensive subject to the less extensive subjects, which together comprise the comprehensive subject, and from each of these to their subordinate subjects, e.g. **Art see also** Painting. Art **see also** Sculpture; Sculpture **see also** Bas-relief.

(2) *Co-ordinate references*: These refer both to and from subjects which are equally extensive and which are allied or serve to illustrate one another, e.g. Arithmetic, **see also** Atheism; Atheism, **see also** Theism.

Systematic catalogues have no need of such a syndetic apparatus since their entries are filed not by alphabetical order of subject headings, but in a systematic grouping of subjects within classes which itself brings into proximity entries for works on similar and allied subjects.

T

Teletex: Teletex is not the same as telex. It is an enhanced telex system designed to take advantage of modern digital packed-switched communication systems. It is 50 times faster than telex.

It is a combination of word processing and telex where information is exhausted among terminals using a common business letter format at the transmission speed of 2400 bits per second. It refers to a particular technique for inserting digital pulses within previously unused scan lines of a normal television signal.

It transmits data partially via a portion of normal television signal, without addressing the question whether a return link might be available. It also transmits data via telephone lines and a cable television system. It is intended for wide public use, carrying information of broad public interest. Content of any frame can be changed, while the system is in operation. It is same as videotex except current system is limited in size. India, however, began the teletex service on Nov. 14, 1985.

Text: (1) The author's work in a book, as distinguished from notes, commentaries, etc. (2) One of the versions of an author's work which may have been published with variations in different editions. (3) The main body of matter on a printed or written page as distinguished from note etc. (4) The type matter of a page as distinguished from the illustrations and margins. (5) The main part of a book as distinguished from preliminaries, appendix, index, etc. (6) A term sometimes applied to block letters or gothic type.

Thesaurus: It is a controlled vocabulary of an indexing language. In methods of assignment the words for document, content and representation are derived from a prepared vocabulary of descriptors, i.e. a thesaurus or an authority list. The word meaning of thesaurus is 'dictionary'. It does not refer to an alphabetical list of words. Thesaurus is an alphabetical list of controlled terms or descriptors, but different from a conventional alphabetical authority of different concepts. It has two kinds of entries: (1) descriptor words, and (2) concept words. It is referred to 'terms', 'used for' narrower terms, broader terms and related terms.

There is a difference between thesaurus and subject headings. Basically, a list of subject headings is complete listing of names of subjects usually arranged in alphabetical order. While thesaurus is a list of terms and not subject.

Three Card System: S.R. Ranganathan evolved a new method of 'Three Card System'. These cards of size 5″ × 3″ are known as register card, check card and classified index card. Register Card is meant to record information about the name of the journal subscribed, its supplier, publisher, frequency of publication, amount of subscription, voucher number and date of payment. It clears the position of the journal whether received and when. Check card is the main card of Three Card System since it facilitates the checking of the receipt or non-receipt of a particular issue of a periodical. Classified cards provides additional information to a reader by making it easier to know as to which magazine on a particular subject is received in library. These cards are kept in typical visible index and are in two sizes of 6″ × 4″ and 8″ × 5″; the other cards popularly used are 'Robot Karded' and Kardex.

Tracking: In a card catalogue, the record of a main entry card indicates the headings under which added entries for that work are filed. On an authority card references are also recorded. The most usual position for tracing is on the reverse of the card, but they are sometimes placed on the front, or an accompanying card. Should the entries for a work required to be recorded from the catalogue for alteration, withdrawal etc., the presence of the tracing on the main entry card directs the attention to all entries and ensures that none is missed.

The most explicit form of tracing consists of the exact heading of each added entry. More usually when the names used for added entry headings appear in sufficient fullness in the main entry, abbreviations are used which indicate the kind of added entry only (except in the case of subject entries, where the exact subject heading is essential to the finding of the entry).

For example:

an. – analytical entry.

comp. – compiler entry.

ed. – editor entry.

illus. – illustrator entry.

jt. – joint author entry.

ser. – series entry.

t. – title entry.

tr. – translator entry.

Transaction Charging: Book issue methods by which the loan record are filled in the order in which the loans occur are known as transaction charging system. Each book issues or receives a serial number, the first transaction of the day receiving the lowest number and the last having the highest number. At the time the issue is made, a numbered 'transaction' card, which may also act as a 'date due' card, is inserted in the book. When the book is returned, the only immediate task is to remove the transaction card. In due course these cards are sorted into sequence, the missing cards include loans overdue.

The library obviously needs to keep a record in transaction number order, so that details of the overdue book are available when needed. This can be done by hand, by having the set of cards made up in duplicate, one card being inserted in the book as described and the other bearing the same number being used to record the borrower's identity and the book number. American libraries usually require the borrower to do the writing on a call slip which is filed with the retained transaction card.

The system as described can be mechanized by using punched card as the transaction cards but, as the filed record could be sorted into book order, the technique is essential to the use of punched cards. Photo charging and audio charging, however, provide a record which cannot be re-arranged and they are, therefore, essentially transaction charging methods. With all versions, the charging system cannot assist in intercepting reserved books since the filled cards, films or tapes do not readily reveal the record of a given book. There is also, as a rule, some additional work involved in dealing with overdue books. The disadvantages must be balanced against the improved speed of services at the library counters.

A recent development, the addressograph-multigraph 'Bookamatic' system, appears to offer the same advantages as other transaction system and also reduces the work of sending overdue notices.

V

Vatican Library: It was established by Pope Nicolas V. in 1450. It is the greatest library of the world. It has made possible the quest, purchase and transaction of manuscripts codices on a large scale in the great papal building.

Pop John XXII (1316-1334) decided to establish the library at the Papal residence. In 1457 about 300 manuscripts reached the Bibiotheque Nationale, Paris. The Papal library had 350 Laline codices besides some Greek and Arabic ones. In 1447 it became Vatican library. Nicolas has been the director of various libraries and he sent persons to France, Germany, Scandinavia, Greece and Turkey to purchase manuscripts. With the development of printing, the collection increased and Pope Sixtus V had to provide new halls to house the collections. Pope Pius XI invited an American Mission to organize the collection on scientific lines in 1927. The library completed 500 years in 1950. It had 1500 codices, 20 lakh printed books, 7500 incunabulas, 15 lakh engravings and maps and several thousand archival documents. There are a number of halls with partially never-ending galleries, thousands of steel shelves with 25 kilometers of self-space, each 120 metres long with 7 racks in a row. The reading space is available for 450 readers at a time. The reading and study area is airconditioned.

W

W.A. Borden: He was Dewey's student and born in Massachussetts (UK) in 1853. He was a teacher in Columbia University Library School. Borden was invited by Maharaja Shivajirao Gaekwad of Baroda to plan for the development of modern library system. He remained as Director of State Libraries in Baroda until 1913. He devised a special classification plan based on Dewey system. He organized travelling libraries. He stimulated the publications of a professional periodical *The Baroda Library Miscellany*, a quarterly (1912-1919). Borden left Baroda for USA in 1913.

Word by Word Filing: One of the two basic methods of arranging entries in alphabetical order in a list, catalogue or bibliography. The method is also called 'Nothing before something' from the principle of regarding the space separating the first word from subsequent words in a compound or phrase heading 'nothing'. Such a word files before a longer word beginning with the same letters, the additional letters in the longer word being something.

For example

Green acres
Green field
Green bank
Green shank

The same entries filed by the alternative letter by letter method would appear as follows:

Green acres
Green fields
Green Howards
Green shank

X

Xerophraphy: A dry photographic method of documentary reproduction which is an electrical process making use of sensitized paper. A document is photographed using a special camera and plate, or by projection from, for example, a microfilm. The plate electrically change into a processor beforehand and on exposure is discharged except at those parts on which the image was projected. A resinous powder bearing an opposite charge to the plate is then spread over the surface, and the powder adheres to the mirror image of the original document. When the plate is placed in contact with the sheet of paper and put in a processor where it is charged again, the resinous powder is transferred electrostatically to the paper. Finally the fixing of the image is carried out by heading the paper to a temperature which melts the resin, thus forming a permanent image.

Detailed Explanations

A

Abstract: It is a summary of the essential contents of a work usually and articles in a periodical together with the specifications of its locus, that is the place of occurrence, (Ranganathan). An abstract is a brief statement of the essential content of the original or indication of the characteristics of the original.

It is a precise summary concerning the main theme of the contents. Abstracting was needed for the following reasons:

(1) Increase in the number of periodicals.

(2) Growing interdisciplinary character of most of the fields of research.

(3) Growth in the technical reports, commission and committee reports.

(4) Increase in the seminar and conference papers.

(5) Limited distribution of papers.

(6) Wide communication of pre-print and drafts.

(7) Need of current awareness service.

(8) Need of Selective Dissemination Information of Literature.

Abstracting is a basic tool to aware the user with latest developments in a subject field and it is produced in the:

(1) Publishers abstracts of articles.

(2) Separate publisher's documents (pamphlets and parts of books).

Abstracting service can be divided into two groups:

(1) Discipline Oriented Service (advance knowing of subject field).

(2) Mission Oriented Service (solution for complex services).

However, Abstracting is a brief statement of the essential contents of the original or an indication of the characteristics of the original with bibliographical details, which means:

(a) Brief statement.

(b) Related to essential contents.

(c) Original concept of characteristics.

(d) Special features or bibliographical detail.

Allen Kent: "An Abstract is a summary of a publication or articles accompanied by an adequate bibliographical description to enable the publication or articles to be traced."

This definition clearly indicates three points:

(a) Summary of a publication or article—the list of thought contents.

(b) Bibliographical description—physical special features.

(c) Search tools—the source of tracing the related publication and articles.

Herman M. Weisman: "Abstract is an announcement medium whose object is to provide knowledge of and an ordered and logical access to new primary literature. It can serve as a tool for both input to and retrieves from a system's information store."

The definition clearly mentions that:

(1) It is a medium of indication/announcement—it is openly published to the user and invite them as a medium of references.

(2) It provides knowledge and that too in order—the information about the micro-document is provided. The information is arranged in a systematic order based on logic. If order of arrangement is not logically sound, the reader may be confused to trace his information or the articles.

(3) It is a tool to input the information storage—the literature of a discipline is accessed to storage and placed in an abstract.

(4) It retrieves from a system of information storage—whatever information is accessed or input, it is retrieved after dissemination and arranged in a system of abstracting. In other words, Abstracting service is a retrieval of information storage.

However, Abstracting is a media to collect, organize, disseminate and retrieve the information storage.

Robert L. Collinson: "An Abstract is the true presentation in the authors own language of all the points made in the same order as in the original piece of primary documentary information—that can be a book, a research report, a periodical article, a speech of proceedings of a conference, an interview etc."

The definition clarifies that:

(1) It is a true presentation in the authors own language —every author write his articles, report, or present papers in his own language.

(2) Points made in the same order—the order of the points or theme is kept in the same sequence in which the author has given in his original work, i.e. book, report, article, speech, paper and interview.

R.S. Giljarevski: "An abstract is a summary of the document specifying its nature as well as the techniques, findings, time and place of investigation. It also indicates the objectives and main theoretical premises of the study, supplies the pertinent figures, formula, tables, charts, and diagrams and conclusions with a number of illustrations, tables, charts, diagrams and references in a abstract publication, as well as the authors name."

The definition explains:

(1) It is a summary of document.

(2) It specifies the nature and the techniques.

(3) It specifies the time and place of investigation.

(4) It indicates the objectives.

(5) It supplies the pertinent figures, formulas, tables, charts and diagrams.

(6) It supplies references in an abstract publication and authors name.

The central theme statement is given with all bibliographical details along with the time and place of researcher.

S.R. Ranganathan: "Abstracting is a summary of essential contents of a work usually and articles in a periodical together with the specification of its locus, that is the place of occurrence."

The definition explains:

(1) It is a summary of essential contents of a work (usually article periodicals).

(2) It supplies the specification of its locus (place of occurrence).

Asworth: An abstract is a precis of information contained in an article in a periodical.

However, Abstracting means:

(1) To draw out an idea.

(2) To determine the relevancy of ideas.

(3) To reproduce the ideas into a contact keyword.

In fact abstracting is different from summary. Summary reduce the length of documents. Precise means to reduce the length to 1/3 of the document. Abstracting document reduce the length to any limit. It depends on the nature of the article.

Abstracting is:

(1) An intellectual work of reading and editing.

(2) A skillful work of shortening the matter.

Purpose of abstract:

Abstract is purposeful in many ways, like:

(1) It saves the time of the user and helps him in his literature search both current and retrospective.
(2) It locates the document skilfully.
(3) Abstracting is always kept up-to-date so as to acquaint the readers with latest developments.
(4) It serves as secondary source of information.
(5) It represents all articles or other documents, no matter they may be of interest, partial interest or no interest.
(6) It promotes current awareness.
(7) It facilitates the selection of document.
(8) It helps to overcome the language barrier. There are more than 80 languages used in the world. There are handlly any engineers who knows more than 2-3 languages. This problem can be solved by abstracting to trace the required articles.
(9) It facilitates literature search.
(10) It informs indexing facilities.
(11) It helps in the preparation of review.
(12) It arranges the literatures into related groups.

Allen Kent identifies three main functions:

(1) CAS services—Abstract are important tools to provide current awareness service as it is up-to-date always.
(2) Abstract provides references of a back file accumulated information, which may be consulted as required.
(3) Abstracting serves as basis for indexing a record.
(4) It serves as substitute for reading the source material.
(5) It serves as means of assessing whether the original, full source material is worth-reading.

Qualities of a good abstract:

An abstract may be good or bad. In other words the abstract may be considered good if it is useful to the users in their research.

A good abstract may have following qualities:

1. An abstract should mention complete information about the micro-documents. Incomplete information cannot be useful to the users.
2. All information given in the abstract should be clear in sense and must be accurate.
3. Information should be precise and reasonably brief.
4. It should present new data, which may not have been reported earlier.
5. It should be as brief as possible.
6. It should not include any criticism.
7. It should also include negative results.
8. It should be written in third person.
9. It should assume that the reader of the abstract has some knowledge of the subject but has not read the paper.
10. It should usually begin by stating the subject unless it is obvious from the title.
11. It should include author's own view.
12. There should be minimum possible time-lag between publication and the abstract.
13. It should include an index.
14. The price of indexing journal is also a quality factor.
15. A good printing, compactness and improved presentation of the text.

Types of absract:

There are ten types of abstracts:

1. Indicative and Descriptive Abstracts
2. Informative Abstract
    (i) Mixed Abstract
    (ii) Listing Abstract
    (iii) Critical Abstract

3. Expended Title
4. Summary and Synopsis Abstract
5. Annotated Abstract
6. Starting with a Slant Abstract (point of view)
7. Pseudo-Abstract
8. Graphic Abstract
9. Telegraphic Abstract
10. Extracts

1. Indicative and Descriptive Abstract

Indicative index contains the description of the document:

(a) It contains general statement of the nature and scope of the document excluding quality and quantitative data.

(b) It will be better or suitable if it covers in a single sentence or phrase, explaining the form of documents.

(c) It provides clues as to whether or not the information being sought.

(d) It should be used only for documents that do not embody information summarisation, explanation, bibliographies, symposium, proceedings, handbooks, reviews, and progress reports.

But in some cases, while dealing with subjects of considerable complexity, and in order to make the abstract meaningful; reference is made to some of the procedures, conclusions and results of more significant investigations.

2. Informative Abstract

It contains principal ideas, methods, arguments and data. It omits excess cordage and detailed explanation.

Such abstracts are used in information retrieval system, e.g. Chemical Abstract and Biological Abstract. Informative Abstract includes:

(a) Explanation of the nature of the document or micro-thought.

(b) Scope of the problem it deals or the situation of the thought contents.

(c) It contains objectives of investigations.

(d) It explains the account of the study or research methods.

(e) It gives an account of major findings or results, conclusions, and recommendations.

(f) It includes incidental information.

There are three types of Information Abstracts.

(i) *Mixed Abstract*

Mixed Abstract which are informative about some particular portion of the document, but indicate the other thought contents. They are usually used for document of mainly peripheral interest.

(ii) *Listing Abstract*

Listing abstract, as clear from its term, lists the contents of the documents. Such abstract covers the conference papers, conference proceedings in which the author or the writer contribute his paper individually. Listing abstract contains the author, title, page and the host documents.

(iii) *Critical Abstract*

It is an abstract in which the abstract functions as evaluator. It does not work as objective reporter and his opinions are excluded. But the function of abstractor is different in critical abstract. Here abstractor functions as a critic giving his opinion and evaluating the thought contents in the light of original thoughts of the author.

The value of critical abstract depends upon:

(a) Subject competence of the abstracts much more.

(b) Extra care has to be taken for the other type of abstracts, example, Applied Mechanics Review.

Comparison between Inductive and Informative Abstracts

	Inductive Abstract		*Informative Abstract*
1.	It is often little more than a broad statement of contents. It is also an extension of title of the original.	1.	Summarises all relevant arguments, data, methods, findings and conclusion.
2.	It discusses the original and is an extension of the library annotation.	2.	Summarises the original, comprising the information.
3.	It is presented in the passive form of the verb in order to reduce such constructions as the another fill than.......... and maintained in personality, present tense, discuss the article, which describes the research.	3.	It denotes 'ideal types' in practice. It is a matter of degree.

3. Expanded Title Abstract

A good title is often sufficient to indicate, particularly to the experienced reader, whether the paper is of interest. All such titles, which are supplement to other papers or which extend the scope of the other referred papers are listed in this abstract.

4. Summary or Synopsis Abstract

It is similar to the indicative abstract, though it is normally sufficiently long to give an outline of the whole of the work described. Many journals require author to write a summary of their papers.

5. Annotated Abstract

Sometimes some additional implications in title are needed, which indicate the nature and scope of the document. Such indicating phrases or sentences are called annotations. They are much shorter like those of digits.

Accession methods and records: Accession records the purpose of an accession's register so as to record officially the existence of books in the library stock, usually in the order in which they are added.

Provision is made for details of accession of number, cost, vendor or other sources, department or branch to which each item is disposed, and dates of addition, binding and withdrawal. Bibliographical details are reduced to a minimum. The accession register is widely used for analysis of statistics relating to expenditure in each main class or by departments.

The traditional ledger, so long used by public libraries, has largely given place to the loose-leaf book or card file. The whole process of accessioning has been so adapted by each library to its own particular circumstances that no single method is in general use. Efficiency requires that purely clerical processes be reduced as far as possible, and in some libraries it has been decided that the accession register can be abolished altogether.

The running number given to every book added to stock provides a link between the book itself and the bookseller's invoice. This may be necessary to satisfy auditors that books purchased have actually been added to stock. The accession number also serves to link the book with the catalogue (or shelf register) and the charging system, and distinguishes between copies of a book when there is more than one. A modification of the running number system is one whereby a separate sequence of numbers is kept for each main class (prefixed by a letter), the numbers being used again when books are withdrawn. The primary purpose of this method is to facilitate rapid stock-taking, but since books cannot be stocked in invoice order, the link between the accession number and invoice is lost and must be provided in some other way.

The application of punched cards to library routine has produced yet another form of accessions register. Libraries adopting this method use the actual punched card as a stock record wherein is provided numerical order the details of author and title, plus other information required for statistical purposes in coded form. A punching machine makes small holes in the cards correspondingly to their position to the figures required to be encoded. Other machines file batches of cards into numerical order, or make tabulations showing totals of expenditure by classes, or by any desired analysis.

The simplest accessions register is a file of invoices arranged in the order in which they were dealt with, each bearing a record or stock numbers allotted to the books listed on it. In practice, the library may be unable to retain the actual invoices, and copies would be used instead. The logical development of this method is the abolition even of this file, and the substitution of a record by invoice details and accession numbers used. In neither of these methods, however, is there adequate facility for statistical analysis. This must be done independently of the accessions record, either by hand or by punched cards. Once the required tabulations have been extracted the punched cards can be discarded.

Added Title Entry: In a book processing more than one title-page is complementary to the one chosen for the construction of the main catalogue entry. The added title-page may precede or follow the main title-page, and may be more general (e.g., a series title-page) or equally general (e.g., an engraved title-page or a title-page in another language).

The choice of title-page for the main entry transcript is governed by definite rulings in the chief western catalogue codes, which agree substantially:

(a) Where the title-pages are of different categories of generality, that is, which applies directly to the book being catalogued is used for the main entry transcript; the other(s) being given appropriate added entry (e.g. series entry) or mentioned in a note.

(b) When title-pages are equally general and in the same language the first is chosen when one follows the other, the second when they face each other.

(c) A printed title-page usually takes preference over the engrave one, and always when it bears a later date.

(d) If the title-pages are in different languages, and the text in but one language, that which is in the language of the text is preferred. When both title-pages and text are in more than one language, a title-page in the original language of the work is preferred.

(e) Where the preference above would lead to the choice of a language employing characters which cannot satisfactorily be reproduced, that in roman or gothic characters may be adopted.

Added (Class Index) Entry: An added entry in the classified catalogue is necessitated by a book dealing with two or more distinct subjects. The book itself may be filed at only one place on the shelves. Normally the classification number is for:

(a) The subject dealt with most fully, or

(b) That which comprises the largest portion of the book, or

(c) Where each is treated equally, the one which occurs first, or

(d) That which is most important to the particular library. The main entry for such a book is filed at the shelf classification numbers representing those subjects.

CCC: Entry other than the main entry.

DC: A work may also get more than one entry, such additional or added entries, as they are called, belong to one or the other three types (Subject Index Entry, Book Index Entry and C.R. Index Entry).

A secondary entry, i.e. any other than the main entry. Added entries may be made for editors, translators, titles, series, subjects, etc., and usually display less information than the main entry, sub-title, annotation and all or part of the imprint of collation being omitted. Where unit cards are used, an added entry is a duplicate of the main entry but with the addition of a special heading for editor, translator, etc., to be distinguished from a Reference.

AGROVOC: The thesaurus AGROVOC was jointly produced by FAO and Commission of European Committees. It is a controlled, structured vocabulary of agricultural technology. It is compiled according to guidelines for the establishment and the development of monolingual and multilingual thesauri in English, German, Italian, Portuguese and Arabic version. In fact, original AGROVOC was developed by European community software package called ASTUTE. INIS adopted AGROVOC as Thesaurus Maintenance system. FAO also adopted AGROVOC with 10,000 description in each language. After all word block developed, AGROVOC represents in each language a file of some 150,000 records.

AGROVOC used following relationship:

(a) Hierarchical relationship (BT and NT)

(b) Associate relationship (RT)

(c) Preferential relationship (USE & UF)

(d) Scope notes (SN)

(e) Scope Note Reference (SNR and SNF).

INIS modified the software and one language was adopted as principal language of maintenance. All changes in the hierarchy are defined in the principal language, the other language versions are adjusted automatically.

AGROVOC consists of four directly accessible disk files, which are the basis for all other files.

1. AGROVOC term—It is maintained in the Term File, a language indicator, the internal AGROVOC descriptor code and an indicator for descriptor or non-descriptor.
2. Descriptor Code—The Dictionary file is arranged by descriptor code and contains all first step relations for the terms, i.e. BTI, NTI, RT, used for scope note, references, etc.
3. Scope Note File—It is sorted by scope note codes and contains the text of a scope note in a fixed length field.

On-Line Project: Since 1975 onwards AGRIS, in cooperation with INIS, carried on-line sets. The necessary equipment was installed and tested for dial-up telephone users. Retrieval courses were held and manuals for retrieval were developed.

CD-ROM: AGRIS experts produced CD-ROM disk of AGRIS database. Two test disks were tested and started producing CD-ROM production disk using UNESCO's Micro CDs/ISIS.

AGRIS has contributed a lot in the field of Agriculture through its retrieval centres. AGRIS have developed fully computerized database of more than 2 million references and covered nearly 150 countries. It is publishing Agrindex.

Alphabetico Subject Catalogue: A catalogue of subject entries arranged alphabetically by subject heading, together with the necessary **see** and **see also** subject references. By the edition of author, title and series entries together with the necessary reference the alphabetical subject catalogue becomes a dictionary catalogue. The principle of specific entry is paramount in a construction, that is, each work entered under the heading algebra, not under a class heading Mathematics, nor under an indirect form of heading such as Science–Mathematics Algebra.

The chief advantage of this kind of catalogue is that single direct consultation under the name of any individual and distinct subject will reveal all the entries for works on the subject. However, such a catalogue will not easily enable an enquirer to survey all the entries for books within a large subject field or class.

In other words, we find all books on a particular subject as the entries are arranged alphabetically. This type of catalogue is useful because all books on a particular subject are put at one place. It uses verbal subject headings to enable readers to find material on broad and specific topics directly without reference to any index. It helps to collect material from different fields under a capital name, and it brings interrelationship together under names in dictionary catalogue. But, on the other hand, it has no index and there is no provision of alphabetization of whole collection.

Alphabetico Classed Catalogue: A catalogue of subject entries entered under class-subject-headings in the indirect form, e.g. Science-Mathematics-Algebra, or Art-Painting-Gouache. The catalogue is arranged primarily into broad subjects alphabetically arranged; these are sub-arranged into their subordinate subjects in alphabetical order, each of these being sub-arranged by specific topics arranged alphabetically.

It is a variety of subject catalogue. Entries are made under class headings and categories with sub-headings for divisions and sections are all arranged alphabetically. First of all entry are made under the name of subject. Specified subjects are grouped under the name of the class.

It was advocated that this kind of catalogue secured the advantages of both the classified and dictionary kinds by combining the systematic subordination of subject classes, sub-classes and topics with the simplicity of alphabetical arrangement that appears complex to the enquirer, whilst collection of related subjects is largely destroyed by the use of alphabetical sub-arrangement.

Such a hybrid kind of catalogue, although possibly of use with a small and largely static stock, is seldom seen nowadays.

Alphabetical Subject Index: An alphabetical list of all the subject named or dealt within a book, or in the schedules of classification scheme, or for which there are entries in a classified catalogue, together with reference to the place(s) where each subject occurs. Where the book, classification or catalogue is one in which each subject is treated in only one place together with all its aspects, subdivisions and relationships, a 'specific' index is possible, i.e. one which will normally need only a single reference under the subject name (or synonym) referring to that single place. The specific index is somewhat of a rarity, the most famous example in the field of librarianship being the index to the subject classification of James Duff Brown.

Most of the alphabetical subject indexs are 'relative' index indicating the relationship, aspect or subdivision of each subject treated in various places. This relationship is indicated by subject headings, e.g.

1. Book Index

Storage	
Archives	65-8
Cabinets	23-5
Maps	46-51
Newspapers	35-7

2. Classification index

Gratings	
Architectural constructions	721-87
Architectural design	729-387
Carved architecture	729-594

Alphabetisation: It means arranging entries alphabeticaly either letter by letter or word by word, in any script, viz. Roman, Devanagri, Persian etc. Canon of consistency should be followed throughout the filling of entry cards. Indian Standard Institute has although framed necessary rules for methods, Dr. S.R. Ranganathan has suggested 'Gestalt Alphabetisation'.

Alphabetisation is not a simple process. It is a complex process, though it follows the dictionary pattern.

Canon of Consistency: There should be consistency in the system adopted in arrangement of entries. Any change in mid of the arrangement or any change in rule of the work, if done, may create problems of tracing the required information in catalogue by the reader. Hence, whatever system is adopted, it should be consistent in nature. There should be no change in the system when already followed.

Necessity of arrangement: Filing of entries in proper arrangement is essential as it helps the readers in locating the book. Penumbral system or a proper system is followed whether dictionary or classified. All precautions should be taken in preparation of cards also so that no ambiguity should be involved in arrangement.

There are three methods of alphabetisation:

(a) Letter by letter

(b) Word by word

(c) Gestalt method

The letter by letter method is known as arrangement, while the word by word arrangement is also known as step-by-step arrangement.

For Classified Catalogue—A Classified Part

1. It depends on the scheme of classification.
2. Class number depends on leading section (main and cross-reference index entries).

Arrangement of value of digits

> → → . : ; , – a b – —   . ≠ 12 – 9A – Z ∠

Alphabetical part

(a) Arrangement strictly by alphabets

(b) No attention is paid to initial articles

(c) Scottish names arranged according to their apparent alphabetical make up.

Prefix Mac
Mc
ST

Superior comma in Scottish name, are to be ignored.

For details see: Letter by letter
Gestalt system
Word by word

Annotation: A note appended to the entry for a book in a catalogue, reading list, bibliography, etc., extending the formal description of the book, detailing its subject, scope, purpose and special features. Originally the term, as used by cataloguers, embraced all notes of any kind following the collation. Modern practice separates bibliographical notes as the fifth part of a main entry, the annotation proper forming the sixth and final section.

An annotation may be purely descriptive or critical. The former, also called characterization or analysis, comprises a factual description of the content of the book, adding information not revealed by the formal part of the entry. It concerns itself with detailing the following kinds of information:

The qualifications of the author or special experience affecting the books authority, the subject theme, theory, etc. and the particular aspect dealt with.

The method of treatment, level of treatment, and the degree of prior knowledge of the subject required by the reader.

The standpoint of the author, the purpose of the book, and the class of reader for whom it is intended.

The relation of the book to others by the same author or others on the same subject.

Critical annotation, called the evaluation or appraisal, states whether in the view of the annotator, the author has successfully accomplished his aim in writing the book, and involves a comparison of the thought content of the book with existing literature on the same subject in arriving at an estimate of the book's worth.

Whilst descriptive annotation is most often used in catalogues within the library, evaluation is nowadays chiefly used in book lists and similar material for use away from the library. S.R. Ranganathan categorised annotation of two types—Verbal Annotation and Pictorial Annotation. Broadly, annotations are of two types—Descriptive Annotation and Critical Annotation.

B

Bibliometrics: With the advancement of knowledge, published material is being produced in huge numbers, like books, periodicals, articles and increase in the number of collections and readers. It requires better management and serve to handle the large number. Ranganathan applied statistical calculus laws. He coined this name 'Librametry' in 1848 at the Aslib conference held in Leamington Spa. The discussion provided the base for calculating man-hours needed in that year for each item of work in the library. This helped to deduce a neat staff formula, which can be used for the determination of the strength of the staff in an objective and impersonal way.

Librametic studies can also help in the most judicious distribution of staff. The work of various sections vary and the work-load of the staff and provision of staff can be accordingly planned. Librametric can be applied for determining the optimum size of a service library, design of library building, size of reading books, helpful facet sequence through readers' queries, use of sampling techniques in listing the accuracy of cataloguing entries.

Biometrica, in concept manner, was being used before librametrics, in the name of statistical bibliography. Biometrica means 'the application of mathematics and statistical methods of books and other media of communication'. In other words, it is a quantitative treatment of the properties of recorded discourse pertaining to it.

Bradford has introduced the Law of Scattering (1934) distributing the articles on a subject in different periodicals. According to the formulation, if the total literature on a subject is contributed by 248 journals, they might be divided into a nucleus zone of 8 highly produced journals, a second zone 5 × 8 or 40 journals of moderate productivity. Each zone contributes about 200 to the total of 600 relevant papers on the subject. This was published in the documentation in 1948, analyzing the periodical literature of two subjects, geophysics and lubrication. If the resource periodicals are arranged in decreasing orders, three zones are created of these periodicals.

V.C. Vickery refined the Bradford's formula as:

$$T_2 : (T_{2x} - T_x) : (T_{3x} - T_{2x}) : : 1 : n : n^2$$

Originally this field of Bibliometrics has been characterized by researchers, mainly traditional librarians pursuing studies in this area in a limited domain, counting papers, journals, citations and concentrating on the parameter of information for publications with routine statistical applications. There has been a vast change in researches and main focus has occurred in search over the years. There are more researches coming in various disciplines and interdisciplines, like mathematics, sociology, psychology, science and technology studies etc. These non-informational parameters are human resources, financial resources, institutions and their relation with informational parameters.

Book Mobile Service: A service for providing library facilities to outlying stations particularly to rural community through mobile van which houses miniature library and is comparable to a part time branch library.

Many people of community may not attend the library regularly on account of their physical disability, lack of time and conveyance. The libraries must try to serve those who do not come to the library for these reasons. The travelling library supply books to the readers regularly.

The best way to extend book service to distant areas is to extend library services to far flung regions where it may not be possible to establish a permanent branch library. The mobile libraries provide services. We call such libraries as 'Library on Wheels' or the bibliobus or the book mobile.

Indeed, the travelling library play an important role in library extension work.

In fact, the mobile library system was first introduced at Baroda when Maharaja Shivajirao Gaikwad invited an American librarian to prepare a plan for rural libraries. Accordingly, rural area was served through mobile system. The other effort was made in Tanjore district when Dr. Ranganathan started rural library service through bullock carts. These bullock carts were used for carrying books to villages for distribution and return. This system was appreciated by all and later on converted to Mobile-Van library under Five-Year Plans. District libraries were established and they were given the responsibility to serve the rural areas. The district libraries were provided official vehicle as and when available. In some districts (M.P.) the Jeep of Inspector of School was given for 2-3 days a week for this purpose. In some states the country type vans were provided, though these vans were not manufactured for library purpose, but for all purposes. It was the effort to provide maximum service at lowest costs. There are instructions not to use such van for other than library purpose.

Delhi Public Library, established in 1952, aimed at providing library service to every corner of Delhi. It was aided by UNESCO. Special library vans were purchased. Library centres were established in every important place in Delhi and its surroundings. The mobile library service of Delhi Public Library is a model library service in India. It has more than 20 vans taking round of library service points of Delhi and providing library lending services regularly and efficiently.

Merits

1. Maximum use of library services at minimum cost.
2. Proper utilization of services will increase the membership.
3. People at long distances are served by mobile services.

4. The local people can suggest the new points of service.
5. Mobile van may be used for exhibition purpose in addition.
6. It encourages reading habits.
7. It saves time of the reader.
8. It is very economical to public.
9. It requires minimum number of library personnel.

C

Catalogue Code: A set of rules for the guidance of catalogues in establishing headings and preparing entries for a catalogue, sometimes including directions as to the filing and arrangement of these entries. The most important and easy code was British Museum Code of 91 rules adopted by the Trustees in 1839. There are few important catalogue codes introduced:

1839	British Museum Code-91 rules.
1852	Jewett, C.C. on the construction of catalogue of libraries.
1876	Cutter, C.A.: Rules for a printed dictionary catalogue and revised in 1889, 1891, and 1904.
1878	Cambridge University: Rules to be observed in forming the alphabetical catalogue of printed books.
1883	Library Association Cataloguing Rules.
1883	Dziatzkio, K. Instriction for doe Ordnung der Titel im alphabetischen Zettelkatalog der Koniglichen and universitiats Bibliothek zu Breslau.
1889	Delisle, L. Instruction elements et techniaues pour la misc et le maintien en order des livers d une bibliotheque.
1890	Linderfelt, K.A.: Eclectic and catalogue rules: Author and title entries.
1899	Prussia. Intruktionen fur dir alphabetischen kataloge der preuszischen Bibliotheken...

1905	Library of Congress: Supplementary rules on cataloguing.
1908	Library Association and American Library Association Cataloguing rules: Author and title entries.
1912	Association des bibliothecaires francais Regles et usages observes dans les principales bibliotheques de Paris....
1923	Bibliotheque Nationale, Usages suivis dans la redaction du catalogue geneerale des livres imprints.
1929	Association des bibliothècaires francais Regles generales.
1931	Vatican Library. Norme per il cataloga degli stampati.
1934	Ranganathan, S.R.: Classified Catalogue Code.
1936	British Museum Rules for compiling the catalogues of printed books, maps, and music.
1945	Ranganathan, S.R. Dictionary catalogue code.
1949	American Library Association (A.L.A.): Cataloguing rules for author and title entries.
1949	Library of Congress: Rules for descriptive cataloguing in the Library of Congress.
1978	Anglo American Cataloguing Rules: Rev. Ed. 2 in 1982.

CD-ROM: It is growing and advancing technology and holds great promise for libraries and as an alternative for both online database and printed sources. CD-ROM is an upcoming technology in the library world. CD-ROM has been built on the success of C.D. Philips and Soni, the companies that first exhibited CD-ROM players at COMPEX. Later Microsoft proclaimed the importance of CD-ROM produced by Library Corporation that contained MARC (Machine Readable Catalogue) record. CD-ROM stands for compact Disc-Read Only Memory. Both disc and drive are based on the computer audio consumer product.

The disc is 120 mm in diameter, single sides and holds upto 660 megabytes of data. One CD-ROM is equivalent to 10 computer magnetic tapes, hundreds of pages of microfitche or millions of pages of CD-ROM challenges current practices of publishing and intimating information in a fundamental way. Its highest storage capacity (200,000 pages of coded text) is major advantage. CD-ROM being based on CD-Audio disks are rugged, portable media and they are capable of being transported via postal services. It is being good for database in libraries particularly in Library of Congress.

CD-ROM contains pre-written data or programms stored in the memory by the manufacturer. The contents of such memory is permanent, i.e. non-erasable. However:

(a) The contents of memory is permanent.

(b) The memory is not erasable.

(c) User has no control on the contents of such memory.

(d) Such memory is suitable for publishing materials.

(e) It does not require input from the user.

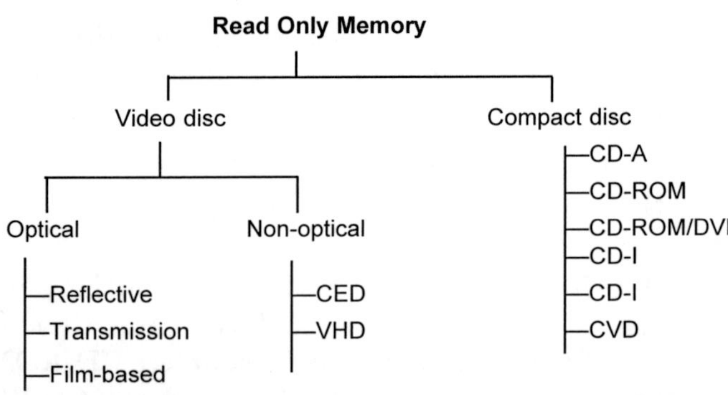

Video disc is synonymous with Laser Version and also loosely termed 'laser video disc' and is a generic term referring to different types of discs. These are manufactured according to different techniques and processes. A video disc is an optical disc which can store colour video pictures and two channel sound along with a spiral track.

Functions of CD-ROM

(i) The main task of the CD-ROM disk writers is the production of master copy from which CD-ROM are mass produced.

(ii) They provide software support to disk drives.

(iii) They allow quick search of databases in various forms.

At present, it is not possible to use the same CD-ROM drive with different softwares of different drives with the same software. This problem may be overcome, the software written for different database requires the use of different makes of drive. Thus, the CD-ROM technology has the problem of non-changeability and non-portability.

CD-ROM Services: Company Disk-Read Only Memory is better known as CD-ROM. It is a storage technology. It permits databases to be made available and searchable at local level. This facility was not available before the introduction of CD-ROM.

The storage technology:

(1) is centered around an optical memory disc.

(2) can store 500-600 mega byte of information.

(3) is not much expensive and available at local work-stations.

(4) builds file processing software at central location to structure the source data.

(5) builds indexes to data through file processing software.

File processing software is an important tool to access data. It prepares instructions to transfer that data to a master disk. Multiple copies of that disks can be prepared from a master disc by mass-production facilities. Such softwares are used with PC and a disc reader is to access and work with the indexes on the disc and to retrieve and display records retrieved from the disc. It works as with abstracting and indexing services. Updating is done monthly or less frequently.

The following equipment configurations are required to use CD-ROM along the lines of the packages:

(i) PC or PC-DOS version (equivalent to IBM PC) 2.0 or higher with 512K RAM.

(ii) Hard storage disc (at least 1.5 mega byte of free space).

(iii) CD-ROM reader with Microsoft extension software or reader.

(iv) A modem (capable for on-line searching).

A single disc has a storage capacity of a lot of data, each consisting of an entire encyclopedia or several years of abstracting and indexing services. Search software can be operated manually or by a command driven mode. The databases are constructed in an inverted file structure. CD-ROM speed is equivalent with on-line searching. The search software can save the search formula and apply it to the next disc of multi-disc database. The search on PC also makes possible to take the search results and use them for part processing programmes and also provide edited version for the user. CD-ROM products have been prepared for in-house use, but generally, widespread public use.

There are many types of CD-ROM for external and internal use particularly for publishing business and the holdings of libraries:

(i) MEDLINE, NTIS, ERIC—for abstracting and indexing services.

(ii) DISCLOSURE, LOTUS—for company financial data.

(iii) Dictionary, Directories, Encyclopedia.

(iv) UMI/INSPEC, ADONIS, PRAVDA—for full text publications.

(v) GEO disc—for illustrations.

Merits of SDI Services through CD-ROM and On-line Services

(i) They contain more information than available in print media.

(ii) Computer-based searching of a database (on-line or CD-ROM) can provide an answer that might not be found in a search of printed index.

(iii) It increases the productivity of a limited number of skilled professionals.

(iv) It is an effective means to search one or more databases and provide prompt and effective responses to a large numbers of queries.

(v) If there are not effective communications capabilities for administrative, financial and technical reasons, on-line searching capabilities can be provided by CD-ROM product. In this way, the users need not be deprived of access to a valuable information source.

(vi) CD-ROM products can be used to provide inexpensive tool for training people to use the counterpart on-line services.

CDS/ISIS: CDS/ISIS is a library software developed internally according to the local needs. It takes time and best suited to the individual library situation. But it may not be suitable to a library participating in a network. It is developed and distributed by NISSAT, India.

CDS is a menu-driven generalized information storage and retrieval system designed specially for the computerized management of structured textual non-numeric databases. A bibliographical database can be a library catalogue or database of dissertations and thesis, research papers, and conferences papers published in technical journals.

CDS/ISIS takes into consideration all the special characters of the bibliographic databases and caters to the specific requirements in its functions. CDS/ISIS remembers each database filed with its tag numbers which is a unique number value in the range of 1-32767 given by the user at the time of creation of database.

CDS/ISIS automatically creates a serial number to each database record as and when it is created. This number is called Master File Number (MFN) and can be used as a field of the record for all practical purposes.

CDS/ISIS allows to define databases containing the required data elements, entry, edit/modify records into the given database, creating and maintaining first access index files from the specialized fields and subfields, retrieve records from their contents through an efficient search language, display the records according to requirements, recalling of queries, their modification etc., sorting and printing the records in the order one wants, exchange the records with others by export / import utility of CDS/ISIS in ISO-2709 format.

CDS/ISIS has also been used as the platform for the development of useful utilities. For example ICRISAT has developed a general purpose programme for the production of SDI outputs based on stored user profiles for use with any CDS/ISIS database and also coordinated a project to produce 'Union Catalogue of Serials'. This is available on CDS/ISIS database. The IARC Union Catalogue as a CDS/ ISIS application has been distributed to more than 1200 agricultural and search centres worldwide.

Chain Indexing: Quality of indexing determine the quality of retrieval of information. Indexing involves mental processes to analyse a subject. The background of indexer and mental string, and users approach are the factors that help in subject determination. Quality of indexing tools available have their own importance in indexing operations. Indexing techniques and systems have tried to minimize the influence of these several factors by prescribing rules and regulations, providing guidance, establishing control and providing the indexer with authoritative indexing tools. It achieves the higher potency and consistency in indexing.

Subject approach to information has been an area of intense study and research for the last hundred years, resulting in the generation of new theories and design of the corresponding new indexing models. Subject indexing is an identification of ideas or concepts in documents and their representation in suitable language. It is usually a constrained language or a controlled language.

Controlled language is an artificial or natural language, e.g. list of subject headings or thesauri subject indexing is not an end in itself but a means to an end.

A semi-mechanical method of producing the requisite subject index entries for a classified catalogue is based on analysis of the classification symbol of each subject. The method was originated by S.R. Ranganathan, being first published in the Theory of Library Catalogue and subsequently modified in the second (1945) and third (1951) editions of his *Classified Catalogue Code.* Although it was originally intended for use with ease to any classification scheme whose notation symbols indicate the subordination at each step of division, and in adaptation for use with the Dewey Decimal Classification it has been demonstrated successfully by British National Bibliography since 1951.

The classification symbols for every specific subject represented by an entry in the classified catalogue is analysed as a series of classes subordinated successively from the main class to specific subject.

e.g. Outline of Sanskrit drama:

0	Literature
01	Indo-European
015	Sanskrit
015.2	Drama

Each member of the CHAIN provides an index entry. Two basic modifications enabling the method to be used with other classification schemes than the colon are, first, that intermediate steps in the CHAIN represented systems unlikely to be consulted are omitted entirely; second, that step produced by faulty subordination in the classification scheme is likewise omitted. These steps of the CHAIN are called respectively 'unsought links' and 'false links'.

Colon Classification (CC): It is an analytico-synthetic scheme. It is not enumerative. It does not enumerate or attempt to enumerate all possible classes in a single schedule as most schemes do. It confines enumeration to about 200 short, independent schedules. These occupy less than 150 pages, and yet the number of class numbers that can be constructed for use in book-classification is of the order of 10^{10} which is far more than in others. The thought content of the books classified gives the prescription. The schedules of connecting symbols and phase relations contain the adhesives and other neutral material needed to integrate the ingredients into a state of consistency. CC is also comparable to a Meccano set; the connecting symbols and the digits for phase relations are like its bolts and nuts.

CC conceive the designing and the applying of a scheme of classification involves work in three planes: Idea, notational and verbal plane. Class, class number and subject are corresponding or equivalent terms in these planes. Isolate is a generic term to denote an isolate or a class or any of its equivalents in the other planes. Facet is a generic term to denote the totality of isolates formed on the basis of a single train of characteristics germane to a basic class. It is also used to denote any single isolate or any basic class.

CC bases itself on a member of postulates, these are not taken from any metaphysical system. They are chosen only because: (i) They secure a more or less helpful sequence among the known classes of knowledge, (ii) They are of use in finding a more or less helpful place for a newly emerging class, among the already existing ones with little disturbance to their own established sequence, (iii) To make the scheme more or less self-perpetuating and this increases its expectation of life. Here are some important postulates as samples, with short annotations, for e.g. any class is either a main or a basic class forming a subject by itself; an integration of it with any number of isolates not capable of forming subjects by themselves; an integration of two or more classes, each of which becoming phases of the overall class.

Any facet or isolate is a manifestation of one of the five fundamental categories: Personality, Matter, Energy, Space and Time. The sequence in which that are mentioned above is the sequence of their decreasing concreteness. They are arranged in the same sequence in any class number.

To implement on the notational plane the above postulates of the idea plane, CC uses a mixed notation: (i) Roman lower case letter to denote phase relations, and for zone one, (ii) Packeted class numbers for zone two, (iii) Indo-Arabic numerals to denote geographical isolates and certain main classes, and for zone three, (iv) Roman capitals to denote chronological isolates and most of the main classes, and for zone four, (v) The digit as a non-significant octavizing digit to secure hospitality in array, (vi) Punctuation marks as connecting symbols, (vii) Local value of a digit as in decimal fraction to secure hospitality in chain, and (viii) The absolute values of digit in such a way that the species fall in ascending sequence as follows:

The procedure in CC is in seven steps: (i) Filling up ellipses in title or name of subject, (ii) Reduction to kernel terms, (iii) Analysis into phases, facets and zones, (iv) Transformation to suit the syntax of the classificatory language, (v) Standardization of the isolate numbers, and if the published schedule is inadequate, shapening foci, or adding foci, or facet according to prescribed rules, and (vi) synthesis of isolate numbers with the aid of connecting symbols.

Chief main classes: Z. Generalia — (1) Universe of Knowledge, (2) Library Science: (A) Natural Sciences, (B) Mathematical Sciences, Mathematics, Physical Sciences, (C) Physics, (D) Engineering, (E) Chemistry, (F) Technology, (G) Biological Sciences, (H) Geology, Mining, (I) Botany, (J) Agriculture, (K) Zoology and Animal Husbandry, (L) Medicine, (M) Useful Arts, Humanities and Social Sciences, Mysticism and Spiritual Experience, Humanities, (N) Fine Arts, (O) Literature, (P) Linguistics, (Q) Religion, (R) Philosophy, (S) Phychology, Social Sciences, (T) Education, (U) Geography, (V) History, (W) Political Science, (X) Economics, (Y) Sociology, and (Z) Law.

D

Database/Data Bank: The database concept is an advancement over the notion of an integrated set of files. The design of database provides table of description, interrelationship (structure) separate from the data (content), mechanisms for accessing the data elements and sets directly and indirectly via indexes, pointers, conversions, or computation, a capability for movement of individual data items or group from the associations in which they are stored to the associations in which it is processed back to the storages.

In many projects, the end-user has a new role, that of a designer or at least co-creater of databases. Mc Clelland investigated the probability of databases, i.e. capacity to transfer a complete database or a subset from one operating system to another without extensive programming or reloading of data. Mainframe computer, minicomputers and personal computers, optical storage devices (CD-ROM or WORM) are connected to computers and the users have passwords to access databases.

Database portability would diminish or minimize abstracts which prevent the most cost-effective use of storage and retrieval systems. For example, small database created on PC could not be transferred to a larger computer when the file becomes unmanageable: CD-ROM would require different search mechanisms from online supersets of the same files; user would have database.

Protection of integrity and security of data items or groups of data items, management control of usage, content structure and optimization data that represent the activity of the enterprise.

A necessary criterion in the creation of a database is that creators must agree on a common set of definitions for all informations in the database, which is not always practicable because of problems of the synonymous, alternative definitions and two different names used to describe different pieces of data with definitions. Hence, database designer should develop the complete dictionary of definitions. Data structure has a bearing in the determination of processing the data and the access procedures. There are two different approaches to accessing the data. These are sequential access organization and direct access. In sequential organization, records are located in sequence. Direct access permits the location of individual record without searching, but is less efficient for maintaining a file with high activity. The store media must be selected on the speed with which access to data is to be provided.

The majority of machine readable database store actual information rather than reference. There are known data bank that provides answers, facts and data in response to a query. The data bank store directory type of data pertaining to business economics, social sciences, education and science and technology. A guide to databases and data banks was first published in 1975 and is updated regularly. Information Directory published in USA in 1980 covers 1,280 database and data banks, of which 565 are bibliographical database and 715 are data banks.

Access to S & T Databases by scientists and engineers is provided through a variety of time sharing systems such as DELNET, MCI, TELNET, TAYMENT, and UNINET etc., and gateway services. The bulk of these database is available round the clock and everyday. Some databases are also available on CD-ROM.

DELNET: DELNET is one of the experiments that are now on-going in the country to network libraries in big metropolitan cities. DELNET will network thirty-five libraries in Delhi area. Participating libraries creating databases of their monograph and serials holdings using CDS/ISIS. All databases created co-operatively are expected to reside on a central computer system and dial up access is provided to all participating libraries. DELNET also is one of the initiatives taken by NISSAT and it was are a project of India International Centre, New Delhi. It is a registered society being promoted by National Informatics Centre, Planning Commission, Government of India and India International Centre, New Delhi. It is in operation since January 1988.

Objectives

1. It helps in promoting resource sharing by inter-library loan among the libraries in Delhi through computerized networking to effect maximum use of resources and offer better facilities for users.
2. Provides assistance to member libraries in cataloguing of books, serials, non-book materials and in cataloguing production.
3. It coordinates the efforts at collection development and ensure minimization of duplication.
4. It establishes referred centre to monitor and/or facilitates catalogue search and maintains a central on-line Union Catalogue of book, serials and non-book materials.
5. It promotes the delivery of documents manually or mechanically.
6. It develops databases of projects, specialists and institutions.
7. It maintains electronic and mechanical equipments and ensures for fast communication of information and delivery of electronic mail.
8. It coordinates with other regional, national and international networks for exchange of information and documents to the users.

Dictionary Catalogue: A catalogue of entries under authors, editors, translators, etc., titles, subjects forms and series which, together with the necessary references, are arranged in one general alphabetical sequence. It may be regarded as consisting of an author catalogue, a title catalogue, an alphabetical subject catalogue and a form catalogue consolidated in one alphabetical file.

A later development than the classified catalogue, in the 19th century, this form achieved a rapid acceptance particularly in the libraries of the United States, wherein 1876 Charles Ammi Cutter published the first edition of his *Rules for a Dictionary Catalogue*. This publication was the first to codify the principles of dictionary catalogue construction and offers rules for the making of every kind of entry, heading and reference necessary. These rules still form the basic code although later codes, notably the Vatican Library's *Rules for the Catalogue of Printed Books* (1st ed., 1930; 2nd ed., 1939) and S.R. Ranganathan's *Dictionary Catalogue Code* (1945) have modified certain rulings and methods.

No indexes are necessary to this catalogue since all kinds of entry are included in a single sequence, allowing direct consultation under any search factor relating to the required book. Ease of consultation is assured by the use of alphabetical arrangement, though the sub-arrangement under a subject heading or an author's name may vary from the strictly alphabetical order.

The success of Dictionary Catalogue in displaying a subject approach to the books catalogued depends largely on the care with which the subject headings (i.e. the terms expressing the subjects of the books catalogued, under which the relevant subject entries are filed) are chosen. The use of this principle in an alphabetical catalogue results often in the separation of entries for allied and related subjects, according to the initial letters of their names. The Dictionary Catalogue, therefore, incorporates a system of subject references which direct attention to the subject relationships and this syndetic apparatus is to some extent a substitute for the systematic arrangement of subjects provided by the Classified Catalogue.

In comparison to the fully-indexed Classified Catalogue, the Dictionary Catalogue is simpler to use, its arrangement being easier to understand and is more particularly suited to quick reference under specific subjects than systematic perusal of subject representation in the library's stock.

Divided Catalogue: It is a catalogue of a single library or collection, which is separated into two or more sequences. Principally applied to a dictionary catalogue, it is divided by the removal of subject and form entries together with their references, into an alphabetical subject catalogue and an author-title-series catalogue (but equally applicable to the classified catalogue—whose indexes or ancillary catalogues are always separate).

The principal advantage of the divided dictionary catalogue lies in the simplification of filing which often results. Fewer entries are involved in each section, long sequences under a subject heading no longer obtrude into the filing of other kinds of entry and filing problems, occasioned directly by the co-existence of subdivided subject headings and inverted subject headings with personal or corporate author headings and title entries are often eliminated for the same reasons. The process of consultation is often easier and faster. (Ency. Lib.)

Division: (a) The process of dividing classes of a classification scheme into smaller groups, i.e. dividing genus into species. (b) One of the above groups. In the **Decimal Classification** a division is subordinate to a main class and a section is subordinate to a division.

This nomenclature, although useful, is not universally accepted and parts of a division are often referred to as subdivisions.

Documentary Reproduction

Non-Photographic

One of the earliest methods of reproducing documents other than by printing was by the use of damp paper. A master was prepared by writing with a copying ink, and copies were produced by pressing the damped master in an iron press in contact with a think translucent paper. The copy was mirror-image and had to be read through the paper or with the aid of a mirror. But basically all methods fall into two categories—the optical, in which a camera is necessary, and the non-optical. Camera methods include the 'photostat' and similar process, and straightforward photography with a good camera. Microfilming and the production of microprint are camera methods. The 'Photostat' has after many years become a household word among librarians and readers, and is indiscriminately used in describing any photographic reproduction of a document. It is in fact a trade name, and a 'Photostat' copy of a document is one produced by the 'Photostat'. At the same time the image, which in normal photography, reversed is 'corrected' by the passage of the rays of light through a prism. The result is a right-reading copy, which, however, has a white-on-black appearance I place of the black-on-white of the original document. This copy may then be photographed to produce a facsimile of the original, but for most purposes the first print is reported. Later models of the photostat which was first introduced in the United States in 1907, automatically develop, wash and dry the prints. Reduced, enlarged or actual-sized prints may be made.

The reflex process is the oldest of all methods of documentary reproduction by photographic means. Successful results may be obtained with no more elaborate apparatus than a sheet of plane glass and an electric lamp, but there are now on the market many different makes of apparatus—some of them very expensive—which ensure perfection of results. Unfortunately, from the librarian's point of view, the librarian is faced with the problem of taking photocopies of pages in books of all sizes and thickness, and in volumes of periodicals where the inner margin of the text is close to the binding. He will find most of the models on the market unsatisfactory, however efficient they are for office use.

In a large library where photocopies are required in great numbers, the librarian may decide that the photostat or similar camera is the most efficient. Such cameras are expensive, and their purchase can only be justified in libraries where they would be in daily use in handling a considerable amount of material. The librarian of the smaller library must make other provision, and has a choice of several alternatives.

Documentation: The author has been unable to trace the first use of the word in its modern sense; it may perhaps be said to have come into being in 1930, when the **Bulletin of the International Institute of Bibliography** was resumed after a lapse of 16 years under the title **Documentation Universalis.** In 1934 Paul Otlet, co-founder with Henri La Fontaine of the **International Institute,** published his *Traite de Documentation.* The word had achieved a recognizable significance by 1937 when the **International Institute of Bibliography** changed its name to **International Federation of Documentation** (with headquarters at Hague) and extended its scope 'to include all aspects of the art of making information useful. Dr. S.C. Bradford (twin apostle with Professor A.F.C. Pollard of the Universal Decimal Classification in England) on pp. 101-2 in his book *Documentation* gives a schedule of the various headings under which documentation is practiced today.

The most authoritative definition of the word is that adopted by **Aslib** in 1945 for the *Journal of Documentation*, namely 'Recording, organization and dissemination of specialized knowledge'. Documentation does, in fact, embrace the whole gamut of operations from the discovery or creation of new knowledge, through its publication, analysis, classification and arrangement to its arrival at the user; that is to say report writing, publication, abstracting, classification indexing, reassembling, presentation and dissemination. While it emerged from librarianship and might be regarded as a part of librarianship in its widest sense, documentation is essentially different from librarianship in a professional sense: 'Documentalists differ from general librarians in that one basic qualification which is specialized knowledge at graduate level of the subject in which they organize their services, and that some of the techniques they use presuppose this qualification'.

Journals of abstracts were produced as the first solution, commencing in 1830 with the Pharmaceutisches Centralblatt (now Chemisches Zentralblatt); these cover fields of knowledge, both broad and narrow, and still constitute a valuable tool in the documentalists' equipment. But the ever-increasing outpouring of information made it necessary to supplement these publications by specialists searchers to serve special interests. Documentation in its present form came into being to serve research establishments particularly in the applied sciences. This type of service has spread into other fields and is employed widely by industry and various organizations in subjects such as administration, social sciences, market research, production engineering, town planning etc. This was followed in 1958 by a similar conference in Washington. The recognition of the new profession in this country was marked by the formation of **Aslib** in 1924 to provide a forum for members to discuss their problems; with its amalgamation in 1948 with the **British Society for International Bibliography, Aslib** became the national representative body of the **International Federation of Documentation.** The attention of the scientific world was drawn to the profession by the highly successful **Conference on Scientific Information**, organized by **The Royal Society** in 1948. The reports and papers 4 & 5 of these conferences constitute a most valuable assembly of knowledge of the problems and techniques of documentation.

Considerable trouble has been taken in developing and standardizing the Universal Decimal Classification so as to facilitate the handling of information exchanged among many centres. The use of microfilm, micro-card and other methods of reproduction have been studied to facilitate ready exchange and dissemination of information. Mechanization of subject indexes and rapid selection devices are constantly under review for the more efficient assembly of information. (Ency. Lib.)

E

Electronic-Mail (E-Mail): Electronic-mail is a means of sending information via a computer-based network between addressed computer workstations. It is available on national and international basis. It is a logical extension of the familiar telex service, with the exception that the destination and original points are no longer centralized in a single physical location within an institute.

Electronic mail user codes (or addresses) can be assigned to individual and are not tied to a physical location. A user on a trip could log on to the E-mail service from several different locations on the trip at any time of the day, and send messages to others and retrieve message that had accumulated since the last log on.

E-mail as Broadcast Message: Current E-mail services can simultaneously broadcast messages to a specified list of addresses. They can also support 'Bulletin Boards' where any interested reader can post a message or respond to an issue. E-mail services can be used to forward copies of receiving mail to other parties.

Merits:

1. It enables all users to transmit and receive mail.
2. The mail service has been custom designed taking into consideration the network architecture and operation environment.
3. It provides an individual service with certain privacy measures.
4. It provides broadcasting and bulletin service.

5. In bulletin service, it provides personal, employment and transport information especially for NIC officers to plan their visit to the headquarters.
6. The transport bulletin service will contain reservation availability for all the trains from Delhi.
7. It is less expensive alternative to telex for international messages.
8. It can be effectively integrated with PC word processing and modem software.
9. It can be used by the institutions that has regular and continuous communication with institutions outside the country.
10. It is time saving than cable or telex.
11. It is almost possible to carry on a conversation by E-mail without taking note of often higher cost associated with a telephone call.
12. It facilitates and speed up document delivery services.
13. This is a very fast way to order publications and useful to librarians.
14. Retrieval citations (on-line search) can easily be forwarded by E-mail to a document delivery service chosen by the searcher.

Encyclopedia Britannica: A new survey of universal knowledge, Chicago, *Encyclopedia Britannica* has been continuously reprinted and revised. It is one of the oldest and most popular English language encyclopedia. A comprehensive index has been provided in a bold face capital letters and the portion of articles covered within the main articles are provided in light face in capital and small letters.

Encyclopedia Britannica was first published in 1770-71 although the publication started in 1768 in 3 volumes. It was published by Encyclopedia Britannica Incorporation, Edinburgh (UK) under the title *Dictionary of the Arts and Science*. The first edition was published by the "Society of Gentleman". The second edition was published in

10 volumes in 1977-80, while the 3rd ed. in 1810 in 20 volumes. In 1899 its authority was taken by M/s Hooper and Jackson and its control change from Britain to America. Its diamond jublee was celebrated in 1968 after the completion of 200 years; 15th ed. was published in 1974.

It is divided in 3 parts:

Vol. 1-12	:	Micropaedia
Vol. 13-31	:	Macropaedia
Vol. 32	:	Propaedia
INDEX	:	In two parts A-K and L-Z.

Micropeadia includes brief factual information. Macropeadia provides knowledge in depth to perform educational functions. Propeadia gives outlines of knowledge and guide to this set.

Since 1938 it is published yearly. It covers 24 major categories of knowledge from an anthology to 24 miscellaneous categories. It is alphabetically arranged and organized. Entry title are in alphabetical manner, i.e. A-Z. Other marks are avoided.

Abridgment: A shortened or curtailed version of a book, retaining the essential character and theme of the original, an epitome. Such books may no doubt miss many informations which are important for few readers, but these are used by small group and have limited scope. Example: There are abridged editions of dictionaries, and also Dewey Decimal Classifications.

Abstract: A brief summary that gives the essential points of a book, pamphlet or article. Abstracting is a brief statement of the essential contents of the original or an indication of the characteristic of pamphlet or article of the original with bibliographical details. An abstract is a condensation that presents succinctly, the objectives, scope, and findings of a document.

F

FID: It is known as International Federation of Documentation/ Federation International-de Documentation. It is situated in Hague. It was founded by Paul Outlet and Henri La Fountain in Brussels in 1895. In 1924 statutes revised and in 1938 it was named as FID under the sponsorship of UNESCO with its General Secretary F. Donkar Knyvis. A conference at Brussells was organized in 1955 to formulate the FID frame. It has 21 members states (16 Europeans, 3 Asians, 1 African and 1 American). Membership increased up to 85 in 1989. It is managed by at Active Council, Executive Committee and nine study committees. Membership is for individuals, document organizations, research councils and one national member from one country. The important publications are *International Forum* from one country. The important publications are *International Forum on Information and Documentation* (quarterly), *R&D Projects in Documentation and Librarianship* (bi-monthly), and *FID News Bulletin* (monthly).

FID performs many functions—coordination on an international level of document activities, classification research and standardization of classification terms, revision of Universal Decimal Classification, promotion of training of documentalists, providing assistance in creating national information and documentation services in developing countries, and to facilitate the exchange of information in member states.

There are few committees which carried the activities of FID:

1. FID/RI – The study committee which prepare an international source of scientific information terms.
2. FID/CR – Classification Research Committee
3. FID/CCC – Central Classification Committee
4. FID/LD – Linguistics in Documentation Committee
5. FID/TM – Machine Technique Committee
6. FID/DM – Operation Machine Techniques and Systems.

In sum, FID has acted as catalyst for cooperation of national and international activities.

Film Library and Librarianship: There are two types of libraries and it is important to distinguish between them. Firstly, there are libraries which are associated with film production and are referred to as a stock-shot library, or sometimes as a film archive. Secondly, there is a library concerned with film distribution and here the term used is film library. The two types will be considered separately here as although they are occasionally combined, the work of each is in fact quite different.

Stock-shot Library is a library in which any film unit exposes a great deal more negative than it used in the final film. Some of them unused, may be of value for subsequent film production. A film unit of average size may produce many hundred shots of this nature a year, and with larger unit and feature film organizations the number will run into thousands. It is a clear problem of library organization to arrange this material and compile the index to it so that it can be referred to again. Film libraries are now to be found attached to feature film companies, documentary film units and news reel companies and the library staff in each case work closely with the members of the unit concerned. They may participate in discussions about a film, in form, its script and in detailed editing so that at all stages the resources of the archive can be fully utilized. For example, a script may call for Egyptian marker scenes; the library may have a number of Moroccan market scene. By slight rearrangement of the script it may be possible to use the latter and spare the expense of speal shooting. Such advantages can be gained only if the library is consulted at all stages.

A sound library can be of great value. Sound can be stored on film, magnetic tape or disc and the library principles involved are similar in all cases. These points are dealt with under sound libraries. **Film Libraries** are quite separate with Public Libraries. Few State libraries and the National libraries have separate section in their libraries. In India Film Institute, Pune has a big and specialized library. Similarly, All India Radio and T.V. Centre have film libraries. Many important Film Studios & Productions have their separate film libraries. Films, like books, deteriorate with use. A book in bad condition may be usable, but a bad copy of a film will not be readily tolerated by a film audience. Libraries issuing bad copies will soon find their loans dropping. It is important, therefore, to check each copies of films for scratches, tears, sprocket hole damage and so on. Hence, an examining section forms an integral part of a film-lending service. It is the channel through which all films are returned and if the library is to maintain its reputation for good quality prints, an efficient examining section is essential.

Film libraries do not have standard methods of procedure although the copies of films are usually given a running serial number to simplify filing and locating copies. Accurate records must be kept of all bookings and confirmation notices as the dispatch note even if a charge is made as an invoice.

The catalogue is extremely important for it is the main link between the library and its borrowers. However, it should not be the only link. Advertising the existence of the library is appropriate. Periodicals will also stimulate enquiries, many of which can be answered at least in part by sending a copy of the catalogue. Direct approaches can be made to persons and organizations likely to be interested in borrowing the films and special subject lists can be compiled if the library is large enough. All steps must be taken to promote the use of film library. But behind the promotion there must be a reliable distribution service supplying good quality prints of the right films in the right place at the right time.

Five Fundamental Categories: Dr. S.R. Ranganathan divided the universe of knowledge in main classes and canonical classes and each class is divided by more than one train of characteristics. Each train of characteristics give rise to one facet of the universe. These facets in the field of knowledge are manifestations of five fundamental categories—Time, Space, Energy, Matter and Personality. These five fundamental categories are symbolized as 'P' for personality, 'M' for Matter, 'E' for Energy, 'S' for Space and 'T' for Time in colon classification.

But the problem remain in deciding which characteristic should be chosen first for the division of genus into species and which one should come next. All characteristics chosen as the basis of division are related to five fundamental concepts which he calls Personality, Matter, Energy, Space and Time. They are arranged in the same sequence in any class number.

In fact the classifier should be able to relate each division of the appropriate fundamental category. Ranganathan terms this order as the Principle of Inversion. Any order of increasing concreteness is considered as a helpful order since it reflects a very common approach to the study of subjects and to the searching for these in a classification. But the problem of order in array remains.

The entire process of determining the facts of a subject is known as Facet Analysis. Firstly, while dividing a subject we break it into different facets and mention therein all possible entities. Secondly, when we have to classify a document, we examine that the entities belong to knowledge classification.

Five Laws of Library Science: Dr. S.R. Ranganathan enunciated the normative principles known as Five Laws of Library Science. They form foundation of library science and for all kinds of library work. These laws are:

(1) Books/Documents are for use,

(2) Every reader has book/document,

(3) Every book/document has its reader,

(4) Save the time of the reader/user,

(5) A library is a growing organism.

It is a fact that books implied knowledge is to be distributed. It is possible when books are used. In ancient period libraries were open for public. In medieval periods books were collected and kept under safe custody thereby establishing monopoly of learning of a small community. In modern times books are made free to all and leading services have been started. The first law says that books are not to shelved but to be used freely by all without any difference of cast and creed. The second law is from the side of the readers/ users of books. The second law plans new libraries containing collections that give information. Books being the tools of education, the law lays that every reader should have his book. The second law presupposes the concept—education for every person. Varied are the requirements of readers and as such, there are obligations involved in an undertaking to provide every person his book. Such obligations are government, finance, legislation, coordination and also choice of book and choice of staff. If all factors are supporting, it is possible that every reader will get his book.

The third law literally means that an appropriate reader should be found for every book. The most satisfying media is the open access system. The other device is self-arrangement, catalogue entries, reference services, opening of certain departments, publicity methods and extension work. In addition to this, the library staff would be required personally to help readers, in the proper use of catalogue and reference tools. Mechanised devices and direct contact would be necessary.

Library systems and procedures should be simple and moderate and easily understandable to the readers so that library services may be provided promptly as it will save the time of the readers, for e.g. open self system, mechanized methods and efficient and skilled professionals save the time of the readers.

Library is a growing organism. Library always grows with the growth in collection, staff and building. It is a continuous process. The realistic attitude in planning and organization, which stipulates a provision for future extension commensurate with its growth. Readers at all levels, using different types of libraries are on the increase, which increase the size of reading room, holding sections, staff and books and other reading material.

Floor and Flooring: The quality needed in floors are that they should be: (a) pleasant in appearance, (b) durable, (c) non-slippery, (d) easy to clean, (e) warm, (f) soft, and (g) (for reading rooms) quiet. At the same time it should not be too expensive. It is only by weighing up these eight qualities that a floor can be properly judged. There is probably no material which fulfils them all. Wood, which may be laid in strips, or in blocks, usually has qualities cited above. However, these qualities depend on method of fixing, polish, wood blocks and wood boards. Cork tiles are recommended for reading books. They are more expensive than wood, but still a medium priced material. They are, however, not suited for very large use. Plastic tiles, a recent material, e.g. 'vinyl', 'acotile' etc., are available in many colours and fulfil qualities, but two of these are inclined to be slippery, cold, hard, noisy, although some of these qualities are now being improved. They cannot be recommended for reading rooms, but may be used for entrance halls. Much the same applies to glass tiles and clay tiles, though these are harder and colder. Terazzo, gralithic and other store composition floors are liable to crack, and are cold, hard and noisy and hence inappropriate for many usages. They are durable, and suitable only for corridors, entrance halls, etc. Linoleum, as a floor covering, is recommended for its qualities, even if not highly polished. It needs to be cleaned with soap and water, and treated with linseed oil. Rubber as linolium is used as floor covering. It has to be cleaned with soap and water, and treated with linseed oil. However, it is considered one of the best materials. It certainly has all the qualities. Carpets have qualities but are not durable and are difficult to be cleaned besides being very expensive. Their sole purpose seems to be as a mark of distinction for the offices of higher ranking librarians.

G

Gestalt Alphabetisation: This system is devised by Dr. S.R. Ranganathan. Ranganathan has shown the following ascending scale of ordinal value in arranging the entries in the alphabetical order:

1. Section space
2. Full stop
3. Comma
4. Numerals in their natural sequence
5. Bracket
6. Words in Roman
7. Words in Italics or underlined
8. The word 'and' or its substitute semicolon.
7. Others

Abandonment of the Rule of "Nothing before something":

1. Uncertainty and inconsistency in the name of the author.
2. Variations in use of space and hyphen between these names:

Examples: Sivashankarnarayan
Siva-Shankar-Narayan
Siva Shankar Narayana

3. In Gestalt alphabetisation, space between words, variations in script, type of letters or digits are ignored.

But in Gestalt alphabetisation ordinal value of 'Word space' and type of letters (capital, small, italics) are given:

Example:

1. CAMBRIDGE
   Their hundred year progress
2. CAMBRIDGE
   See also
   Cambridge
3. CAMBRIDGE, BIBLIOGRAPHY
4. CAMBRIDGE, EDUCATION COMMITTEE
5. CAMBRIDGE Psend
6. CAMBRIDGE (City)
7. CAMBRIDGE (John), DRAMA
8. CAMBRIDGE (John), Tr.
9. CAMBRIDGE (John) and ROSS (EB).

I

International Standard Book Numbering System (ISBN): This system was first introduced by the British book trade in 1967. Its main objective is to simplify billing, inventory control warehousing and royalty accounting operations not only in inter-firm but also with the libraries. British Standard Institution approved and finally issued the standard and 'BS 4762: 1971'. British National Bibliography used to mention these. SBN corresponding to the title entered therein. The growing use of computer did accelerate the adoption of a system similar to ISBN and hence we have ISBI. About 20 countries have adopted the scheme and are operating their own National Book Numbering Agencies.

ISI in collaboration with the ISBN agency compiled and issued a standard guide on the system entitled "IS:8310-1977/Guide to Standard Book numbering in 1977. An ISBN is represented by ten digits. It is divided into four distinct parts, e.g. group identification, title identifier, check digits and publisher identifier. The first part is allocated by the ISBN agency (e.g. 0=United Kingdom/USA, 3=Germany, 81 = India, etc.). The national/regional agencies usually allocate the suitable digit/block of digits representing the second part or the publisher. The publisher assigns digits of the third part of the title, the total of these two part is always 8 digits. The last and the fourth part, which consists of the tenth digit is called the check digit. It is a measure against the mistake that may arise due to the incorrect transcription. It is calculated on the modules of "(i.e. 11) with eights 10 to 2 from left to right." Each digit is multiplied by their respective weights than added and finally divided by 11. Now the remainder is substracted from 11 to get the check digit, which always lies between '0' to '9' (i.e. 0<check digit<10). When the result comes out 10, then only it is represented by 'X' and in all other cases (i.e. from '0' to '9') the same is represented by the digit itself.

ISBN is displayed by printing the set of digits representing it, on the verso of the title page, foot of the back cover and also at the same place on the jacket, preceded by the letters 'ISBN' and each part is hyphenated or letter spaced, e.g. ISBN 0-07-026814-2 or ISBN-0910608 33 4. This number is also included in the cataloguing in publication data (CIP) or any other commercially produced catalogue cards as well as on all the publicity materials, viz. trade catalogues, pamphlets etc.

Imprint: Imprint is publishers' statement which includes: (1) the place of publication of a book, publisher's and/or printer's name, and publication date, usually printed at the foot of the title-page of a modern book. Before the separation of the businesses of printing and publishing, the term applied only to the printer's name and place of business, normally forming part of the colophon. (2) A catalogue entry giving the publication details as follows:

(a) Place of publication

(b) Publisher's name

(c) Publication date

For example, Delhi: Metropolitan Co., 1973.

Ranganathan defined imprint as a record, in a document or a volume of it, of the name(s) of its publisher(s), of the name(s) of the place(s) of its publication, and of the year of the publication. CCC has not made provision of imprint as entry element. According to Dr. Ranganathan, imprint is generally not demanded by the readers. In exceptional cases such information may be provided by accession register. In AACR-II, imprint area is used to record all information about the place, name, and date of all types of publishing, distributing, releasing and issuing activities. Information relating to the manufacture of the item is also recorded in this area (AACR, 1.4 A-B). This information is taken from the chief source of information or from any other source specified for this area. Information supplied from any other source is enclosed in square brackets. If the publication, distribution and other details appear in more than one language or script, the record of such details are kept in language or script of the title proper; if this criteria does not apply, the details that appears first are recorded.

Imprint Date: It indicates the year of publication as specified on the title-page or publisher's statement. It does not necessarily give the actual date of publication owing to the trade custom of pre-dating, e.g. autumn books.

It is record of the name(s), of its publisher(s), of the name(s) of the place(s) of its publication, and of the year of publication in a document or a volume of it.

In CCC imprint date is omitted. S.R. Ranganathan has not given any weightage to it as it never attracts the reader directly for information. In CCC it is contained in call number. It is left to a local code to prescribe the edition of the year of publication as an additional sentence at the end of the title section either when the call number does not indicate the year of publication or in all cases.

In AACR there is a provision of separate mention of imprint date as a part of Imprint Section (Publication statement). Imprint date is preceded by a fullstop and a dash and followed by a colon and then the name of publisher.

Indexing of Books and Periodicals: The tendency to index books and periodicals has always existed, but in most cases what has been produced has proved inadequate for the purpose. The index has taken various forms at different times; not all of these are readily recognizable as types of index though they are undoubtedly intended to fulfill that function. Thus, the chapter headings in early books and manuscripts, the illuminated initials (particularly those which illustrate relevant scenes in the text) and the line of contents all played their part in enabling readers to find their way quickly about the books they used. The development of counter lists was especially favoured as a means of quick reference. For instance, in 18th Century volumes of the Statutes these lists run to several pages of great detail. Even earlier examples are known: Thus, a 1640 book on arithmetic and geometry has a 14-page Index capitum in which the chapter headings and those of the sections of this 440 page volume are set out in the order of the text. A 1635 book on theological matters had an alphabetical index rerum et. verborum, but the alphabetisation is correct only to the first four letters of each word, though such words as in, non, bene, ad, etc., are ignored when used initially. Another system which proved very popular was the use of inset—or even marginal—paragraph headings, which even after the evolving of the modern alphabetical index has survived in some works with exceptionally long chapters. The evolution of the alphabetical index has been slow to reach any effective form: at first the tendency was to index names and occurrences rather than ideas which, of course, are more difficult to define. Also the concept of the choice of the significant word for entry came very late, just as the system of ignoring definite and indefinite articles as entry words are yet to be universally accepted.

The contemporary aim in indexing is to ensure that everything which can possibly be regarded as useful is indexed if space allows. Thus, a modern book may well include index entries for illustrations, matters mentioned in forewords and appendices etc. In the case of periodicals it is usual to omit advertisement, brief new paragraph and such features as minor correspondence. The ideal is to make entries not only for proper names, places, events and other easily-identifiable points of this type, but also for subjects and ideas treated in the text. This is one of the most difficult aspects of indexing and is therefore one which is most often shirked: thus many periodicals issue so-called indexes which are nothing more than simple contents-lists rearranged in alphabetical order. Others purport to provide sound indexes but in fact ignore almost everything but proper names: a philosophical idea, a spiritual development or a difficult technical process are omitted. Indexing of this kind is rife today and involves a vast amount of time and money to trace material which has not been indexed.

The standard index entry describes its subject accurately, briefly and under the initial heading where the majority of people seeking it will most naturally look. Against this heading appears all the page references where information on the subject is to be found; if there are many of these, they are subdivided according to period, aspect or evolution, so that the right place can be found without delay.

Even now the average index is only approximate in its references: few indexes refer to more than the page, though some encyclopedias refer to an approximate position on the page and concordances and edited texts usually refer to numbered lines. Atlases are more efficient in this since they give references to both latitude and longitude. The numbering of paragraphs is occasionally used as an aid, but this rarely occurs outside scientific and technical works.

No speedy method has been discovered by which indexes can be constructed: each indexer has his favourite method, and it is not possible to say that one of these is best in all circumstances. Making the index entries on slips or thin cards is probably the most popular, the slips being 5″ × 3″, although many indexers prefer larger slips (8″ × 5″) or long narrow slips (3″ × 2″). A separate slip is made for each heading, references are entered on them and when the indexing is complete, the slips are sorted into alphabetical order and the entries edited: this involves the amalgamation of entries under headings, the elimination of inconsistencies and the checking of references and cross-references. A good index is a complete analysis of the book, in which each entry is related to similar subjects; the evolution of thought is properly demonstrated and no significant idea or fact is left unmentioned. Other systems of indexing include making entries on sheets of perforated paper, the strips being subsequently separated and treated as above: this method is particularly suitable for typewritten entries. Some indexers use gummed strips of paper which can be sorted and mounted in correct order on backing sheets, thus eliminating the necessity for re-typing.

Indian Library Association (ILA): ILA was founded on 12 Sept. 1933 during the course of the conference which was inaugurated by J. Leitch Wilson, the then Education Commissioner, Govt. of India, and held in Asiatic Society Hall in Calcutta. Founder members are K.M. Abdullah, S.R. Ranganathan, Kumar Munindra Deb Rai Maharaja, R.V. Sabnis, S. Basiruddin, Labhu Ram, G.S. Mishra, M.O. Thomas, T.A. Chapman and Justice Sir Abdul Qadir ILA organize national conference every year at different places of India. Various library problems and development planning is discussed in conferences and Govt. of India is persuaded for making rules, providing adequate budget and increasing the status of library and librarian. The Indian library association is now the apex body of the profession and includes in its fold, librarians of all types of libraries interested in organization and promotion of libraries. It works through its council, executive committee and thirteen sectional committees. Association publishes a quarterly journal called *ILA Bulletin* on symposia, seminar and conventional proceedings. It celebrates the 'Library Week' on 14th November every year. It organizes Annual ILA conference every year in Jan.-Feb. and conduct the elections after every two years.

Indian National Library: Its genesis can be traced to the Calcutta Public Library founded in Aug. 1935 at the public meeting presided by Sri John Peter Grant, a judge of Supreme Court. J.H. Stocqueter, editor of *Englishman*, was its first secretary with 24 members of management. The nucleus of the library was formed by private donations and by the transfer of 4,675 volumes from the Fort William College. The library was opened to the public on March 21, 1836. Lord Curzon declared it Imperial Library by amalgamating Calcutta Public Library by purchasing its assets and rights of its proprietors. It was set up on the line of the British Museum.

After Independence the Govt. of India declared it as National Library in 1947. J.A. Chapman was the first librarian from

1910-1930. Delivery of Book Act passed in 1954 by which four copies of each book published in/for India will be sent to National Library. V.S. Kesavan was first librarian after independence. INL launched Indian National Bibliography in 1958. It is housed in Belvedere building. It has special private collection like Jadunath Shankar collection, S.N. Sen collection on history, Bukar collection of Arabic and Persian material, Vaiyupuri Pillai collection in Tamil, the Sapru papers of Tej Bahadur Sapru. This library has a collection of more than 25 lakh books—4 lakh books in Indian languages, 7 lakh under Delivery Act, Indian Official Publication 4.5 lakh, 4.5 lakh gifts, manuscript 4.5 thousand, maps 1 lakh, current periodical 24,000 and bound volumes 120,000. The library is open on 362 days in a year. It is one of the four depository libraries under Delivery of Books and Newspaper Act 1954, amended in 1956. Other three libraries are Carnemera Public Library, Madras; the Central Library, Bombay; and Delhi Public Library, Delhi.

Information Retrieval: Information is a communication channel and retrieval is the operation by which documentations are selected, information called in response to search questions. Catalogue, mechanic selector or electronic data process of information is a retrieval device. Information retrieval system represents a requisition, including organization of files, question of handling (search methods) and dissemination.

Current awareness service is one of the aspects of information science activities. It is a direct link between the user and the communicator through communication system or communication devices. CAS (Current Awareness Service) involves time lag information that should reach the user as soon as possible. CAS can be divided into two categories, SDI services and SPEED services. CAS is given through conventional sources (books, catalogue, abstracting and indexing), CA tools like CA lists prepared by international agencies, professional organizations, research institutions; important lists that are current contents; chemical abstract service, current chemical papers and local current awareness lists.

Information scientists keep in touch with users and review their needs time to time. User is the one who uses information. Its demand may be the demand for specific documents, demand for specific data, retrospective search, current awareness demands, demand for exhaustive search. User's survey is conducted to know the user's demand through survey technique, questionnaires, interview schedule, observation method, diary method, by general survey, specialized direct and indirect survey, sample survey, primary and secondary survey, postal survey and Ad-hoc survey.

National information system has been initiated to share the nationwide resources, and development to fulfill all information-requirements of users of all levels. It may be National Information System, State Information System and Local Information System like—NISSAT, INSDOC, VINITY, FID, IFLA etc.

Information Science: Information is a shape of behaviour, voice and language. There are three sources of communication: expressions, voice and languages. Written communication is called information sources, and where information is communicated to the needy persons in systematic way it is called Information Science. It is a process in which both the factors physical and social, are involved. Information cannot be effective unless it is communicated to others. It is an interdisciplinary science. Georgia Institute of Technology in its conference in 1961 rejected the term 'Documentation' and adopted 'Information Science Retrieval System'.

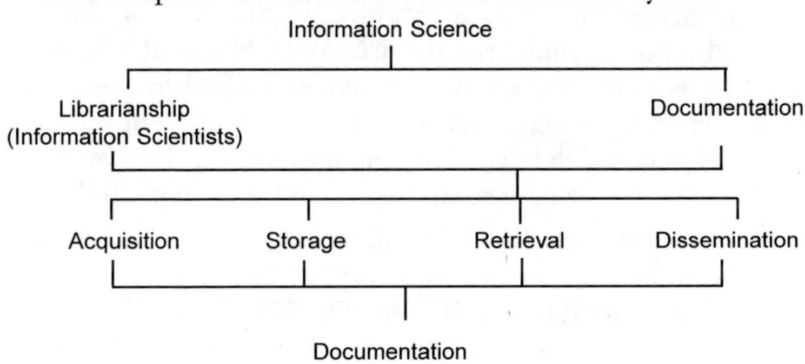

Information science is a new scientific discipline which concerns with the study of properties of information for optimum accessibility and usability. "Information Science is a multi-discipline science which includes maths, logic, language, operational research, management studies and librarianship. Mezal in his survey divided the study of information into three categories—communication behaviour studies, use of communication medium (use studies) and flow of information. There are various approaches to information like current approach (periodicals, abstracts etc.), every day approach (data, method, formula), exhaustive approach, catching up approach (specific subject area), and information survey techniques.

Information System—Automation: The first step in the world of library automation has been taken as the special libraries of the country. These libraries/documentation centres are the R&D institutions under the Council of Scientific and Industrial Research, Indian Council of Medical Research (ICMR), Indian Council for Agricultural Research (ICAR) or the Defence Research and Development Organisation (DRDO), Notable libraries belonging to the private sector and public sector, industrial R&D organizations such as BHEL, R&D and Steel Authority of India (SAIL) and other international organizations like International Crops Research Institute for Semi-arid Tropics. These libraries were supported by the Department of Scientific and Industrial Research (DSIR) by extending Sectoral Information Centres established in some of the CSIR laboratories under the auspices of the National Information System for Science and Technology. NISSAT has also funded several training programmes and software development projects which have played an important role in improving awareness of new technologies and their potential.

During the last five years library automation software has been developed in various ways and spheres. Some special libraries notably at BHEL, R&D, SAIL, ICRISAT, INSDOC, NIC, Defence Science Information & Documentation Centre

(DESIDOC), IIT, Kanpur, have successfully developed software for library automation. These centres have concentrated on applications in their specific environments, and there they pay off in terms of better control, new services, or more efficient operations was seen as important. It also developed its application in the field of books, serial acquisition, computer assisted cataloguing, Union Catalogue, SDI and current awareness, computer assisted cataloguing. CMC Ltd., a computer company in public sector, has built an integrated software package called MAITRAYEE suitable for a library network. This package will be applied in CALIBNET. DESIDOC has built an integrated application using Micro CDS/ISIS as the software platform. It is public domain software package like CDS/ISIS and the free distribution of such a package could be more useful for small libraries in the country.

The Department of Telecommunications has established a nationwide public packet switched data network called I-NET. I-NET will have nodes in 8 cities connected through high speed (9,600 and 64,000 bytes per second) links. It is an ideal NET and suitable for users whose data traffic volumes do not justify a dedicated network. Database mounted on I-NET hosts are an obvious application of interest to the library community. Similarly electronic mail is possible on I-NET. Indian overseas communications service at Bombay, Madras, and Delhi has been supported by I-NET for data networks. PADS (Packet Assemblers/Disassemblers) at these cities ensure access to 300-2400 bts to the gateway and to external networks. I-NET is less expensive and reliable computer communication in the country.

INIS (International Nuclear Information System): International Automatic Energy Agency of United Nations appointed a study team to draw a design for INIS that resulted in its establishment in Vienna in April 1970. It started Atomindex in 1973. It covers Physical Science, Chemistry, Material Science, Earth Science, Life Science, Isotope, Radiation, Application, Engineering and Technology etc. India has been participating INIS. The Bhabha Atomic Research Centre (BARC) inputs its data to INIS through Magnetic tape, paper tape, bibliographic and abstract of files, Bibliographic error file, Indexing file, and Indexing error file. INIS publishes INIS circular letters, INIS technical notes and INIS newsletter.

INIS is computer based. It is an international IR system that ensures quick communication, operates on the principles of decentralization at input stage, develops its thesaurus and offers machine readable information service. INIS output products are INIS magnetic tape service, INIS Atomindex, INIS Non-Conventional literature.

International Federation for Documentation (Federation Internationable de Documentation) (FID): The 'Institute International de Bibliographic' (IIB), predecessor of the present FID, was founded in 1895 by Henri LaFontaine and Paul Otlet, both lawyers (one a politician and the other a barrister) in Brussels. Both were internationalists and pacifics and may be considered as modern 'encyclopedists' conscious of the unity of knowledge and searching for the synthesis of the totality of sciences.

They wanted to create a comprehensive world bibliography on cards. For this 'universal repetory' they wanted a standard classification in order to classify the bibliographic material according to subject matter, and also they wanted to standardize the size of the cards. For the first purpose they chose the decimal classification of Melvil Dewey and expanded it not only in so far as the scientific contents are concerned, but also with a view to the theory of classification so that the 'Classification Decimale Universelle' (CDU, UDC) was developed as the first polydimensional classification. In introducing the 'colon' as classification symbol, their classification was at the same time the first colon classification. On the suggestion of Henry Field (the founder of the Concilium Bibliographicum in Zurich) they adopted the American postcard format as standard size (now well-known as the international bibliographical card). They considered the 'Classification Decimale Universelle' not directly for general standardized use but as a main tool for their repertory. The first edition of the classification was therefore called **Manual du Repertoire Bibliographique Universel.** It appeared in 1905.

The IIB also treated other problems of bibliography and librarianship, e.g. an attempt was made to standardize cataloguing rules. In 1905 the IIB published a proposal of Goldschmidt and Otlet to make use of microfilm (the invention of Dagron in 1870) for library and documentary reproduction purposes (**le livre microphotique**).

Various congresses were organized by the IIB, as an association of individuals supported by the Office International de Bibliographic (being an institution founded by the Belgium Government).

In 1905 Zaalberg (Zaandam, Holland) applied the UDC to the classification of archives and written records. This made the world 'bibliography' less appropriate in the circumscription of the International Institute but only in 1931 was the word 'documentation' accepted by the Institute by its name at its 10th Conference at the Hague. Hence the name was Institute International de Documentation. The word documentation was then defined as the collection, classification and distribution of records of any kind. In a more strict sense the word documentation indicated the methods and means for rendering the scientific contents of a document accessible to the user, as opposed to librarianship which is the management of collections of books, periodicals and other printed documents.

The modification of the name in 1931 was not the only change in the character, such the IIB. After the First World War, IIB got into serious difficulties, mainly of pecuniary character, such that the world card catalogue of 14,000,000 cards had to be stopped. F. Donker Duyvis (Holland) suggested to transform the association of individual persons into a federation of institutions and conformly the statutes were recast in 1924 so that the IIB acquired a federative character consisting in the beginning of five national members and three international members. Explicitly, this modification came to expression in the name of the organization which since 1938 is called the 'International Federation for Documentation'. In its present form members of the federation are national institutions or associations which act as national members (29 in 1959) and the representatives of which form together the Council of the FID; Associate members (81 in 1959) are admitted and also international associations (3 in 1959) or international specialized groups (6 in 1959).

Conferences or congresses were held in the following years: 1895, 1897, 1900, 1908, 1920, 1924, 1928, 1929, 1930, 1931, 1932, 1933, 1935, 1938, 1939, 1946, 1947, 1951, 1952, 1953, 1954, 1955, 1957, 1958 and 1959.

Committees have been established on Classification (in general and in special fields), Bibliography and Abstracting, Copyright in connection with reproduction, Information services, Technical means of documentation, Mechanical selection and Training of documentalists.

Periodicals issued are the quarterly *Revenue de la Documentation*, the monthly *Informations FID* and the half-yearly *Extensions and Corrections to the UDC* that are issued or prepared in English, French, German, Japanese, Portuguese and Spanish.

Official abridged editions of the U.D.C. have been published in the following languages: Czech, Dutch, English, Finnish, French, German, Japanese, Rumanian, Spanish, and Swedish. A trilingual standard abridged edition in English-French-German appeared in 1958. Various selected editions treating special domains were published. Various studies on documentation have been published by the FID. The most important of these published with the aid of UNESCO are: *Index Bibliographicus*; *Manual on Document Reproduction and Selection; Directory of Photocopying and Microcopying Services, Library and Documentation Periodicals, Handbunch der Classification, Bibliography of Standards on Documentation.*

A complete listing of all FID publications is given in the catalogue of August, 1958.

Since 1938 the central office of the FID is in Hague, 6 Willem Witsenplein.

International Federation of Library Association (IFLA): The aim of the Federation is to promote co-operation in the field of libraries and particularly to carry out investigations and make propositions concerning the international relations between libraries, library associations, bibliographers and other organized groups all over the world.

IFLA had its origin over 30 years ago. At the International Conference of Librarians and Book Lovers, held in Prague in June-July, 1926, the proposal of setting up an international committee which should represent the various national library associations was considered of topical interest and was unanimously adopted.

On the occasion of the 50th Anniversary Conference of the American Library Association held in Atlantic City in October 1926, an international committee recommended to the ALA to take the initiative and to invite the delegates authorized to study the creation of an International Library Committee to Edinburgh for following year on the occasion of the 50th Anniversary Conference of the (British) Library Association. This was held in September 1927, and as a result of its deliberations the 'International Library and Bibliographical Committee' was definitely constituted.

Its first meeting took place in Rome in March 1928. Fourteen national associations had signed official letters of adhesion and the Committee was thus regularly constituted. It accepted the invitation of the Italian delegation to hold an International Congress in Italy in 1929. A second full meeting of the Committee was held in Rome, Florence and Venice in June 1929. The draft statutes were approved and accepted by the General Assembly of the Congress held in Venice. Some modifications were introduced in the sessions at Stockholm in 1930 and Copenhagen in 1952.

In the course of time the figure of members went up from 14 countries in 1929 to 75 members in 45 countries including four international organizations in 1959.

The proceedings of the Congress in Italy in 1929 were published under the auspices of the Italian Local Committee in six volumes: *Atti del Primo Congresso Mondiale Delle Biblioteche e di bibliografia* (1932).

The next International Congress was held in Spain from May 20-30, 1934, in Madrid and Barcelona. The **Actos y Trabajos** was prepared jointly by Secretariat of IFLA and the Local Spanish Committee. The composition having disappeared for a large part during the Civil War in Spain, only Volumes 1-2 and combined Volume 3 were published in 1936 and 1949. The remaining reports are deposited in the IFLA archives. The third International Congress of Libraries took place from September 10-16, 1955, in Brussels. The proceedings were published in three volumes. The IFLA Council (International Library Committee until 1952), which governs the affairs of the Federation, met after its preparatory meetings annually with the exception of the war years.

The proceedings of these sessions have been published in 26 volumes under the title *Actes du Conseil de la FIAB*. Volumes 1-8 of it are out of print. Volume 6, 11 and 16 contain the cumulative indices of the matters dealt with in respect of its member associations.

These publications are distributed to the member associations and are obtainable from Martinus Nijhoff at the Hague.

The communications of the Board to the member associations from 1953 are published as a separate chapter in the international library periodical *Libri*.

The activities of the Federation are performed by the following committees:

1. Parliamentary and administrative libraries
2. Union catalogues

3. Unification of cataloguing principles
4. International loans
5. Periodicals and serial publications
6. Professional training
7. Exchange of publications
8. Hospital libraries
9. Rare and precious books
10. Statistics.

A session deals with Public Libraries, another with the problems of the National and University Libraries and a third with the Libraries and Museums of theatrical Arts.

There are four international associations members of IFLA: International Association of Technical University Libraries; International Association of Agricultural Librarians and Documentalists; Association of Libraries of Judica and Hebraica in Europe; International Association of Theological Libraries. Since 1958 there exists an Ibero-American Committee of Librarian Associations with the specific object to incorporate the different associations of librarians of the Ibero-American countries, together with Portugal and Spain, in the universal library movement of IFLA.

L

Library Association in UK/USA: The association is responsible for the examination and certification of library workers, the accommodation and dissemination of general information concerning libraries and the establishment and propagation of general standards in librarianship.

The International conference of librarians held on Oct. 5, 1877 in the London Institution proposed the establishment of library association. A draft was prepared for UK Association. Its object was to unite all persons engaged in or interested in library work, for the purpose of promoting the best possible administration of existing libraries and encourage bibliographical research. Of the first council of 19 members, only five were from rate supported public libraries. By Sept. 1878 the Association possessed 168 members, 207 by 1879, 240 by 1880, 365 by Sept. 1882 and in 1927 its constitution was passed. The phase of associations history was soon over. Its character was changing. With the growth of free libraries grew the proportion of municipal librarians in membership, and of town councillors. Simultaneously, the attention paid to purely scholarly and bibliographical matters declined. When the Association received its Royal Charter of incorporation in 1898, three of its ten stated aims related specifically to public libraries. The membership was divided into fellows Chief librarians, and others of distinction, Honorary fellow —members—personal and institutional, and Associates—library assistants, entitled neither to vote nor to head office. A separate bibliographical society was founded in 1893. The status of fellowship offered some incentives to membership, while increasing attention paid by employing authorities to certificates gained in the Association's examinations. The Association had its own staff in its London offices.

The by-laws were adopted at the meeting of Sept. 1909. When the country libraries developed after 1918-19, the librarians were appointed from outside. The Irish Rural Library Association was founded in April 1894. In 1926 Special Development Committee was appointed to consider the constitutional and administrative reforms necessary to extend and strengthen the influence of the library association under the Chairmanship of E.A. Savage, city librarian of Edinburgh. In December 1931 the Headquarter committee held its first meeting under the chairmanship of Mr. Savage in May 1933. The converted Malet Palace building was formally opened with a full-time secretary. The cumulative effect of the Development Committee's proposals throughout the succeeding decade was great and greatly needed.

Library Building: It is an important factor for the development of the library. Library is a growing organism and it grows in all spheres of services and researches, staff, collection and building. Similarly, libraries have different nature—public, academic, children, adults, research, business, technique and scientific and different collections; reference and non-reference material, photographic equipment, different services—reference service, computer service, lending service and inter-library loan service, different readers—general public, scientists, research scholars, blinds, students, labourers, children, women etc.; different staff—technical and semi-technical staff.

All libraries have basically similar pattern of organization but differ in function. A college library needs reading room, university library, seminar room and research subjects etc. A good library building is always purposeful for efficient function, maximum service, conservation of reading material, specialization, departmentalization etc. A library building should have accommodation for reading material, for reading community, and for library staff. A library building is based on some principles of planning. It should be multipurpose and utilized by all without consideration of cast, creed and sex. It should be multipurpose and utilized by all without consideration of cost. It should be functional but not ornamental. It should be simple in construction but effective for efficient service, the reading room should be near the stack area. It should be built keeping in mind future growth. Planning of library should be based on total collection of the library—journals subscribed, specialized collection, non-book material, number of books added every year, acquisition programme, technical work done, circulation statistics, reference service provided, reading capacity, special service provided, number of library staff in various capacities, stackroom capacity, and rate of growth in each section. All big countries have formed some library building standards. There are National Standard Institutes, viz. British Standard Institute, American Standard Institute and likewise in Russia, China, France and Australia. Indian Standard Institute is also working in New Delhi. It has two committees (1) Documentation sectional committee and (2) Committee for library building, fitting and furniture. Ranganathan was the Chairman of the Committee. There are standard institutes functioning at international level, i.e. FID, UNESCO and International Standard Organization.

Indian Standard Institute has published the following standard IS-1553-1960: Code of practice relate to primary elements in the design of library building.

IS-1829 (Part I)-1961 Library furniture and fitting; Part I: Timber.

IS-1661=1964 Libraries (Mobile Library).

IS-2662-1964 Packages for use of libraries.

There are general precautions taken while organizing a library building. Location on ground floor, convenient access to loading and shipping area, banking facilities, adequate floor space, adequate lighting, telephone located at the point of higher use, proper heating and ventilation, a treatment of working area, sound proof, location of stack area, provision of rest room, staff lounge, laboratories at out-part of building.

Library of Congress Classification: The Library of Congress was founded in 1800, burned out in 1814 and restocked in 1815 with the private library of Thomas Jefferson. This was arranged in 44 classes based on Bacon's Chart of human learning. With modification the method lasted until 1897, when the library was rehoused, and the consideration of new scheme was begun.

The Congress Library has to serve two masters. It is the deposit library for the consideration of national states covering almost a continent and also the research workshop for the federation legislature. The schedules consist of a series of separate main classes each of which has its own relative index. There is no index to the whole, but the list of subject headings used in dictionary catalogues of the Library of Congress can be a constituent. The debt this outline owes to cutter may be seen by comparing it with the one to be found in the article on the expensive classification.

A. General Works Polygraphy
B. Philosophy and Religion, Pt. I., B-BJ; BL-BX
C. Auxiliary Sciences of History
D. History: General and Old World
E. CF America
F. Geography Anthropology
G. Social Sciences
H. Political Science
I. Law
J. Education
K. Music and Books on Music
L. Fine Arts
M. Philology (language and literature)
P-PA

PB-PH

PG

PJ-PM

PN-PR-Ps-PZ

PQ Part 1-2

PT, Part 1-2

N. Science

O. Medicine

P. Agriculture

Q. Technology

R. Military Science

S. Bibliography and Library Science

Letters up to a maximum of two are used for classes and divisions, then numerals up to four are used serially to indicate subdivisions. The subdivisions are mostly minute and the depth of classification obtained are not unduly long or complicated. Auxiliary tables and similar mnemonic devices, as used in other schemes, do not exist. Grcat usc is made of alphabetical arrangement within subdivisions where that order is suitable. Class numbers are put on all printed cards sold by the Library of Congress. (Ency. Libnshp)

Library (Information) System for Serials:

(a) ***OCLC's SCS***: Online computer library centre has housed the conversion of serials (CONSER) database. OCLC's SCS provide librarians with local serials control as well as access to OCLC online Union Catalogue which contains over 6 lakhs serials bibliographical records. SC-350 developed for use with the OCLC M350 workstation, a modified IBM personal computer support a full range of technical services, including bibliographical record selection and transfer, automatic check in and claiming routine, binding, financial control, OCLC user, the MARC, SC350 maintain links to the OCLC online system.

(b) **LINX:** It is designed and marketed by F.W. Faxon Co. LINX is an online, remote access serial management system that integrates customer-vendor acquisitions and interrelated services are Datalinx and SC-10.

(c) ***CHECKMATE***: It is a California library authority systems and services. It stands along SCS using a TRS-80 model II micro-computer with floppy disk drives. It is for special collections. It uses 80 inches floppy diskettes. The first diskettes contains CHECKMATE programme and TRSDOS operating system. The second diskettes contains the keyword index to the data. Special features include keyword searching using Boolean operators and field modification techniques. The function includes check in claiming, routine, accounting, subscription exploration alerts and production of titles and subject lists.

(d) ***EBSCONET***: It is a communication network allowing a library's computer terminal to be online to EBSCO's host computer in Birmingham. The SCS handles any serially received material regardless of medium or source. IT performs checks in claiming, binding preparation records. On line retrieval flexibility is one of the most striking features of the EBSCONET SCS. Any type of teletype terminal or any IBM 3278 terminal can be used with the system.

(e) ***NOTIS-3***: NOTIS is designed to run on IBM compatible equipment cathode—ray-tube terminals are used to access a file of records at the university administrative data processing centres. It was MARC format, which helps to produce data and catalogues by the computer NOTIS offer all the SCS like check in claiming binding, accounting, full record display.

(f) ***PHILSOM***: It is a network intended for medical school libraries. PHILSOMS on-line programme are written in Standard MUMPS. It does not follow the MARC format accessed by the ASSN number, title key or a keyword search.

(g) *STACS*: Information dimensions Inc.'s STACK is BASIC SC application which is used separately or in conjugation with TECHLIB. It is a DBMS (Database to manage the SC operator by tracking serials titles from ordering to building and weeding).

(h) *PERLINE*: A SCS provides fully comprehensive integrated suits of programme covering all aspects of book and journal selection, check-in, circulation or routing, claiming, accessioning, binding etc.

Library Softwares: There are few important library softwares used:

(a) *CDS/ISIS:* It is a mini-micro conversion applied in more than 200 libraries. This package enquire deep study and understanding. The package is highly versatile, flexibile and excellent for integrated database management. It is developed by DSIR.

(b) *LIBRARY MANAGER*: System Data Controls Ltd., Bombay has developed the software (Library Manager). It needs IBM PC XT with a minimum of 384 kb core memory. The software takes care of maintaining a file of books, details of members, complete range of circulation control, including issue-return, updating, reminders, reservations, queries on book file, membership file, transaction file. The software is fully menu driven and user-friendly, developed on relational database concepts.

(c) *SALIM*: This software is developed by Uptron India Ltd., New Delhi. It is known as software for automation of library information management. The software caters to circulation control, stock verification, catalogue card, painting, serial control etc. It recommends a hard disk of 40-80 mb.

(d) *INTEGRATED LIBRARY MANAGEMENT SOFTWARE*: It has been developed by Pragati

Computers Pvt. Ltd., Madras. The software provides for database creation and all aspects of circulation control. It also includes a user initiation/orientation module which helps the new user of the library to get to know rules and regulations of the library. The software has been developed employing relational database similar to dBase by works in concurrence with CM/M-86 environment on ATLAZ series of micro-computers.

(e) *ULYSIS*: It is developed by WIPRO Information Technology Ltd., Secunderabad. It is a comprehensive library software standing for universal library information system to take care of acquisition control, serial control, circulation control and a powerful quering function.

(f) *LIBMAN*: It is developed by Data Pro Consultancy Services, Pune. System requirements are IBM PO/ XT with 20MB-DOS Ver 2.1 or higher 640 kb Ram. The package provides for creating database of books, members, circulation control, inter-library loan, overdue lists, computation of files etc.

(g) *LIBRARY CATALOGUE SYSTEM*: It is developed by Ultra Business System Pvt. Ltd., Bangalore. The library catalogue can be developed on a floppy disk. Data entry is done through interactive filling up of forms at the terminal. The system needs ultra-micro-computers which are CP/M machine.

(h) *SDI PACKAGE*: It is developed by Radig Cybernetics Pvt. Ltd., Secunderabad, using PSI micro-computer based on CP M86 and dbase II. This has been developed for an organization called Central Institute of Tool Design, Hyderabad. The programme provides journal articles only, each article may be indexed by 22 keyboards.

(i) *ARCHIVES*: It is a library management system developed by Minifax Electroc System Pvt. Ltd., Bombay. It is suitable for use on any standard IBM,

PC XT. The vendor supply both hardware and software. Archives is a comprehensive package offering acquisition control, serial control, circulation control, SDI, cataloguing etc. The system also takes care of acquisition cataloguing and search of non-book materials.

(j) *LMS*: It is developed by U & I Software (P) Ltd., Bangalore. It is library management software for generalized user friendly package for IBM PC XT users. Database creation is through inbuilt data entry screen. Data entry provides for data security, data validation and error recovery proceedings, book ordering. Database quering on various keys, exception reporting, pending orders, budgeting and funds management are all available. The whole system is developed in dbase and user 80 modules using 10 databases.

(k) *LIMBAN*: It is developed by Kasbah System Software, Madras. Package takes care of database building, circulation control, searching, book ordering, collection of fines and reminders. Reservations are also included.

(l) *WILISYS*: It is integrated library information system, developed by WIPRO Information Technology Ltd. WILISYS is a family of comprehensive software for library computerization. WILISYS consists of two major modules—MILIMAX (Library Management System) and MILLTRAX (Library Abstract System). Both uses 'C' language under UNIX operating system using UNIFY-RDBMS for data storages.

(m) *INNOVAC*: It is an interface between the bibliographic network and a stand alone circulation system that was developed by Innovative interfaces. The system operates on multiple processor computer system. INNOVAC serials modules provide check in claiming, routine and binding with acquisitions functions provided by the acquisition modules.

M

Main Entry: It is the principal catalogue entry for a work, giving all the information necessary for its complete identification. As a rule, the main entry is the author entry (since the author is responsible for the book's existence and the work is not likely to be looked for this name). A standard main entry comprises five sections, each concerned with the provision of particular items of information:

1. ***Heading***: Determines the place of the entry in the catalogue sequence. Chosen by the cataloguer, normally in conformity with a code of cataloguing and to choice and rendering. Usually the name of the author.
2. ***Title***: Identifies the work, and differentiates it from other works of the same author and other editions of the same work, by giving a transcript of the title page giving all title and subtitle, the name of the author and any editor, translator etc., and the statement of edition if other than the first.
3. ***Publication***: The place(s) of publication, name(s) of the publisher(s) and the publication date.
4. ***Physical description***: Supplies a description of the physical composition of the work by stating the number of volumes comprising the work, or the statement of pagination if in one volume, the numbers of each kind of illustration included, the size (height of volume and width of unusual shape) and the name of the series.
5. ***Notes***: Specification of the contents, additional bibliographical information and annotation.

In a card catalogue the main entry bears also tracings indicating all the other headings under which the work in question is entered in a catalogue. When used as a master card it may carry in addition tracing of references and a record of other pertinent data concerning the cataloguing of the work.

Melvil Dewey: Youngest of five children of Joil and Eliza Dewey, Melvil Dewey was born on December 10, 1851, at Adams Centre, New York. When 17, he became a teacher on a meagre salary. In 1870 Dewey entered Amherst College, Massachusetts, graduating in 1874. While a student there, he became Assistant Librarian of the college. No sooner did he begin work in the library than he was employed for the wasteful practice of reclassifying books to maintain subject allocation every time a library grew beyond its walls. Dewey loved numbers and among numbers he had deep affection for Indo-Arabic numerals when employed as fractions. On May 8, 1873 Dewey presented to the library committee of the college his plan. In 1876 the classification was known to public at large. In April 1876 Dewey left Amherst College for Boston where he assisted the editor of American Library journal. In a conference of librarians on Oct. 4-6, 1876 he was appointed Secretary of American Library Association. On Oct. 19, 1876, Dewey was married to Anni R. Godfrey, Librarian of Wellesley College. By 1883 Dewey moved to Columbia College. He founded co-education library school in Jan. 1887 and two more edition of DDC appeared. In Dec. 1888 Dewey became Secretary of the Board of Regents of the University of State at New York. In 1892 he founded New York Library Association. Dewey moved to River Lake, New York. In 1927 the editorial office of DDC moved to the Library of Congress in Washington D.C. DDC was entrusted to Forest Press. The 12th edition (1927) was the last to come under Dewey's scrutiny. In Aug. 1922 Anni Gofrey Dewey died and in May 1927 Dewey married a family friend Mrs. Emily Kckey Bea. Dewey died at the age of 80 from a stroke on Dec. 26, 1931. He was a crusader and reformer at an early age.

Dewey was a charismatic man with a vigour. He was genius, skilful, and an educational leader of marked originality.

Mobile Libraries: Mobile libraries are collections of books arranged in vehicles and so staffed as to provide a library service capable of being directed to communities which are often though not exclusively, rural. They are used by some municipal and many country library systems in the UK. In many areas abroad they are making notable contribution to the development of library services particularly in large parts of Asia, Africa and Middle East. There is a distinction between mobile branch libraries and travelling libraries. The mobile branch library is a medium-to-large vehicle with a shelf stock of upwards of 2000 books used over reasonably good roads to serve villages and towns. The travelling library is smaller vehicle with a limited stock used in the service of scattered communities and providing, in some cases, a house-to-house service in remote areas. Mobile and travelling libraries vehicle are made with specific provisions. The shelves face inwards and generally run round three sides of the vehicle. The fourth is usually reserved for the issue desk. The books facing forward in the rear of the vehicle pose a special problem since heavy braking will dislodge them. Even titled shelves, hinged slabs and sliding grills are sometimes used to prevent this. Issue desks normally cross or partly cross the front of the vehicle. Adjustable seats allow the librarian to face inwards to attend to readers at halts and to face forward while the vehicle is in motion. Roof lights are provided which may be flush or of the projecting lantern variety.

Visits are made in rural areas at weekly, fortnightly, or monthly intervals. The duration of the mobile library visit depends on the size of community served. The mobile library has played a notable part in the development of the country library system. Rural community had been largely served by village library centres with limited book collections and usually an untrained librarian. The mobile library provides a considerable larger stock and a trained librarian in towns. In India mobile library system was introduced in Baroda at the time of Raja Shivaji Rao Gaikwad and then in Tanjore district of Tamil Nadu. Delhi Public Library is providing mobile library service to the community of Delhi and its remote area. In states district libraries are providing mobile library services in states like Madhya Pradesh and other south Indian states.

N

Newspaper Libraries: A newspaper library is a collection of reference material and sometimes of consultations planned to serve the daily needs of a newspaper. It is expected to provide a quick reference service on any of the diverse topics forming the news of the day. It may be as near self-sufficient as is economic because it is regularly in use when other libraries are closed and experts are not available. Newspaper libraries have three fundamental characteristics: emphasis on recent information, brevity and conciseness in its presentation and rapidity of service. These essential characteristics naturally have considerable effect on methods and arrangement, and within that framework the library observes normal practice. Only some of its tools are different.

It serves chiefly the editorial staff: leading writers, reporters, sub-editors and specialists, each of whom has his individual approach to a subject. If, as is frequently the case, both morning and evening papers are served, the department may be called upon at almost any time of day or night. It does not follow, however, that the library staff is present during the whole of this time. Some smaller libraries would find this uneconomic and therefore allow enquirers to help themselves during slack times; a factor which discourages any tendency towards over-elaboration.

It is pity that at the present times only a few of the newspapers libraries employ trained librarians. Their numbers are growing, however, and the influence of professionalism is making itself felt, in movies towards standardization and a closer study of this branch of librarianship. The size of staff varies from 20 or more in the libraries of some national newspapers to many one-man organizations in the provinces.

The library stock comprises books, bound newspaper files, pamphlets, Government publications and Press cuttings, the last being by far the most important item. In addition, many libraries also store photographs, maps, half-tone blocks, photographic negatives and microfilms. Some maintain an index to their own newspaper. Book stocks vary considerably in range and size. The stock of most libraries consists of quick reference books supplemented by statistical complications and works of biographical reference. Several duplicate copies of books in daily use act as desk books. Pamphlets and Government publications are variously dealt with, sometimes being filed with the cuttings and sometimes forming a separate section, with more important of them being bound and treated as books. Many books and pamphlets reach the library in the form of review copies which present their special difficulties.

Partly because of the demand for information too recent to appear in books and also because of the primary need to preserve the contents of the home newspaper, Press cuttings are the most heavily used class of material in the library. Towards their organization the larger part of the routine is devoted. Most libraries cut their own newspaper extensively and take exclusive and fuller stories from others. National newspapers cut almost everything, from political and foreign news to the apparently unimportant 'oddities' of life. The proportions reflect the newspaper's contents. All pay much attention to contemporary biography, while the recording and indexing of crime is a preoccupation of some of the libraries of the 'popular' Press. Sports and speeches (arranged by speakers'names) are important sections. Provincial newspapers naturally emphasize local events and personalities, and commonly leave most of the foreign news to the news agencies.

Press cuttings are usually stored in folders or envelopes in vertical filing cabinets. Quarto size is general, although some prefer shallower index drawers or pamphlet boxes. An important recent development is the use of lateral suspended files on an open framework of rails. Whether or not to mount cuttings is a matter of local decision, bearing in mind size, usage and quality of newsprint. Different coloured mountings are sometimes used to indicate main classes or year of publication.

Methods of selecting and filing cuttings are chiefly designed to ensure that nothing potentially useful is missed and to provide for consistency in classifying. The paper is usually 'marked up', with subject headings allotted, by a senior member of the staff who passes it to a junior for cutting, or the whole operation may be carried out by the same person. Where several copies of the same item are required a different keyword or heading is indicated on each (usually by underline) of the copies.

In view of the lack of contract between newspaper libraries it is significant that nearly all employ the same general arrangement for cuttings—alphabetical by subject. Foreign news is subdivided under country of origin and most of the remaining headings are British in emphasis. The extent of subdivision and choice of main heading depend on local usage. The plan of subdivision is empirical and follows the development of the subject from the point of view of the newspaper. Existing headings are frequently changed in conformity with current phraseology and new ones interpolated as they arise.

Biography forms a separate sequence in all but the smaller libraries' practice varies in case of those no longer living (the 'morgue'). The storage (and sometimes the preparation) of advance obituaries of the well-known living is usually the library's responsibility. Sport and sporting biography are also sometimes separately dealt with.

Newsprint being cheap, has many duplicate cuttings depending on its necessity and may be filed at different aspects of a story. Where this is undesirable, slip references on coloured papers are placed in the files under alternative or associated headings. It is desirable that the subject headings in use should be controlled by an index—either of cards, in manuscript or on flexible display stands. Although many libraries manage with one. The alternative is to list *see also* references on the files themselves and to use dummy folders for *see* references. Continuous and systematic discarding is an essential part of library routine. The removal and separate storage of material earlier than defined period plays an important part in the process.

Most newspapers also find themselves supplying a number of auxiliary services designed to assist the provision of news and information. These include such items as an index to experts and the addresses and telephone numbers of some of the less easily located societies, lists of approaching events (in chronological order) and certain special groupings of news items to assist a specific purpose (e.g. domestic accidents involving boiling water).

The future may hold some interesting developments. Microfilming of bound files is becoming general and at least one newspaper is available on microcards. In America the microfilming of the cuttings themselves is being carried out. Wire photo-apparatus is reducing the need for each newspaper to hold large collections of pictures. The Telex system and the tele-printer enable the library to be exploited more fully by its overseas and country correspondents.

NICNET: A unique infrastructural networks with a history that goes back to 1978 is the National Informatic Centres (NIC) network, also called NICNET. It is a satellite based communication using low cost roof-top micro-earth statics to connect 450 district headquarters and 32 states and Union Terriroty capitals with a central hub at Delhi. It uses 500 very small operative terminals (VSATs), each of which is connected to specific outbound and inbound channel on a satellite's transponder. VSATs have been used to connect computers, terminals, telexes and other devices to other computers/devices via the satellite. NICNET is desired primarily to be a government information network. Its objectives are to promote the collection, storage, analysis transmission, and exchange of data at district, state headquarters and central ministries and departments at New Delhi for use in planning, management and monitoring of projects and government sponsored programmes.

Ninety-one rules: It is a name given to the catalogue code prepared, at the instigation and under the guidance of Sir Anthony Panizzi, by a committee consisting of Thomas Watts, J.M. Parry, J. Winter Jones and Edward Edwards. The code is so called because of the 91 rules it contained, prescribing the methods of entry, choice of headings, added entries and references to be used in compiling the British Museum catalogue of printed books. Its importance lies in the fact that it was the first major code providing detailed rules for the consistent entry of books, logically according to their authorship circumstances, and setting the catalogue pattern of main entries, added entries, and references now firmly established in cataloguing practice.

The code received the approval of the British Museum Trustees in 1839, being published in 1841, and was used for compiling the General catalogue of printed books of 1881-1900 and the subsequent supplements. The latest revision (1936) of the British Museum code contains, in all, only 41 rules, yet nearly all of the 91 decisions remain valid. It is a tribute to the work of the committee, and especially Panizzi, that all subsequent codes of rules for author entry have been based largely on this code. During the present century much criticism has been voiced against certainty of the class entry rulings embodied (such as the entry of periodicals under Periodical Publications, orders of divine service under Liturgies, etc.) and against the treatment of anonymous works. Certain original rules have therefore been discarded in British Museum practice.

O

Online Information System: Online information system is one in which information is fed to a computer and computer is operated with a set of programmes that enable users to retrieve specific parts of information according to their requirements. This system was developed in USA. For the first time in 1963 two projects were taken up in USA by Massachusetts Institute of Technology and System Development Corporation. By 1964 SDC succeeded in developing a rapid bibliographic system called ORBIT (Online Retrieval of Bibliographical Information-Time). National Library of Medicine also developed online system in 1971 called MEDLINE. Online systems are used commonly now in European countries. The development of low cost communication networks for data transmission has played a significant role, known as SALINET, SOLINET, TELENET, TYMNET, EURONET, NELENET and DOALOG (in 30 countries). India has also taken keen interest to develop online information facilities to its scientists. UNESCO and UNISIST sponsored project RECON aims at linking the world source. It is information organized by Department of Science and Technology. In India, at Tata Institute of Fundamental Research, NISSAT is also working on it.

Online Information System has wide scope, speed accuracy and exhaustiveness, and high retrieval power, browsing and iteration, and good sorting capability. Online services are used for variety of purposes, viz. preparing bibliographies for scientific research, use for inter-library loan, gathering information for sports, speeches, proposals, serving patent literature, avoiding duplication of research, developing educational programme, forecasting business trends and research. A number of studies relating to evaluation, effectiveness, performance and cost-effectiveness have been carried out.

P

Pre-Natal Cataloguing: Dr. Ranganathan introduced Pre-natal technical work which includes:

1. Pre-natal cataloguing.
2. Pre-natal classification.
3. Works to be undertaken by National Central Library for each book before its release by the publisher. The National Library prepared a master stencil of catalogue card for each book before its release and provide:
   (a) Call Number,
   (b) Catalogue entries for each book.
   (c) Class number that can be printed on the back of the title page, and
   (d) Catalogue card that can be printed even when the book is released. This is called Pre-natal cataloguing.

All the above methods CIS, CIP and PNC are the same having the objective to prepare catalogue cards before the release of the book. CIS fails to serve this purpose. CIP proves more successful.

Prerequisites for Centralised Cataloguing

1. Uniformity of cataloguing and classification:
   (a) Catalogue code,
   b) Classification scheme, and
   (c) Physical form.

2. Duplication of stocks in libraries.
3. Establishment of some machinery by which new documents can have a quick and speed access to information of books by publishers or other agencies. Any delay may result in failure of the scheme.
4. Proper finance.
5. Economical:
   (a) Sophisticated machine,
   (b) No waste of labour,
   (c) No waste of material, and
   (d) Quick disposal of work.

BNB and Centralised Cataloguing

BNB (1951) is an organization supported and controlled by:

(a) Council of Library Association,
(b) British Museum (through copyright),
(c) Publishers Association, and
(d) Booksellers Association.

BNB started card system in 1956. BNB also publishes CBNB (Books of periodicals) weekly (cumulative monthly) that started in 1956. There is another catalogue published by BNB in 1950, entitled 'British Catalogue for Music' (Music score).

Special Features

1. DC applies in BNB centralized cataloguing.
2. AACR is applied by BNB.
3. PRECIS is applied for indexing.
4. Computer assisted techniques were started by—
   (a) National Cash Register
   (b) Photochromic Micro-Image (PCMI)
   (c) Computer output microfilming.

LC and Centralized Cataloguing

LC started card system in 1901 and indexed in cumulative book index through which cards are ordered and also the National Union Catalogue.

LC used classification scheme for entry purpose. It has also used ALA/AACR with modifications.

Public Libraries in USA/UK: The term public library had and still has many different connotations. It is not even possible to say that a public library is one which is not private or, that it is one which is available generally to the people or it is the one supported substantially by public funds. The public library is concerned with all materials of value to the individual and the community. Public library must offer comprehensive, general services to all sections of the community. It should be a free service in that no user should be required to pay any fee, subscription or other charges.

The concept of public library service is rather more than 100 years old. In USA the state laws enabling towns to establish and maintain libraries by taxation were passed in 1849, though the first free public library in USA was set up without any specific legal basis as early as in 1833. As a result of private benefaction, however, a few similar libraries came into being in 17th century. The foundation of the British Public Library services owes much to William Ewart, M.P. from Salford, and Edwards who were largely responsible for the passing of the first public libraries bill and establishing first public library at Manchester in 1852. The 1850 Act applied only to England and Wales. The 1919 Act gave library powers to country councils and it made substantial grants and gave invaluable guidance and encouragement.

In 1986 public library service was given by 1200 independent local library authorities. Service was given from at least 47000 points and also 700 mobile libraries. Registered borrowers from lending libraries totaled 42% of the total population, and annual issue for home reading numbered 89 crores. Total expenditure was 3.50 crores of which 2 crores were on books. Staff employed in public library work totaled 37 thousand.

Nevertheless, the British Public Library services is one of the best in the world and is steadily improving as yet. The pattern of library service in the United States is basically similar to that in the United Kingdom. The libraries of United States have accomplished more than probably any other nation. The next best public library service in the world is probably that of New Zealand. In this vital work of promoting worldwide public library facilities both as a means of securing fundamental education, both social and economic, and in gradually creating decent standards of living and intellectual opportunity and freedom, UNESCO is playing a great part and needs the fullest support of all those who realize how essential good public libraries are in the consolidation of genuine civilization.

Public Library movement in the United States took place in 17th century. In 18th century the movement started in its own soil. Benjamin Franklin is considered one of the founders of the social library in the United States. The support of these libraries depended upon voluntary subscription. There were few subscription libraries left in metropolitan area such as Boston, Philadelphia. In 1835 the New York legislature passed a law supporting school district libraries. In 1838 the Federal government offered matching funds. Today the 17 thousand public libraries potentially serve 78% of the population. They own 37 crore volumes and more than 2 crore patrons registered. The total expenditure is 35 crores. There are 37 thousand full time and 19 thousand part time professional librarians. In recognition of the interdependence of the educational force of the public library, renewed activity in the field of international relations shows increased importance. Librarians representing all fields are advising foreign governments on American library procedures and assisting, when invited, in development of library schools buildings and services. The International Relation Committee of the

American Library Association coordinated activities in the field. Librarianship in the United States is changing. There is a new respect in the United States for librarians and profession they represent.

R

Reference Libraries: Reference Library is the oldest form of library in the history of the world. Even in the days of clay there were temple libraries in which tablets were available for consultation, and lists of them were inscribed on the walls. To define a reference library as one where the material may not be removed from the building would however be wrong: the true concept of a reference library is rather a collection of written and printed sources to which people may report for information. It is in fact better to look on the reference library as a living encyclopaedia which in itself is a summary of the aims and ideas and achievements of mankind which attempts to provide a complete picture of current information on the subjects within its field. From this it may be seen that as long as a reference library is able to provide adequate information on any topic at any given moment, it is reasonable that it should be allowed to lend secondary material whenever it is necessary or desirable to do so.

The material of which a reference library is composed has no bounds; all sources of information come within its scope—not only books and periodicals, newspapers and pamphlets, but also maps and charts, gramophone records, motion and strip films, lantern, slides, microfilms and many other objects (such as actual examples of textiles, etc.) which may conceivably add to the information contained in the more conventional reference works. This is, in fact, what constitutes a reference tool. Rejecting the accepted idea that a true reference work is one which is built on the lines of a dictionary, encyclopaedia, glossary, etc., it is best to think in terms of something from which individual items of information may easily be extracted, a condition which presupposes either a scientific arrangement of contents by some recognizable scheme such as alphabetical, chronological or evolutionary order, or the provision of detailed indexes. Thus, a given book may be at the same time acceptable for both reading and reference use: to one reader it will appeal as a work which he wishes to read completely, while to the others it may seem eminently suited to reference use owing to its orderly arrangement of facts and illustrations, tables, appendices, indexes, etc.

In more recent times the reference library has tended to become a department of much larger organization, and at that not always the most important section. Today reference libraries are to be found in all types of libraries—university, special, public etc.—but they are usually subordinated to a system which may embrace many other features such as lending and travelling libraries, branches, information services, extension work, etc. The function of the reference library has scarcely changed, but its position and its methods have altered and developed. Thus, in the larger public and university libraries the reference service is co-ordinated with all the other activities of those libraries, to the benefit of the system as a whole. This co-ordination affects many things: choice of material is made on lines which ensure that collections in the different departments complement and strengthen rather than merely duplicate or overlap each other; members of the staff are frequently changed from one department to another so that their experience is varied and enhanced; readers in one department are advised of the resources of the others. In all this it is true to say that the reference library gains more than it loses, and that the reference which largely remains a watertight compartment is both an anachronism and also an indication of serious inefficiency.

A reference library not only includes many types of material, but it may also consist of several different departments; it may for instance have, in addition to the general collection of reference works, such departments as Commercial,

Technical, Government Publications, Maps and Atlases, Art Music or other subject divisions. Even small public reference libraries usually have, if not a separate Local collection, at least a section on this subject which may form considerable part of the total department. And with divisions there may be staff with special qualifications in the appropriate subjects. While the basic desirable qualification of a reference librarian is undoubtedly a thorough knowledge of all aspects of librarianship, it is equally important to possess a specialised qualification of the subject wherever there is a definite concentration on one subject-field. Training in other departments before coming to reference work is of great importance; the librarian with a good knowledge of cataloguing and classification procedure is an asset to his colleagues when he joins the reference staff.

In a reference library the demand of space made by both readers and material must necessarily result in a compromise; once the stock of the department exceeds that of the available open-shelf space, it is essential to realize that only a token collection of reference material can be displayed if sufficient room is to be left for readers. Thus, the majority of new additions to a reference library will be consigned to the bookstack immediately, if so demanded by its readers and only after its reputation has been firmly established, a process which may take some years. Even more than in other branches of a library service, it is therefore necessary for a reference library to be thoroughly catalogued and classified: material which is not so treated is practically worthless. A reference library's efficiency depends, in fact, on the detailed organization of its contents, and on adequate rooms, i.e. well-lit, dry and convenient storage space. Few reference libraries can boast of such facilities.

As the modern reference library cannot operate independently of other departments in the same library system, it would be foolish to carry out its work without intimate knowledge of day-to-day contact and co-operation with other sources of information. For example, reference libraries are becoming increasingly dependent on huge files of periodicals: it is possible for several libraries in the neighbourhood to build up sets of the same titles, and it is desirable when, by cooperation, they can collect different periodicals on the same subject and thus increase the total resources in the area (the best example of this being the Sheffield scheme). In the same way, reference libraries in a number of areas throughout the country are collaborating on such questions as the division of subject-fields, the purchase of expensive works, the compilation of union lists of periodicals, the disposal of withdrawn material, the temporary exchange of staff and other points which help to make their services mutually more efficient. Nationally, cooperation occurs in such forms as union catalogues of periodicals, directories of subject resources, the formation of subject groups, the preparation of annotated lists of the best reference items, etc. Future developments may well take such forms as the joint provision of regional reference libraries in area where now there are no comprehensive co-operative coverage of material and compilation of bibliographies in given subject-fields and the more efficient pooling of resources. Basically what is needed is a standard reference services recognizable as such by readers, so that they can confidently enter a reference library in the same way as they now enter a post office. This would imply that every small library should be well equipped with catalogues and bibliographical aids so that what has been written on a subject and the whereabouts of individual copies of books can always be discovered. The provision of these, and also of the larger and rarer reference items, comes nearer for every library with the rapid development of the microcard and the microfilm; very shortly it should be possible to equip small country library branches with micro-copies of the reference aids appropriate nowadays to a city library and with this step forward a real public reference service will begin.

Resource Sharing: No library is self-sufficient at any time. No library can hold all the literature which is demanded by the readers. There has been tremendous increase in scientific and technical knowledge during the 20th century. Resource sharing is the only media to fulfil the readers' demand. It is necessary because recorded information and knowledge is a human resource and the shared information technology is complex, specialized and costly and the revising cost of conventional library operations require cooperative arrangements, and rapid, effective improvement/extension of library services.

Resource sharing in academic libraries is even more important because the financial condition in academic libraries in India is far from satisfactory. In spite of recommendations of Radha Krishnan Commission, 1948 and of Kothari Commission, 1964 that the academic libraries should be given at least 6.26% to 10% of the total budget of the institution, most of the universities and college spent only 1.5 to 2.3% of their budgets on libraries. Termite (1850) has suggested the accumulation as stereotype blocks of the catalogue of Smith Sonian Institution for other libraries for their use but this proposal was not implemented. In 1966 Calorade Council of Libraries examined the feasibility of establishing a book processing centre to serve all states of USA Dr. Ranganathan suggested the inter-library loan scheme among university libraries.

Resource sharing can be applicable in the field of acquisition work by co-operative Acquisition Programme, storage problem by co-operative storage centre, cataloguing by processing problem by book processing centres, inter library loan by Inter-Library-Loan Programme, computer service by library network, internet programme, readers service by bibliographic centres, documentation centres, and information centres. Union catalogue is also a resource sharing media if it is revised and made upto date.

S

School Libraries

1. General

Purpose and uses: The need for a school library arises from the nature of eduation itself, with its concern for the development of the whole personality. The school library serves many ends: enrichment of teaching by provision of illustrative background material; instruction and practice in the use of books and of a library; reference; 'extended reference' (project and research work); development of pupils' personal interests; recreative reading. It also gives opportunity for the exercise of various administrative responsibilities.

Teaching the use of books: The school library has a special position among libraries in that it is possible to ensure that every member of the community it serves becomes familiar with it and is given help in its use. Help may be given to individuals incidentally as the need arises; to groups for some special piece of work; or by a course of systematic organized instruction. For this, classes may be given regular definite periods in the library (library periods). The objective in all 'library work' is to help the pupil to use books and library independently, to train him to discover facts, check and compare evidences and form judgements for himself.

Library periods are periods in the time-table allotted regularly to classes in secondary schools, for use of the library and not for work that can as well be done elsewhere. Younger pupils may use such periods to browse the library resources, to take out books for home reading and return them. Later systematic instruction in using the library for various purposes may be given and practiced. Such teaching must be given gradually, and never in bulk and should be linked with a clearly understood objective. On no account should it become a school 'subject'. Skill thus acquired in using books may serve personal interests as well as school work. Its value in advanced work cannot be overestimated; and it is a skill (and an attitude) that can be carried over into adult life.

In view of whole school curriculum and the wide field of children's personal interests, the library must be comprehensive in range, and must cater to the needs of the school **at all levels**, from the junior most to the senior most and most backward to the most advanced.

The Teacher and the Library: All good teaching involves cooperation between teacher and pupil and seeks all the time to increase the pupils' own part in the process of learning so that his responsibility grows progressively. This principle has always been accepted in good Sixth Form teaching; it is clearly applicable at earlier stages. For this a good library and training in its use is indispensable. Full exploitation of a library depends directly on the character of teaching. Teachers need to understand fully themselves the contribution the library can make to their own work; and it is extremely important that this shall be kept in view in Training College work. The extension of the training college course to three years should provide more time and opportunity for the student both to develop his own personal use of the library, and to realize more fully the different ways in which his teaching may make use of the school library.

1. *Primary*: Important principles are: (a) That the child's first introduction to books shall be pleasurable; (b) That he shall throughout the primary period have books constantly in hand as familiar companions. Book provision, therefore, may take the form of (a) bookcorner or library corner at the infant stage (age 5 to 7), where attractive books are displayed and are available for any child to take and look at; (b) Classroom libraries—some books (not sets of readers I) should always be kept in the classroom or lend to it temporarily, covering many subjects and interests (stories, poetry, nature, Bible, simple reference, personal interests); (c) A general library (central collection) of at least some hundreds of books covering the widest range of subject matter, kept together in some place (not a classroom) where children can consult them at will. This is of special importance at the middle-school stage (aged 9 to 11), when the child's rapidly growing thirst for knowledge demands satisfaction. From the general library loans may be made to classroom libraries as well as to individuals for home reading. In small schools provision is naturally simpler, but the same principles hold good.

2. ***Secondary***: Common practice is to provide a library room; this is obligatory by Ministry of Education regulations for all new secondary schools. Here the collection is kept as a whole, and library activities take place. Some large schools have a senior and a junior library, each comprehensive for the ages it serves. Some large grammar schools have developed considerable subject libraries for advanced use, housed where the sixth form subject groups are taught. Though this practice has certain advantages for the specialists served, it tends to withdraw them from the main library, and it may detract seriously from its unity and comprehensiveness, particularly in subjects which have a wide general appeal. Extensive duplication of stock may be necessary.

Book Selection: Fundamental principles are: (a) To provide a comprehensive range, suitable to capacity of pupils; (b) To provide for all ages and levels of intelligence; and (c) As funds are limited, it is particularly important to make sure that each book is as good of its kind as possible.

Subject to this provision, each school should develop its library to suit its own needs; there is no 'standard school library'. The library will reflect local conditions (e.g. of occupation or industry), and above all it will represent the schools' own character. In all schools it is important that the less gifted members of the school, and the younger ones, shall receive satisfaction. A library committee is useful to formulate general policy (e.g. allocation of funds). For actual choice of books the librarian will naturally refer to whatever expert opinion is available for school subjects. This will no doubt be mainly found within the school, for other subjects each school will find its own method, using all information accessible (staff, pupils, parents, public library, bookshops). The librarian will keep in touch with booklists and reviews. Within the library the general reference section is of special importance. Attention should be given to building up a rich collection of material in the school itself and in its neighbourhood.

School Libraries in India: Ranganathan stressed for establishing better school libraries. A habit starts from tender or early stage that becomes an integral part of life at later stage. New education policy started from 1986 on the principles of distance education, open school, operation block, board and model schools, viz. Navodaya Vidyalaya in every district. Higher education cannot be qualitative unit unless school education is well qualitative. Computer education has been made compulsory from Class IV particularly in Central Schools, Navodaya Vidyalaya and Public Schools.

In the present school system up till Class 5 is primary school, till Class 8 middle school, till Class 10 year secondary school and until Class 12 is senior secondary school. Primary education is free and library services are available to every students at all levels.

Secondary and senior secondary schools have good libraries manned by professional librarians. Secondary Education Commission (1952-53) stressed for good school libraries. Teachers are usually available for school students but there is non-availability of literature for general reading, particularly in local languages.

Sears List of Subject Headings: The Dictionary catalogue consists of a single alphabetical sequence in which are filed entries and references under headings for authors, titles, series and subjects. Thus in one sequence, there is facility for bibliographical search (author, title etc.) and international search (subject), sentiments subject entries are removed from the general alphabetical sequence to form a subject catalogue. Whether or not the entries are physically removed, the subject entries can be considered as an entry which we can refer to as an alphabetic-specific subject catalogue. 'Alphabetic' because the arrangement is alphabetical; 'specific' because headings are used which exactly cover the subject of the document and only that subject. It is this specificity which distinguishes the alphabetic-specific subject catalogue from other alphabetical subject catalogue.

In common with all other types of subject catalogue, the alphabetic-specific has as its objective the ready indication and identification of relevant subject information and the arrangement of the total subject file in a helpful, known order. Also in common with other systems (though more so than most) it relies on the use of ordinary languages, and is controlled by the use of a 'standard language' (with its special levels of grammar, semantics and subject).

It is also applied in information retrieval through three processes. First matter is to be named with the subject to which one has classified it. Three processes are (1) Naming—the examination of the document and the selection of words, phrases and sentences which collectivily are an exact and equal representation (are co-extensive with) of the subject of the document. (2) Selection—the selection from this description of these elements of the subject which are relevant either to the community to be served or to the information system used. What, in other words, is needful of record. (3) Translation—the element of description is transformed/translated into the standard language used by the system. All these apply to the alphabetic-specific subject catalogue. A standard language (list of subject heading or thesaurus) is here used to avoid the consistencies of more form or meaning to reduce the length of the subject descriptor. All standard languages aim to describe the subject of documents in terms which will be used by future enquires (sears list).

Shelving: In a short article on book stacks it is only possible to give a brief description of the developments which have taken place within the past few years and the many changes which have been made in planning and equipping libraries. Therefore, to ensure an efficient and economical scheme it is necessary, when planning a new library, that there be same collaboration among the architect, the librarian and the equipment manufacturers. Briefly:

(a) A library must be designed to accommodate books and folios of every description.

(b) Planned such so as to give ready access to every volume and easy communication with cataloguing, reading and delivery rooms.

(c) A ventilating system ensuring adequate fresh air, free of dust, with temperature and humidity control.

(d) A lighting system whereby the titles of books are easily read.

(e) Adequate provision for expansion. Many libraries in the past were designed on the monumental scale and furnished with bookcases in hard wood as high as 10 ft, making access to the upper shelves very difficult.

The general practice today is to use steel book-stacks of such a height that all volumes are within easy reach.

The better quality stacks are furnished in a variety of colours in stove enamel which is exceedingly durable, easily cleaned and affording no room to pests.

The Standard Stack: The steel bookcase sometimes called the standard stack is designed for use where architectural appearance and fine finish are of importance and is especially suited for use in open access stacks. The bookcases are made with a continuous shelf base which supports the double sheet-steel division panels and at top the stacks are finished with a corniced cover plate. The shelves are adjustable at

1 inch intervals. Special features such as paneled or rounded ends to conceal columns or radiators can be incorporated and sloping shelves for display purposes can be fitted. Glass or wire mesh doors may be included to protect rare books. Sliding shelves for quick reference are an advantage.

The Bracket Stack: This is one of the most economical and efficient stacks obtainable and is designed for use in stack rooms.

Tubular columns into which the shelf brackets engage are supported by a heavy shelf base and the shelves are easily adjusted in 1 in. intervals. Closed end panels and top covers may be fitted to give a more finished appearance, and various types of shelves or work desks to form study carrels may be fitted.

Tower Stack: One kind of arranging of many shelves on one another, thus raising the shelf capacity.

Rolling Stack: They are used to meet the scarcity of space for stacking purpose. There are metal stack units mounted on wide tread ball-bearing wheels.

The Multi-tier Stack: Vertical storage has become a necessity on account of the scarcity and high cost of land and the multi-tier system had been adopted in many countries.

This system is constructed with a self-supporting metal framework extending from basement to roof, and designed to carry the weight of the book load, with the weight of the deck floors and line load. The close spacing of the supporting columns which are slotted to support the shelf brackets permits the use of thin slab concrete or metal plate floors.

Model by-laws restrict the use of this system in parts of Great Britain and it is necessary to obtain consent from the appropriate authority, but in other countries this system is permitted, and many stack rooms have been erected using prefabricated all metal construction thus saving valuable time in erection.

In stack rooms fitted with conventional stacks as previously described, Fremont Rider points out that the aisles which give access to the bookshelves take up about 65 per cent of the space in the stack. It is, therefore, desirable when planning a library with limited space, to consider the following methods of the book storage.

Economics in space can be achieved by rolling cases. These are metal stack units mounted on wide tread ball-bearing wheels. These cases are placed side by side forming a solid bank of books and by the use of this system about 50 per cent more books can be stored in a given floor area than is possible by the normal fixed shelving system. Individual cases are easy to pull out provided a hard level floor exists. A recent Swedish invention—already in use in Britain—enables rolling cases to be manipulated by electric power.

Compact Storage: Even more space may be saved by the installation of the compact storage system designed by Snead & Co.

This system consists of units of three stacks, the centre row of fixed double-sided stacks having hinged double-sided stacks at each side. Each hinged stack is hung on ball-bearing pivots without rails or guards and is easily swung into the aisle to give access to material in the inner shelves.

An elaborate system of compact storage is manufactured in America. This has the appearance of a normal stack from the front, but each individual shelf is mounted on runners and may be pulled out for access to volumes at each side.

Vertical shelf adjustment is arranged to place volumes of varying heights. These ranges may be fixed back to back thus forming a solid bank of books. (Ency. Libnship)

Soviet Classification: Over a period of some years a new scheme of Soviet Library Classification has been worked out by three of the largest Soviet Libraries, the Lenin Library in Moscow, the Saltykov Shchedrin Public Library in Leningrad, and the Library of the USSR. Academy of Science for their classified catalogues. The aim was to create a unified scheme which could be applied in all the libraries of the Soviet Union, first of all in the learned and special libraries and the bibliographical publications of the central book chamber. For this purpose the Ministry of Culture of the RSFSR set up a commission consisting of representatives of the three libraries mentioned above and of the Fundamental Library of Social Sciences and of the Book Chamber. This commission has now accepted and approved the main divisions of this classification, which is based on the Marxist-Leninist classification, of the sciences. The following principles were laid down:

(1) Marxism-Leninism, as the science of the general laws of nature, society, and human thought, takes first place.

(2) All the other divisions are arranged according to the historical development of the action of nature on society, and divided into two cycles—the sciences of nature and the sciences of society.

(3) The natural sciences are arranged according to the Marxist-Leninist classification of the natural sciences. The applied science, technology, agriculture, and medicine, which are concerned with how man harnesses nature, stand between the natural and the social sciences.

(4) The sciences of society are arranged according to the Marxist-Leninist teaching on foundation and superstructure.

(5) The general section for literature of complex content comes at the end of the classification scheme.

The agreed and approved main divisions are as follows:

The science of the general laws of nature and society	A	Marxism-Leninism Natural sciences in general.
The sciences of society	B	Physico-mathematical sciences. Chemical sciences. Geological and geographical sciences.
	E	Biological sciences.
	H	Technological sciences.

The sciences of the action of man on nature	II	Agriculture and agricultural sciences.
	P	Medical sciences.
	C	Social sciences in general.
	T	Historical sciences. History.
	Y	Economical sciences. Economics. Communist and worker's parties. Organization of labour.
	X	Government of law.
The sciences of society		Military science. Learning Education. Pedagogy.
	III	Philological sciences. Literature.
	III.,	Art Religion and atheism Philosophical sciences; Psychology. Literature of universal content.

This outline was approved on 11th June 1959, by the Library Commission attached to the Presidium of the Academy of Sciences of the USSR (It should, of course, be remembered that the Academy of Sciences embraces also the social sciences in the same way as does this new classification). *Sovietskaya Bibliografia*, 1959, 3, (55), 102-4 (Aslib Proc., 1960, 12, 47-8).

Standardization in Documentation:

(A) *Background and organization*

Defined here is a document in which are formulated the agreed requirements of a product or process for a given purpose with the object of reducing unnecessary waste (of material, labour, time, etc.), a standard may contain recommendation on any of the following features:

(1) Quantity, dimensions, shape, weight, etc. to reduce unnecessary variety and improve interchangeability.

(2) Quality, performance, to ensure fitness for the job.

(3) A method of test, including sampling and analysis for comparing materials or products.

(4) Terms and symbols, for simpler and clearer communication.

(5) A code of practice or guide to procedure for greater simplicity and efficiency by saving time and labour.

Although standard formulae and units of measure, among other standards, were known in Roman, Greek and even earlier times, it was only the exigencies of the rapid industrial expansion from the turn of the century onward that encouraged preparation, publication and use of the now familiar British and other national standards for the most varied ranges of materials, products and procedures. The British Standard Institution (BSI) is the approved British body for the preparation, promulgation and keeping up-to-date of all British Standards covering the features (1) to (5) above, and the principles it observes are:

(a) That every British standard shall fulfill a recognized want not only of producers for industrial production, science and technology, but also of consumers;

(b) That the interest of both producer and consumer shall be considered.

More recently, increasing international communication in commercial, cultural and other fields has created the need for international standardization, and this is carried on through the **International Organisation for Standardization (ISO)** and the **International Electrotechnical Commission (IEC)** in both of which the B.S.I. is the British National member body, helping to promote simplification, increase efficiency and interchangeability with consequent prevention of waste.

Standardization is the interplay of national and international discussion, more significant than in documentation and, although most documentation standards take the form of guides of efficient practice, library materials and equipment equally require widely agreed and clearly formulated standards that will enable the reader, librarian or other user to get what he wants to the standard required, whatever the source.

(B) *Published Recommendations and Work in Hand*

Classification: The only systems so far which can lay any claim to being standard classification are the **Decimal Classification** (**q.v.**) published in the United States, and the **Universal Decimal Classification** (**q.v.**) sponsored in many languages, not by ISO but by the Federation International de Documentation (FID) and edited and published by the B.S.I. in its English version as B.S. 1000. There are moves to prepare a new general **faceted scheme**, but it seems unlikely that any such system will quickly be accepted as a 'standard'.

Abbreviation of Titles (of Periodicals, etc.):

ISO/R 4-1953 was the first published ISO recommendation in documentation, but consists only code of rules. A new British Standard, in an advanced stage of preparation, will include a select list of several thousand words with their recommended abbreviations amplifying its code of rules, some of which are modifications of the rules in ISO/R 4.

Transliteration: Alphabets for which standards have been or are about to be issued are:

Other standardizing work in documentation: Two other ISO recommendations have resulted from ISO/TC 46 activity:

(a) ISO/R 18-1955 (Short contents list)

(b) ISO/R 30-1956 (Bibliographical strip-'mauchelle').

In addition, and of greater interest, are two further documents likely soon to become ISO recommendations are:

Presentation of contribution in periodicals,

Abstracts and synopses.

Several other problems are on the current programme of work of ISO/TC 46, notably.

Book prelims (form and presentation aspects)

Index cards, bibliographical and publishers cards, form, layout, etc.

Punched cards.

Document reproduction: This is a specialized branch of work, much concerned with photographic materials and equipments Standardization is a matter largely for experts in the photographic industry, both at national and international level; here, too, there are links between many British (and other national) standards and the international recommendations prepared by the special subcommittee ISO/TC 46/SC 1 (Document reproduction).

Two international (ISO) recommendations are now ready on:

(a) Sizes of photocopies on paper

(b) Sizes of bases for microtransparencies and several others in various stages of preparation:

  (i) Essential characteristics of 35mm microfilm readers.

  (ii) Microcopy legibility tests—ISO, that character, 'mire' and micromire'.

  (iii) Microcopy—35mm and 16mm microfilm.

  (iv) Terminology of Microcopies (and their bases) and of Microcopy reading apparatus.

Standardization in library documentation in India have been initiated as early as in 1870, in the field of material used in the libraries. The section committee of Indian Standard Institutions (1947) was appointed under the Chairmanship of Dr. S.R. Ranganathan to formulate standard for documentation. The committee finalized 48 standards in the area of Bibliographical references. These are as under:

IS	4-	1949	Practice for make-up of periodicals.
IS	18	1949	Abbreviations for titles of periodicals.

IS	382	1952	Practice for alphabetical arrangement.
IS	790	1950	Specifications for general structure of preliminary passes of a book.
IS	791	1956	Specification of half title leaf of the book.
IS	792	1956	Specification for title leaf of a book.
IS	793	1956	Practice for author statement in the title page of the book.
IS	795	1956	Canons for making abstracts.
IS	796	1959	Glossary of cataloguing terms.
IS	1250	1958	Proof corrections for printers and authors.
IS	1275	1958	Rules for making alphabetical indexes.
IS	1358	1959	Practice for layout of library catalogue code.
IS	12381	1963	Recommendations for bibliographical References.
IS	795	1976	Guide for preparation of abstracts.
IS	1275	1976	Rules for making alphabetical indexes.
IS	2381	1978	Recommendations for bibliographical References.
IS	2661	1978	Mahila Library Room (Libra clive).
IS	2692	1978	Package for use of libraries.
IS	1553	1976	Primary elements in the design of library building.
IS	4116	1976	Steel Shelving cabinets.
IS	1879	(Pt.T)	1978 Library furniture and fittings.
IS	9400	1980	Guidelines for presentation of information in technical terms.

Subject Classification (of James Duff Brown): This holds a unique place among classification schemes. It is the only general scheme of any moment to be compiled by a United Kingdom librarian and is a mixture of ideas, some of which have developed well, some of which have developed badly. It is used in about 40 British libraries, mostly medium or small ones of long standing. It is not now adopted by new libraries for reasons given below:

The mistakes apparent in his own and Dewey's Decimal Classification caused Brown to try again and to produce in 1906 the Subject Classification. A second edition, revised by the author, was published shortly after his death in 1914, by his nephew James D. Stewart.

Its use was continued by most of the libraries which adopted it originally and a third revised edition was published in

1939 by Stewart. Note was taken of suggestions for revision and a fourth edition was contemplated.

The scheme may be seen in operation at Bermondsey, Ilford and other public libraries. Lack of extensive funds and of a standing revision committee have contributed greatly to the difficulties encountered in keeping the scheme alive, but more has been done to perpetuate it than the Expansive Classification of C.A. Cutter in rather similar circumstances.

Principles and outline: It is basically simple to understand and reasonably proportioned, but suffers from authors' over-indulgence in a personal theory, which results being ill-placed for modern needs in many classes.

Two important principles are employed:

(1) The constant or concrete subject should be preferred to the more general standpoint or occasional subject;

(2) Every class is arranged in a systematic order of scientific progression, as far as it seemed possible to maintain it; while applications directly derived from a science or other theoretical base, have been placed with that science or base.

Brown protests like other classifiers, that practical usefulness must take precedence over theory, but a perusal of the schedules has caused his critics to decide that he has, in fact, pursued his theory too far.

The 'concrete subject' has tended to become the 'object written about, rather than the subject of the book. The author has attempted to make a one place scheme, avoiding the network of relationship to be found in Dewey, but with partial success. Books are ideas in relationship.

The placing of derived subjects with their parents is admirable in many instances and has been adopted in the most modern schemes but, carried to excess, it separates groups of subjects which are sought together and used together. Brown brings together in practice subdivision which are only remotely connected. A look at the detailed schedules will make this clear.

The order of classes is based on the idea that everything derives from a definite sources and is briefly:

1. Matter, 2. Life, 3. Mind, and 4. Record. This expands into:

Table of main classes:

A.	Generalia	
B-D	Physical Science Matter and Force	
E-F	Biological Science	Life
G-H	Ethology and Medicine	
I	Economic Biology	
J-K	Philosophy and Religion	Mind
L	Social and Political Science	
M	Language and Literature	
N	Literary Forms	
O-W	History, Geography	Record
X	Biography	

There is no useful or fine arts class as such. Language and literature are combined at M-N, history and geography at O-W.

Class A Generalia is unusual as it contains subjects which 'qualify or pervade' others, such as education, logic, mathematics, graphic and plastic arts and general science—subjects usually considered major divisions of other classes or main classes in themselves.

The index is specific. As the scheme attempts to provide one place for a subject in all its relationships, there is normally one index entry. This is not always possible, as the entries for children, church and colour will show.

The notation consists of a single capital letter of the alphabet followed by numbers which can be treated decimally if required. The base is reasonably broad and well-allocated, bearing in mind the date of compilation. Letters A-X, including O, are used, Y may be used for Special Local Collections.

Auxiliary tables: The **Categorical tables:** table of categories, forms, etc., for the subdivision of subjects, are numbered from .0 to .980 (ed.3); .0, .00, .02 and .1 to .980 (excluding .37, .502, .694, .695, .698) are used, giving 979 standpoints and subjects which may be combined with any subject number in the main tables, e.g. M520.877, English grammar. The dot is a separating device, not a decimal point. While many of these categorical tables cannot be combined sensibly with many of the subject, some one always combine with some. They are a pioneer attempt at synthetic combination, a problem which still exercises the minds of classifiers, although more elaborate systems have been devised, notably by Bliss and Ranganathan.

An alphabetical index is provided.

National numbers: Subject may be qualified to show locality by adding the members from classes O-W or, where necessary, language numbers, e.g. L185W328, Free masonry in Texas. (Ency. Libnship).

Subject device: Division or formation of an isolated by borrowing the isolated number from another class to indicate temporary occurence.

Subject Specialization: Local autonomy in book selection is essential of effective librarianship, but results in gaps in overall provision. There is a tendency in public libraries, accentuated by attenuated resources, towards under-representation of expensive and unbound materials, books on minority interests and those outside the usual book trade channels—pamphlets, import from overseas, private and government publications besides music, periodicals and maps while in special libraries concentration on essentials leads to mutual neglect of materials on marginal subjects. The fluctuations of demand and the vagaries of publishers, all add to the problems of the selector. An item rejected on publication acquires a subsequent cachet when it is out of print; of three books on similar subjects issued at one time and one initially rejected, is specifically requested at a later date. Reliance on the inter-loan agreements has been proved an ineffectual guarantee of provision; on average, throughout the country, approximately 25 per cent of all items requested are not able to be located within the region originating the enquiry. It is also known that borrowing a book from the region outside of one's own adds approximately one month to the time taken to obtain it.

To meet these problems there have been developed 'subject coverage' schemes of varying form in six regions in recent years. Three of these incorporate provisions for co-operative storage on a subject basis, serve the need for guaranteed provision and at the same time enable the saving to storage space through the prevention of wasteful duplication. They check the unnecessary growth of libraries and enable stock weeding to be undertaken with confidence and boldness. Subject specialization, coupled with co-operative storage, extends the range of total provision, ensuring that at least one copy of works within defined limits shall be obtained and made permanently available; it brings all such resources into use throughout a wider area; reduces the demands on the National Central Library, and tends to reduce the average time taken to obtain requested items. It also enables the smaller library to play a proportionate role in inter-library loans, and helps the conscientious public library book selector to avoid creating a demand for the unworthy book, since it gives him confidence that on request it will be available on loan. A useful additional feature of subject specialization is that the individual with a minority interest is enabled to obtain his requirements, even though he lives in a small community. (Ency. Libnshp)

U

Universal Decimal Classification: U.D.C. or C.D.U. (Fr.) or D.K. (Ger.): Derived some 60 years ago from the D.C. or Decimal Classification of Melvil Dewey and developed by Otlet, La Fontain Donker Duyvis and others, the U.D.C. is a comprehensive scheme for classifying every branch of human activity and knowledge. It can be applied to any special subject and used for all kinds of recorded information (literary, pictorial, etc.) and references thereto, whatever the form of document (e.g. books, papers, letters, samples and specimens) or the method of storage (e.g. shelving, filing). Sponsored by the "Federation Internationale de Documentation" (FID) and published in many languages by the respective standardizing bodies or other national U.D.C. organizations, it is continuously being revised and extended by a network of international (FID) and Central Classification Committee (C.C.C.), which consists of the editors of the full national editions. Among the more important section newly designed or thoroughly revised in recent years are 539.1 and 621.039 Nuclear physics and technology, 621.37/.39 Electronics & Telecommunication, 65 Management, whilst new schedules are being worked out for such rapidly developing subjects as Aeronautics and aircraft engineering and Control theory and techniques (cybernetics), including Computers and data processing equipment. The U.D.C. has recently been adopted by the International Organisation for Standardisation (ISO) for a Card Index exchange scheme and is now widely recognized as a standard classification especially in technical documentation or information centres, scientific and other special libraries.

Principles, structure and notation: The U.D.C. is a subject classification in the strictest sense, depending on the analysis of thought content and based on the principle of proceeding from the general to the more particular, so that related concepts are brought together in more helpful array than can be achieved by alphabetical or other arrangements. The term 'universal' does not, as often supposed, refer to its international or worldwide use, but to the attempt made in U.D.C. to treat all fields of knowledge as a unified pattern of interrelated subjects rather than changed patch work of countless special classifications, each more or less independent and self-sufficient as in so many other general schemes.

The notation consists of Arabic numerals, internationally more familiar in a standard sequence than letters or other symbols, and the whole of knowledge (regarded as unity) is divided into domain, preliminary generalia and more main sections, denoted by decimal fractions .0 to .9, each further divided and subdivided into any required degree. Thus, social science and its main division Law, denoted by .3 and .34 may be subdivided as follows:

.3	Social Science, Sociology
.34	Law, Jurispredunce
.347	Civil Law
.3477	Commercial law
.34778	Copyright, Performance rights
.347781	Literary copyright
.3477815	Kinds of literary works.

For convenience, the initial point I is omitted in practice, though it is the fact that the numbers are in reality all decimal fractions less than unity that determines their sequence; on the other hand, 'points' are arbitrarily inserted as a visual aid usually after every third digit. So the numbers .347, etc. become 347, 347.7, 347.78, 347.781.5. Occasional deviation from this 'triplet' pattern, for mnemonic or other reason, does not alter the order of filing, for which purpose these 'points' are ignored. In its main structure, the U.D.C. thus resembles the D.C. while greater flexibility has been attained in its Auxiliary notation of distinctive signs, which permit the formation of combined or compound numbers for the widest range of complex notions. The most important auxiliary devices are:

(a) The colon (sing of relation) to link two or more main members representing independently classifiable concepts, e.g.

534	Acoustics	GIVING
781	Musical theory	534.781 (physical basis of music)

so that separate cards or entries are automatically made for each number separated by colon and complex subject can be located from the different points of view inherent in it.

(b) Common auxiliaries of language, form, place, time, etc.

Usable with any main number of the U.D.C.,

e.g.

34 = 30 Law, literature in German Language

16 (03) Logic, encyclopaedia or dictionary

629.12 (42) Shipbuilding, in England

531.16. Mechanics, in the 17th century.

(c) Special auxiliaries for elements, details etc. restricted to a particular subject (and usable only with the corresponding number for the subject), e.g.

669.14-42 Steel, bars and sections

678.632.32.21 Phenolics, phenol-formaldehyde composition

726.03 Church architecture,

Availability of U.D.C. publications: All U.D.C. publications are obtained from the FID (6 Willem Witsenplein, the Hague) and from the various national U.D.C. organizations. In Britain the body concerned is the British Standards Institution (B.S.I.) which published the English edition as B.S. 1000.

The issue of the full English schedules, which in recent years has progressed rather slowly, is being accelerated and it is intended that these should be completed by about 1965.

At present the only published sections are C1.5 (complete) Mathematics and Natural Sciences.

621.3	Electrical engineering
622/623	Mining, Military engineering
669	Metallurgy
678/679	Rubbers and plastics, etc.
69	Building

For pending publication of more printed schedules, the usual practice is for librarians to use either the Abridged English BS1000A or the trilingual Abridged Edition BS1000B as a basis for all schemes and to obtain sections from BSI. Such relevant full sections may be available in draft form.

University Library: University presents a major contribution in the growth of human resources. Library promote means of communication and advancement of knowledge. The University library is expected to contain research collection, variety of subject books, a large and complex catalogue; reference staff, large building and open-self device. There were stupas, caves, viharas constructed by the ancient rulers. They were having well-equipped libraries, Nalanda and Taxila were main viharas which established separate university with separate university library with monumental building with rare collection. The Nalanda library was housed in three huge buildings including one of nine storied called Ratna Bodhini which contained manuscripts and several tantric works. The library of Bidar College was built by Mohammed Gawan (1463-82). With the change of time gradually a true appreciation and understanding of university libraries has been forthcoming, chiefly due to growing need and independence of the scholar on the rich and varied book sources. Three universities were established in 1857—Calcutta, Bombay and Madras. University development started slow after independence. There were

8 in First Plan, 11 in Second Plan, 18 in Third Plan, 25 in Fourth Plan, 30 in Fifth Plan, 20 in Sixth Plan, 32 in Seventh Plan and until now there has been a tremendous addition to the total number of universities in India.

Organisational structure: Efficient administration requires forecasting and planning in relation to library's objectives, sensible organization and grouping of appropriate activities. Organisation is a framework of management. The library organization is a process of establishing the pattern of relationship by assigning duties and responsibilities to each department and groups. Organisation is an end in itself but it promotes efficiency and coordinated the various activities. There are six principles of organization: (1) Specialisation (2) Unity of direction (3) Unity of command (4) Delegation (5) Scalar chain or chain of commands and (6) Leadership.

Organisation can be divided into two kinds—formal and informal. Library organization is structured in such a way that it may strengthen the relationship among various departments to provide optimum service. These are: (a) Line organization (b) Line and staff organization and (c) Functional organization. Line unit denotes the qualitative aspects of organizational pattern.

Taylor's system of functional organization can be applied to university library in allotting functions and duties to each person in library by the type of job and specialization a person has. Line and staff organization maintain balanced relationship among different aspects of a library. It is much practiced in big libraries. It is a suitable approach to staff coordination.

Departmentalisation: It is related with the division of labour. A University library has many departments, i.e. Order department, Archives department, Binding department, Photo department, Periodical department, Circulation department, Reference department, Reserve department, Reading room, Computer department, Audio-visual department etc.

Planning and Control: Taylor says, management should take higher responsibility of planning and control. Library is a growing organism. Planning and control have four important functions: Undertaking of risk and handling of uncertainty, coordination, administration and control and routine supervision.

Ranganathan has divided the planning into four categories—series plan, parallel plan, functional plan, and divisional plan.

V

Videotex: Videotex is also known as taxonomy. It is the computer based information storage and retrieval system. Videotex may be categorized as under:

1. Broadcast Videotex (Teletex)
2. Interactive Videotex (Viewdata)
    - (a) Public viewdata
    - (b) Private viewdata

Teletex: In this system information is transmitted from the computer to the receiver by radiowaves. This form of Broadcast videotex has been classified as under (Deeson, Eric)—

(a) Carrier-broadcast signals (Radio or T.V.)

(b) Access serial

(c) Channel-one way

(d) Choice-small

(e) Access cost free

It is a combination of word processing and telex, where information is exchanged among terminal using a common business letter format at a transmission speed of 2,400 byte per second. It is often considered as a part of the videotex/ teletex phenomenon because it brings together computerized information system for mass market. It is more a data transmission procedure than anything else.

Teletex essentially refers to a particular technique for insulting digital pulses within previously unused scan lines of a normal television signal. It transmits data via a portion of normal television signal, without addressing the question of whether a return link might be available (via telephone line or a cable television system).

Specific Features of Teletex

1. Data under teletex system are broadcast within T.V. signals.
2. It is a non-interactive (one way) form of videotex. In other words, it is a method of transmitting text or graphics stored in a computer database, as a part of broadcast, for display on T.V. screen. Thus, user can only receive messages.
3. It is intended for wide public use, carrying information of broad public interest.
4. In teletex the terminals link to the database computer via broadcast channels.
8. It has no reverse links, hence it does not allow direct communication with the computer.
9. It does not employ sound coded signals. Signals travel within the narrow bandwidth of telephone circuits. Instead, the coded character signals are sent as part of T.V. picture signals.
10. There are possibilities of change of contents of any frame, while the system is in operation.
11. It is same as videotex except current system is limited in size.
12. There is no provision of access to other network.

Great Britain first broadcast teletex service in 1974 and India on Nov. 14, 1985. In India it is still under experimentation.

Videotex (Video-based Information System): Today libraries have started video technology for the purpose of recording and displaying visual information. Commonly two equipments are used in this technology—Video-camera and video-cassettes recorders. Some libraries with cable television facilities have started establishing video studio facilities and broadcast programmes on public access channels relating to their opening hours, various services, special collections, and training programmes. There is a close link between the video technology and computers. Microcomputers use television sets as their display devices and television manufacturers use a broadcast or monitor mode. Some libraries have also started using of cable television systems as a link between home television receives and an online catalogue.

Videotex is a computerized information system using home television such that the display device is connected to a central computer via telephone lines with the information divided into distinct page containing both text and graphics in about eight different colours—the users would be able to select subsequent pages by observing a numbered list of options on the screen and pressing the desired number of a keypad (menu system). It is interactive in nature. It covers full T.V. screen.

Special features of Videotex

1. Videotex is a concept of designing information system for the market.
2. It refers to any electronic system that makes computer based information available via VDU or T.V. sets to a dispersed and reasonably numerous audience.
3. Videotex is applied to interactive (two way) systems for transmitting text and graphics stored in computer databases via the telephone network, for display in television screen, i.e. Time saving computers, E-mail etc.
4. View data are transmitted via telephone lines.
5. It is an interactive (two way) system for transmitting text or graphic stored in computer databases via telephone network for display on T.V. screen.
6. It is simple to use low cost information system, catering to a large number of users.

7. Its hardware consists of a central database computer linked to a large number of T.V. displays via telecommunication network.
8. In this data are organized as 'frames', each containing a screenful of alphabetic, numeric and graphic symbols.
9. It can be considered as potential distribution media for all kinds of digitally-coded data.
10. Users link terminals to the database computers via telephone network.
11. It has the reverse link which allows the direct communication with the computers.
12. Employs sound coded signals as a system mode of operations. It assumes that the user has a telephone, to which a T.V. monitor or T.V. set can be connected via electronic interface.
13. The content of any particular frame can be changed while the system is in operation.
14. The system is under continuous development, thus database is capable of great expansion.
15. Access to other networks through 'Gateway' e.g. Telex.

Development: International Telecommunication Union, (ITU) an institute for standardization and tariff structures in telephone, telegraphy and data-transmission coined the term 'Videotex'. The system was introduced in early 1970. The world's first view data PRESTEL was introduced for commercial operation in 1979 in Great Britain.

Videotex system is a computer based information storage and retrieval system. Videotex is a distributed database and categorized as under:

1. Broadcast Videotex.
2. Intractive Videotex (view data)—It is of two types—public view data and private view data. Video data is also known as Interactive videotex like PSNT

(Phone System) or cable, direct, two ways, large and free based (changed).

The following equipments are used in videotex system:

(a) a telephone
(b) an electronic interface with a control keyboard and a modem
(c) an auto dialler
(d) a circuit
(e) a printer/or some recording device.

We can enumerate the following functions of videotex system:

(a) For connecting a TV monitor/TV set via an electronic interface.
(b) For converting data signals to and from the form used for telephone transmission.
(c) For calling the database computer and identifying the calling terminal at the press of a button.
(d) For generating the displayed picture from the receiving data.
(e) For sorting the received frames by the user.

Systems applying Videotex and Teletex

1. PRESTEL videotex system (1978-79): 960 characters, 1200 bits.
2. Autiope videotex and teletex system (French 1981): 16 bits, 2400 bits.
3. Teledon videotex and teletex system (Canadian 1978): used upto 100,000 cells.
4. Captain videotex system (Japanese 1983): 192 rows × 240 columns, 4800 bits.
5. Oracle (UK 1974): 920 characters.
6. LEXIS videotex system (USA).
7. West-law videotex system (USA).

W

Word by Word Filing: It is one of the two basic methods of arranging entries in an alphabetical order in a list, catalogue or bibliography. The method is also called 'Nothing before Something' from the principle of regarding the space separating the first word from subsequent words in a compound or phrase heading 'nothing'.

For example

Green acres
Green field
Green bank
Green shank

The same entries filed by the alternative letter by letter method would appear as follows:

Green acres
Green fields
Green Howards
Green shank

Proper Names:

Single name	-	Ramlal
Compound names	-	Ramesh Kumar Singh
Names with prefix	-	Lord Curzon
Differences in Spelling	-	Anderson Andersson

A. When the same word, or combination of words, used as the heading of different kinds of enries, arrange the entries in the main groups.

(a) Simple surname entry: arrange alphabetically by fore names.

(b) All other entries: arrange alphabetically word by word, disregarding kinds of entries, form of heading and punctuations.

B. Arrange subject entries under a personal or corporate name immediately after the author entry.

Examples

Love, John L	Love POETRY
Love, John L	Love Songs
Love, William	Love THEOLOGY
Love and beauty	Love your neighbour
Love, MATERIAL	

Note: Headings in capital are subject headings.

Personal Name Entry

Smith	Smith, Captain
Smith, 1641	Smith, J
Smith, Adam	Smith, Jobu

Corporate Entry

(a) Author without subheading

(b) Subject without subheading

(c) Name with subdivisions intensified alphabetically with title.

United Nations

UNITED NATIONS

United Nations and how it works (Title)

UNITED NATIONS—BIOGRAPHY

United Nations, Economic Commission for Europe

Place

(a) Author without subheadings.

(b) Subject without subdivisions.

London, Jack (Author)
London (Place as author)
LONDON (subject)
London and Londoners (Title)
London, Central Criminal Court (Author)
London Scene

Subject

(a) Subject without subdivision
(b) Period divisions
(c) Alphabetical extension of main subheading

EDUCATION
EDUCATION - 1945
EDUCATION - AFRICA
EDUCATION - AIMS AND OBJECTIVES
Education and American Civilisation (title)
EDUCATION - US
EDUCATION - US-1945
EDUCATION - US-BIBLIOGRAPHY

Part-II

Essay Writing

A

Agris Database: International Information System for the Agricultural Sciences and Technology is an international cooperative information system. AGRIS is a cooperative system and its membership reached to 130 National and 17 International/Regional centres. All members report their literature published within its boundaries. Data is submitted to the APU on magnetic tapes, floppy disks or on input sheets for Central Processing. Most centres sent their input on floppy disks. The monthly increment of the AGRIS database is 10,000 references. AGRIS began its operation in 1975 and total database contained 1.5 million references. AGRIS is fully computerized. AGRIS has helped to develop the necessary infrastructure with reference to computer utilization in the centres. Many centres have developed their own documentation system based on AGRIS methodology. Some centre process the AGRIS magnetic tape for making a large retrospective database.

In cooperation with INIS, online task were carried out from 1975 onward and on IBM/STARIS. The necessary equipment was installed and tested for dial-up telephone users and for non-European countries' connection to international telecommunication networks were established, the most important being TYMNET of USA.

Special Features

1. It is a cooperative system. It has a membership of 130 national and 17 international/regional centres.
2. All participant centres report to AGRIS of all agricultural literature published in their area.

3. It prepares bibliographics in the field of agriculture.
4. Data is submitted to the APU on magnetic tapes, floppy disks or on input sheets for central processing.

Organisational Chart

FAO
(Food and Agriculture Organisation)
|
AGRIS Coordinating Centre
(Rome, Italy)
|
AGRIS
(International Information System for Agricultural Sciences and Technology
|
AGRIS Processing Units
(Bierma, Austria at International Atomic Energy Agency)

AGRIS started computerization in 1975. It rendered in services equally to developed and underdeveloped countries. It was designed to serve all countries fully. It allowed wide range of input media—from magnetic tapes to data on input sheets. In fact, AGRIS received a part of the total data, i.e. 10% in the form of optical character recognition sheets. These sheets were used for developing countries. Later on optical character recognition sheets were replaced by micro computers and also input on floppy disks which is presently in practice.

AGRINDEX published by AGRIS was made available on various AGRIS participating centres. AGRINDEX was published in English for 12 years, but later on it was published in French and Spanish version. Subject Index was somehow different from English version.

Food and Agricultural Organisation (FAO) supported AGRIS, CARIS and filed projects to establish documentation centres in the participating countries. It took the responsibility to train the people in AGRIS methodology to retrieve the document references from large databases. It resulted in many documentation systems and also infrastructure for proper computer utilization in the centre.

AGRIS developed thesaurus for agricultural terminology called AGROVOC and published in three languages—English, French and Spanish. The output tapes contained the descriptions for all references.

AGRIS Processing Centre: AGRIS basically started fully computerization system. Being the centralized collection of input data, the manual checking was assisted by a range of computer checks for quality database.

About more than one lakh entries are used in computer system.

Prerequisites for designing a system

1. The system designed had to be independent.
2. International standards are to be followed.
3. Provision for future extension.
4. The system should allow for future technological change, i.e. CD-ROM technology, photo-composition and microcomputer.
5. Time consuming feedback countries.

AGRIS information system was designed on the model of INIS (International Nuclear Information System) and modeled in 1970. Checking procedure is designed as a cycle with checking stations. The system has following features:

1. Input data is fed in system and checked in a cycle.
2. Data is stored in a large file of references or documents.
3. Old data are updated.
4. Final checking is done by computer.
5. Good and updated file is sent to production programme and bad file is used for feedback.
6. A print out is distributed to centres for immediate action.

Checking Points

1. Format errors particularly the structure of record, minimum and maximum length, are verified.

2. Bibliographical errors are checked, i.e. use of parentheses, matrix errors, syntax errors and errors on table.
3. Duplication check, i.e. identification number, author, collation, year against the authority file.
4. Index checking, i.e.
   (a) Validation descriptor based on AGROVOC descriptor.
   (b) Automatic correction. One error is corrected automatically and non-descriptors are replaced by descriptor for use in indexing.
   (c) Subject validity—Descriptors with scope notes in AGROVOC are flagged for the proofreader in order to draw his attention to a possible error.

Participating Centres: Computer processing on participating centres includes the work of generation of local databases and the checking and store of raw data on a floppy disk. Small centre send the data on floppy disks. The most frequently used software is Micro CDS/ISISI, a software package for microcomputers developed by UNESCO.

AGRIS also receive output tape and floppy disks based on ISO-2709 standard. Output on floppy disks can only be used for a limited set of data. All participating centres (30 in number) receive the monthly AGRIS tapes and they are used for implementing a complete online database for producing National Bibliographics.

Anglo-American Code: The name of the Cataloguing rules; author and title entries compiled by committees of the Library Association and of the American Library Association. Often quoted as the A.A. Code and the Joint Code.

The code was published in 1908 as a result of four years of cooperative effort on the part of the two committees as the first International cataloguing code. Its origin lay in the fact that in 1900 the American Library Association appointed a committee to revise the A.L.A. Catalogue Rules

(1883) with particular reference to securing agreement between the revised rules and library of congress cataloguing practice. This committee held its first meeting in March, 1901 and by 1902 an advance edition of the revised rules was printed for distribution inviting suggestions and criticisms. Since 1900 British librarians had advocated revision of the Library Association's Cataloguing Rules (1883), and following the Association's annual general meeting in 1902 a committee for this revision was constituted, and produced a draft of the proposed revision in 1904. At the suggestion of a member of the American library committee, Melvil Dewey, the two associations agreed in 1904 that their committees should cooperate in the production an Anglo-American Code with a view to establishing uniformity of practice throughout the English speaking world. Within four years an agreed code was produced containing 174 rules relating to the entry, heading and description cataloguing of works for an author and title catalogue.

The code may be regarded largely as a synthesis of the most practical and convenient ruling contained in the original code of the two associations, those of the British Museum Cutter, Dziatzk, Linderfelt and Library of Congress. In only eight cases were the committees unable to agree on a joint ruling (Rule, 16, 32, 40, 41, 116, 118, 121) and here both rulings were included as alternatives. Nevertheless, the rapid acceptance of this code in all kinds and sizes of libraries in both countries has since been instrumental in achieving a great measure of that uniformity of practice sought by the two associations. The extent of this use threw light on various inadequacies and this, together with advances in cataloguing techniques and methods, let in time to demand for its further revision, particularly in the United States. In 1930 a sub-committee of the American Library Association was set up, and made independent of the Association in 1932 to make necessary revisions with authority to cooperate with the Library Association of Great Britain and with such other national library associations as it may think appropriate. With the aid of Carnegie Corporation grant, work proceeded and a preliminary edition was published in 1941. This was divided into two parts, (1) Entry and heading, (2) Description of the book, that contained 375 rules in greater details, making greater provision for the cataloguing of serial publications, publications of religious bodies, anonymous classics, music and maps, whilst the British alternative rules were omitted.

This preliminary edition met with the criticism of being over elaborate and likely to increase the cost of cataloguing but further revision was referred until 1946 when the A.L.A. Division of Cataloguing and Classification assumed responsibility. Revision of Part-II was abandoned and the second edition of Part-I was eventually published in 1949. Extensive re-arrangement of the rules was made in order to emphasize basic principles and secure a logical arrangement. The total number of rules were reduced to 158 and rules applying to particular circumstances were given as subsections to the basic rules.

The latter, although used frequently in British libraries as an amplification of the 1908 code, may no longer properly be called the Anglo-American code since little cooperation with the library association took place and it has assumed a largely American emphasis.

Aslib: Aslib was founded in 1924 with the title of Association of Special Libraries and Information Bureaux as a result of a conference held at Hoddesdon, Hertfordshire, on the initiative of a group of people working in the metallurgical research associations. The purpose set for it was to facilitate the coordination and systematic use of knowledge and information in industry and commerce and in all the arts and sciences. While circumstances since its foundation have dictated that science and technology should prove the chief field of Aslib's activity, its aim to take all knowledge for its province remains unchanged.

As with many organizations, the early years of struggling existence were years of solid achievement on infinitesimal material resources. In 1928 Aslib compiled and published, with financial help from the Carnegie United Kingdom Trust, the *Aslib Directory*, a guide to sources of specialized information in Great Britain and Ireland. It also contributed to the development of the Central Library for students into the National Central Library, The establishment of the Union Catalogue of the London Borough Libraries and the Guilt Hall Library, and to the movement leading to the 1925 Committee on Patent Law Reform during the Second World War, Aslib undertook such diverse tasks as having irreplaceable scientific periodicals, preserved from the salvage drive, compiling, with support from the Royal Society and the Rockfeller Foundation, location indexes of European and Russian scientific journals, and establishing in 1942, a microfilm service to supply on demand, from master negative, microfilm copies of any foreign technical publication available. This wartime work led to the decision of the British Government in 1944 to assist Aslib's work by annual and special grants to be given through the Department of Scientific and Industrial Research. In 1949 the Association and the British Society for International Bibliography united to form a new body with the registered title of Aslib but without fundamental change in objectives. Members of both organizations had, in the previous year, taken an active part in the important scientific Information Conference organized by the Royal Society; at this conference, methods of disseminating, abstracting, televiewing, classifying, indexing and selecting scientific and technical literature were reviewed for the first time on an imperial scale.

Membership and Organisation: The membership of Aslib is now nearly 2,400 compared with 300 in 1940 and 1000 in 1950 and 25,000 in 1985. Roughly 80% of the membership is in the United Kingdom, though most countries of the world are represented and the United States and Canada together have about 130 members of the British membership. Approximately 44% are industrial and commercial concern, 12% are Government Departments and Government sponsored organizations, 8% learned societies and other non-profit organizations. The remaining 16% consists of individuals interested in information service.

The controlling authority of Aslib is Council, the majority of whom are elected by the British members. A director is responsible for carrying out the Council's policies and both the council and the director are assisted by the advisory committee. These are concerned with conferences and professional education, with Aslib's international relations in publication and with research in information work and connected subjects. Local and specialist activities are encouraged by the existence of local branches—at present there are three, covering Scotland, the north of England and the Midlands and subject groups. Nine groups now exist; they embrace aeronautics, chemicals, economics, electronics engineering, film production libraries, fuel and power, furniture and textiles. Both branches and groups enjoy considerable autonomy.

Service to reader: As the principal focus of special library activities in thc United Kingdom, Aslib assists the special librarian or information officer in two principal ways: by supplementary information services depending largely on cooperation by member organizations, and by corporate activities such as meetings and conferences.

A comprehensive collection is maintained of material on all aspects of special librarianship and information work, including the collection, recording and retrieval of information, translation, documentary reproduction and dissemination of knowledge, as well as certain related fields such as office management and the book trade. Some 2,500 periodicals on these subjects are received regularly from various countries, and much of the material held is not available elsewhere in the United Kingdom. Members may borrow freely from the library and may ask for information on special library and information matters. In this field, Aslib does evaluate the information supplied and is willing to offer advice.

Firms and other organizations wishing to establish or re-organise a special library or information department may engage Aslib as consultants to prepare recommendations and supervise their implementation. Individual information processes may be similarly investigated. The service covers premises, staff, planning of services, basic stock, records, routines and other aspects.

There are five serial publications of Aslib:

1. *Journal of Documentation.*
2. *Aslib Proceedings.*
3. *Aslib Book-list.*
4. *Index to Theses.*
5. *Aslib Yearbook.*

Automation in Acquisition Work: University of Missori Library has developed books ordering system on IBM in 1957. Chicago University Library computerized the acquisition system on IBM 1401 in 1964. For the bulk of books ordered, which are received without problem, it is likely that computerized acquisition system in isolation will show significant saving in staff time. In computerized library the file should consist user number, user name, user address and telephone number. Library keeps the file for current orders and file containing name and address of booksellers. Records are often indexed by ISBN, ASSAN, LC, or BNB number. The acquisition system may be MARC based and important software used are Blackwell's PERLINE, PEARL.

Automation in Administration: In all libraries there are letters to be written, reports to be typed, references for present and former staff to be given, guides and booklets to be produced, accounts to be kept locally, budget to be prepared, interim statements to be prepared, final year account to be presented and possibly receipt from photocopying, fines, reservations, charges, online search charge, and sale of publications, postcard or badges to be recorded. In university libraries electronic typewriter were preferred to a full word processor. A really high speed printer is pointless here. The majority of work is in single letters, but is costly and unsuitable where work load is heavy. Computer may be used for library processor for filing. Such spare capacity technique may exit in a dedicated academic library with capacity for statistical analysis of large files. In such circumstances software will be sufficient for chosen machine in general office. The ability to perform library operations and office file work from a single terminal is obviously of great advantage.

The library accounting system, large number of payments in advance, their queries, and problem of double payment, are facing every library. Similarly, payments of bills and transactions in foreign currencies further completed the system, book purchasing, ordering of books, which turn out to be unavailable. A computer can give a pattern of spending for each department, that can be analysed. Local fields of MARC or other catalogue records may be used to record details of the suppliers, price and invoice number, normally entered in accession.

Automation in Circulation Work: Computers are very effective for circulation work in libraries. This requires a computer with the progressive capacity to handle such sorting of a large file. By the time one is contemplating online access to circumstances or online access to circulation records through bibliographic description in any form, one is, for reasons of file size and processing capacity, moving away from the possibility of microcomputer based system. The theft prevention can be worked out by ALS system united with SENELCO. The introduction of the SWALCAP online circulation system in 1982 involved repeat of this exercise with decoded labels. The mark 3 telepen units used, inter alia, by SWALCAP electronic works as network, or terminal rather than microcomputers.

Automation of Libraries: Automatic work is used for automatic technical process. Information is defined as recorded or communicated knowledge. There is a great demand to provide such information quickly on demand for which efficient and accurate devices or tools are introduced, which are based on mechanized process. There are many fields in a library where automation can be applied, i.e. acquisition work, receipt work, maintenance of accounts, cataloguing, maintenance, circulation control, serial control, documentation and information retrieval, stock verification etc.

Automation is very much needed to create efficient service to provide accurate service, to control the rapid growth of information, capable of satisfying the users and being operated by all users, to link the system into other existing system, which proved to the economical.

B

Barriers to Information: Barriers to communication and information are as under:

1. Language
   - (a) Man-Man
   - (b) Man-machine
2. Jargon
   - (a) Neblogist
   - (b) Synonym
   - (c) Acronym
3. Presentation
   - (a) Level
   - (b) Style
   - (c) Form
4. Communication problem
   - (a) Multiplicity of sources
   - (b) Seepage and scatter
5. Media problem
   - (a) Comprehensive
   - (b) Perception
   - (c) Alien to reality
   - (d) Misunderstanding
6. Socio-culture problem
   - (a) Culture
   - (b) Level of development of countries
7. Over population
   - (a) Primary papers
   - (b) Rehash
   - (c) Abstracts, disserts

8.	Pollution (Noise)	(a)	Propaganda
		(b)	Redundant data
		(c)	Errors
9.	Delay in handling	(a)	Publication
		(b)	Postal transit
		(c)	Translation
		(d)	Processing
		(e)	Searching
		(f)	Accessing
		(g)	Document delivery
		(h)	Feedback
10.	Economical barriers	(a)	Direct tax
		(b)	Overheads
11.	Political	(a)	Instability
		(b)	War
12.	Regulatory	(a)	Foreign Exchange
		(b)	Customs

Bibliographic Classification: The bibliographic classification (BC) is the chief product of Henry Evely Briss's (1870-1955) lifework and is based on a profound study of the nature and history of classification and of the proceeding attempts at general classification of knowledge and of books. The results of this study are given in the works published in 1929 and 1933 and in the prefaces to the volumes of classification. Although BC is regarded as modern scheme, the following shows its long history:

1891: H.E. Bliss joined the library staff of the college of the city of New York.

1903-1908: Classification work started in 1903 and was applied to college library in 1908.

1929-1933: Publication of the organization of knowledge and the system of the sciences and revised in 1939 as org. of knowledge in libraries and the subject approach to books.

1935: A system of bibliographic classification, published.

1940: Bliss retired from the city college.

1941-53: The scheme extended by auxiliary schedules for composite specification and notation. (Vol. 1) Introduction, (Vol. 2) Classes H-K—Human Sciences, (Vol. 3) Classes L-Z—the special human studies, history of peoples and nations, religion, ethics, special social studies, languages and literature, bibliography and libraries, and (Vol. 4), General Index.

BC is not based on a rigid and unadaptable view of the order or knowledge.

The order of main classes is as follows:

Reading room collection.

Alternative for bibliology.

Special collection.

Departmental collections.

Documents or archives of Govt. Institutions, etc.

Periodicals.

Miscellania.

Collection historic.

Antiquated books.

A. Philosophy and General Science
B. Physics
C. Chemistry
D. Astronomy
E. Biology
F. Botany
G. Zoology
H. Anthropology
I. Psychology
J. Education
K. Social Sciences
L. History

M. Europe
N. America
O. Australia
P. Religion
Q. Applied Social Science and Ethics
R. Political Science, Practical Politics
S. Jurisprudence and Law
T. Economics
U. Arts
V. Fine Arts
W. Philology
X. Indo-European Philology, Language
Y. English or Other Language and Literature
Z. Bibliology, Bibliography and Libraries.

The anterior neutral classes include the subject usually found in the Generalia class of other schemes. The separation of pure and applied sciences has been avoided, though class 'U' would be unduly large in many libraries. The title of class 'H' is misleading.

The main notation is literal. This kind of notation is easy to use, and permits useful mnemonics. Bliss considered that a main class mark need never exceed for letters. In most classes marks longer than three letters are rare. These short marks are usually obtained by dividing the subject into two stages for each letter added to the class mark. Thus 'UA' is agriculture, 'UC' animal industries and products, 'UCJ' cattle, 'UCJD' dairying, and 'UCJF' milk production. Further subdivision beyond four letters is by no means excluded, and the scheme is provided with 22 auxiliary schedules and 24 supplementary adaptations of these. Three of these schedules can be applied wherever their use is appropriate. Schedule for form is distinguished by numerical sub-division, e.g. C4 biography of a chemist, 07 a miscellany of education.

The relative index to the schedules given in Volume 4 contains approximately 46,000 entries, compared to 43,000 index to the 14th edition of *Decimal Classification*.

Comparison suggests that the index to BC is better balanced geographically and nationally and by subject. It is one of the most flexible classification systems ever produced, and the use of alternative placing contributes notably to this. Libraries of different sizes can use it easily in various degrees of detail.

Book Selection: Book selection principle is one of the most important techniques with which librarianship is concerned, for it is the bookstock which gives a library its character more so than either staff or buildings. The term is generally understood to mean the selection of books for addition to stock, but frequently the practicing librarian is required to choose books for other purposes such as select bibliographies, reading list, displays, etc., and many of the principles to be outlined here are equally valid.

The selection should be according to the nature of the library, e.g. for university library, the teaching departments should be concerned to provide books to the students for research purposes. Secondly, the selection should be limited by the aim and purpose of the organization it serves. Selection of public library must be related to such factors as the size of the system, the standard of education and the interest of the population served.

Demand theory: The selection of books is also influenced by demand, potential demand is dependent on the type, purpose and scope of the library concerned, and is judged most effectively by constant study of the use made of the shelf stock. Volume of demand is more difficult to assess as it is stimulated very often by incidental factors such as book reviews in the popular press, or recommended reading for lecture courses. Not all subjects or books are of equal merit, and it is important to evaluate demand in order to avoid waste. Every books' existence in the stock should be justified, standard works are assured of this, provided they fall within the scope of the library, and they ought not to be rejected for purpose on the grounds of cost alone.

The ultimate aim of all books selection is to make the most effective use of the allotted book fund. The idea of sufficient funds to buy every book felt to be justified is rarely encountered, and even with the application of the principles broadly outlined here, limitations need to be imposed. A policy is required on the purchase of new edition.

There are book selection tools for newly published books, and as guides to the literature of a subject, for example, book reviews, annotation appear in periodicals, trade bibliographies, national bibliographies, reading lists, and publishers catalogue.

The authority to purchase books varies considerably in different libraries. Library committee, the librarian, subject experts and public dignitaries are the authorities to purchase the books. A staff committee is more likely to offset the effect of personal bias or opinion, and jointly being a broader outlook to bear on the subject. Collaboration is also useful for another reason. Large libraries encounter the problem of attracting all the books and related material which they can usefully acquire. Much of it may be fugitive or published abroad, and unless a large number of sources are checked, there is all possibility that books which the library should have escape notice. Team work is important for the work, and by coordinated effort a large number of specialist reviews, accessions lists of other libraries, booksellers lists, etc., can be checked regularly.

Book Selection Policy

1. There should be a relation between book selection and the objectives of a library.
2. There should be a relation between book selection and the book budget.
3. Book selection policy should involve the library staff and the faculty and combination of both.
4. Means of selection should involve the personal contact of the user and the reference tools.
5. The nature of the collection should be decided in advance to book selection.

Traditional principles of book selection:

There are basic factors, which determine the book selections:

1. Select the right books to the choice of the reader.
2. No consideration should be made of race, nationality, culture, profession, religion and caste.
3. Library collection should be based on broad general foundations.
4. Demand is governing factor in selection.
5. Material selected should meet high standard high quality in content, expression, and significance of subject, sincerity of authors purpose and responsibility of authors opinion.
6. Keeping in touch with publishing activities.
7. A medicare book, if read in performance of a superior books should be given preference.
8. It is necessary to know the community of two kinds of informations—general and specific information.

Prerequisites of book selection

1. The selection of library material requires constant and extensive reading, a broad background of knowledge in the different field of study.
2. The book selector should have high degree of judgement.
3. Final selection should be based on suggestions and specialized knowledge.
4. A coordinated policy should be adopted.
5. Declare the book selection policy in advance.

Five Laws and Book Selection

Dr. S.R. Ranganathan, the father of library science, has given an account of book selection in Five Laws of Library Science. First three laws are concerned to readers and the book relation, fourth law with the time and fifth law with the development of the library.

First Law of Library Science—Books for All: All books are artificial commodity and appeal to intellectual man. The format of a book has an important part of work selection:

1. **Popular size:** The size of the book should be normal and proper to handle. It should not be bulky size.
2. **Good Shape:** The book selected for library should have a good shape, the shape in which reader can easily consult and handle.
3. **Good Printing:** The book should be nicely printed. The letters of printing should be such that can be read and understood without difficulty. Printing should be clean and letter should be clear.
4. **Proper Binding:** The book should have proper binding. Preference should be given to hard binding. Paperback binding should be avoided in a library as it requires hard binding after its little use.
5. **Space:** While making book selection the available space should be kept in mind. The quantity of books should be restricted to the space available in stock area. Sufficient space should be arranged before book selection is made.

Textual Features: Textual features are important features to be kept in mind while making book selection. While a book is selected and considered for selection, its physical features are consulted whether in booksellers' catalogue, bibliographies or the lists submitted by the faculty members. Title page gives full details about the author, title, publishers, copyright year, edition, and price etc. If title fulfills all requirements, it serves the time as well as the subject idea of the book. Language book should be selected on demand. We have to interpret language not only in the commonly understood way but also is the stage in the evaluation of language. Book should be in simple, transparent and dynamic style. Book with short sentences should be prepared. The book is readable if it is arranged in short paragraphs observing the principles of unity of thought. As regards illustrations, the book, which is illustrated adequately with well-drawn, well-printed, apt pictures, diagrams, histograms etc. and appropriate to the standard, style and subject of the book, should be selected.

An index is the indispensable key to every book of information. Index is a fine achievement of intelligence, precision, and effective organisation.

Paper of a book should be durable with satisfaction to the eye and touch. Book selector should have some knowledge about the quality of paper.

Contributors have an important place in reference tools like Encyclopedias, etc. Edition should be latest and up-to-date. In case of selection of yearbooks, reliability should be the basis.

In public library, informative, creative and inspiring books should be selected. In general library, book selection should pay attention to biographics, travel and history books, and literature books.

Second Law of Library Science

Thc law implics that thc book sclection should be based on individual want. Books or their lists should be displayed before the reader for their valuable suggestions for book selection. It is done by:

1. Padler Method—Taking lists of new books to potential users.
2. Shopkeeper Method—Discussing the book need of each reader coming to the library.
3. Reference Initiative—The reference librarian should also take initiative in estimating the wants and accumulate the requirement of the readers.
4. Readers Initiative—Readers should be invited to suggest the useful books.
5. Standard Evaluation—The standard of the books should be evaluated regarding to its subject, language etc., the name and fame of the publishers, booksellers, and research organizations helping in the valuation of the standard of the book.

6. Anticipated Wants—In large libraries like University and Research libraries anticipated want/demand should be considered in consultation with search scholars, heads of the departments, persons of the locality, subject experts, and other meritorious scholars related to various subjects.
7. Reference Work—With reader's consultation reference books should be selected. In University libraries the authoritative reference books and in college and public libraries general reference books should be selected.
8. Periodical's Help–All serials of umbral discipline of interest and a few appropriate ones in the penumbral discipline of interest should be selected. In public library general periodicals of popular variety and specialized periodicals of the main vacations of the people of the locality should receive priority.

Third Law of Library Science

The third law of approach to book selection includes the following factors:

1. Open Access System—This system helps in book selection. Reader consults the books on the shelf and know the availability and non-availability of the book. His suggestions are much valuable in book selection method.
2. Penal of Experts, Consisting of Subject Experts—There are experts, known as subject expert. Sometimes library appoint a penal of subject experts to suggest the best books on their subject. Their suggestions are always valuable.
3. Librarian and Library Staff—Librarians and the library staff are also conscious about the demand of the readers of the books. They keep in touch with the readers. Suggestion box are also placed on the gate for students or the readers. Personal contact also help in book selection.

4. Publicity Media—Book reviews, new books, columns in newspapers, magazines and journals are also helpful in book-selection method.
5. Publisher's catalogues and their bulletins published from time to time also help the librarian and the subject experts to select the best books.

Fourth Law of Library Science

(Save the time of the reader)

Best books are always helpful in saving the time of the reader. Best books means such books which are exhaustive, pinpointed and complete in all respect so far information is concerned. Reader is satisfied by such books. We have to take help of some aids in selecting best books within lesser time. Aids are chronological lists, minute classified lists, subject lists, catalogues, bibliographies and pamphlets. The work may be more easy and less time consuming if open access is adopted in the library. Learned periodicals may be selected by the help of indexing and abstracting of periodicals.

Book selection system should be time saving. It should be based on the size of the staff. If there is small number of staff, the selection should be made in more than one phase. Book selection should be made according to the space available. If space is not sufficient, first necessary arrangement of space should be made. There should be sufficient tools of book selection. All precautions should be taken to approach the subject experts, readers, public and the staff for selecting the best books. All adequate, prompt and efficient system will save the time of the staff and subject experts. It will enable the library to procure the required books without losing more time. All aids like bibliographical aids etc. should be available in the library.

Fifth Law of Library Science

(Library is a growing organism)

Growth of library have played an important role in book selection. Best books→large reading and large number of readers→more staff=Development of the library. The whole system of growth depends on the best and proper procedure of book selection. A library is best known by the collection building. Library is a growing organism, adopting the appropriate book selection procedure. It is said that a single book is sufficient to attract the reader if it affects the need of the readers.

C

Centralised Cataloguing: It is catalouging by one library or cataloguing office within a system of libraries, of all books acquired by all those libraries so that the results of each cataloguing are used by the individual libraries. Centralised cataloguing may be carried out at local level (i.e. within a single library system) or at national level. Within a library system its introduction often coincides with the setting up of a cataloguing department and an acquisitions department which together receive a catalogue of all books destined for each single library, department or service point. At national level the most common form of centralized cataloguing is that of a commercial or state organization which, having access to all or the majority of books published, performs the cataloguing and makes the results available in the form of printed cataloguing cards to libraries requiring them. It is economical, avoid duplication, and maintain consistency.

Library of Congress started printed cards and introduced centralized cataloguing in USA. Other countries also started centralized cataloguing. Council of British National Bibliography started the publication of BNB and a catalogue card service.

Centralised Cataloguing is one such which has recently witnessed considerable development. The centralized cataloguing being limited to that method of cataloguing which is commonly adopted by a large system of libraries, wherein all the cataloguing, classifying and possibly other operations are carried out at a center point in the system, usually the central library (A Henry Sharp).

It means:

1. Centralised cataloguing is a large system of libraries.
2. It is commonly adopted method.
3. Technical works (cataloguing, classification and other related operations) are carried out at central point.

"The cataloguing, by one library or cataloguing office within a system of libraries of all books acquired by all those libraries so that the results of such cataloguing are used by the individual libraries" (*Encyclopedia of Librarianship*).

It explains that:

1. There should be a system of libraries (libraries more than one).
2. Cataloguing by library or cataloguing office.
3. Books of all the library should be included under operation of cataloguing.
4. Results are used by individual libraries.

"Centralised cataloguing is defined as cataloguing services to its clientele from a central point" (C.P. Needham).

Need of centralized cataloguing:

1. There is a shortage of well-trained cataloguing manpower in the country.
2. Libraries are growing in number.
3. There is continuous explosion of knowledge.
4. It is estimated costly to understand separate cataloguing work in separate cataloguing section or unit in all libraries.

In view of the above, centralized cataloguing is an important system mostly started and introduced in Great Britain and USA. Centralised cataloguing is possible through:

1. An agency at central point.
2. An organization at central point.
3. A centre at national level.
4. A centre at state level.

5. A centre at district level.
6. A centre at city level.
7. A centre for special type of material.

All the above centres will work as central cataloguing body for the books in language or more than one language.

In view of the above, centralized cataloguing activity is limited to a library system, which has a number of branches or departments. There is no commercial basis involved in production and distribution. The entire cataloguing process is carried out at the central and headquarter library, just as the book for all the branches is purchased and distributed.

Centralized cataloguing was first brought in the United States in 1901 in Library of Congress, who started the printing of catalogue card of each book. These cards are available for sale. There are many countries where centralized cataloguing work is being done, e.g.:

1. Central Book Chemleer, USSR.
2. The State Lemin Library, USSR.
3. Pansk Bibliogralisk Kontor (Denmark).
4. The Swedish State Library Committee (Norway).
5. Rumanian Ministry of Culture (Canada).
6. Derbyshire County Libraries Headquarters (Derby).
7. Middlesex County Libraries Headquarter (Honslow, Liverpool etc.)
8. Delhi Public Library System.

There are private agencies working in the field of centralized cataloguing printed card system—

1. H.W. Wilson printed catalogue card service.
2. The Deustche Burcharci Publication in Germany.
3. BNB also follow printed catalogue cards since 1950. It can supply printed cards within 48 hours of order.

Objectives

1. It is economical as it reduces the cost of cataloguing.
2. If libraries undertake or carry their cataloguing work

separately and independently, it can be duplication of work. But centralized cataloguing avoid duplication of work.

3. Centralized cataloguing is done at a centre and experienced and expert personnel are appointed and engaged for catalogue work. Thus, it raises the level of quality of cataloguing.
4. Centralized cataloguing provides accurate and systematic cataloguing, which enables the member libraries to provide better services to users.
5. This system achieves uniformity in classification and cataloguing.
6. Cataloguers are put to effective use.

Merits

1. It is a large library system and involves any number of libraries.
2. It is done in centralized system which gives relax to individual libraries in the field of cataloguing.
3. There is no commercial basis and all books of the branches or headquarter library are purchased, catalogued and distributed. It minimize the cataloguing staff. Only books of local variations are dealt in individual libraries which are very few in number.
4. It saves the time and energy.
5. Centralized cataloguing is most relevant to countries like India where different and terrible cataloguing is the order of the day.
6. Cataloguing staff engaged in individual library can be released for performing other services in the library.
7. The most important advantage in introducing this service would be possibility of training a whole generation of librarians in India in the art of true cataloguing.

Documents

Books on local problems are not included in centralized cataloguing.

Forms of centralization

There are five physical forms of centralized cataloguing:

1. Card or Sheaf Service

It means that central organization produce the actual physical entries (unit entries) which individual library can buy. BNB introduced this service. Printed cards are distributed to individual libraries who file them in their catalogues after adding the appropriate heading to the basic unit. BNB card/sheaf service and printed catalogue cards are distributed. Library of Congress also give such services. They distributed proof sheets which can be produced. *Example*: BNB cards, LC-proof sheets which can be reproduced.

2. MARC (Machine Readable Catalogue Service)

It is a production of cataloguing data in machine readable form (e.g. Magnetic tapes). In fact the central organization/ agencies catalogue the document and record the data on magnetic tapes and supply them to the libraries. These tapes can be computerized and printed catalogue can be produced. Library of Congress started this operation in 1969.

It aims to:

(a) minimize and eliminate a problem of card bring out of stock and the storage and inventory of card production.

(b) provide system cards automatically through the use of computer drives, photo composition machine and offset printing machine.

MARC has been modified to automation replacing card catalogue through magnetic tapes. NASA—National Aeronautics and Administration is following the MARC system.

3. Information Service

Bibliography is an important tool. It is the production of bibliography from which libraries can construct their own catalogue either by cutting out the entries and pasting them on cards or by using the information provided as a guide in their own cataloguing or possibly by using the bibliographies as a substitute for the catalogue.

BNB services were of this kind before the starting of card service in 1956. Such bibliographies are also useful for book-selection and acquisition, identification and location. INB has the same nature. BNB and INB are giving this service jointly.

4. Cataloguing-in-Source (CIS)

Under this service cataloguing of books is done by central organizations, in association with the publisher, before publication as catalogue entries and then printed in book form. This is only possible with the collaboration of book trade. LC stated this work in June, 1987. It published 1,203 publications of 157 publishers on a cost of dollars 25 per publications.

The entry generally appears as the version of the title page in the form of facsimile of LC card catalogue entries. This preparation is called cataloguing-in-source entries. This system could not be continued because of its high cost. LC was also not interested as it could heavily strain the cataloguer owing to the close schedule.

5. Cataloguing-in-Publication (CIP)

The system began in July 1971 by Library of Congress. It was a Galley proof system and data return of publisher. Information recorded substitute imprint and collection are omitted, but complete record of description is entered in MARC. CIP cataloguing was undertaken from folded sheets and pre-publication bounded copies are verified. CIP is a modern method. It attracts the publishers and encourage them to send Galley proof of their yet published book. This is a system of optimistic nature but its success depends on the association of publisher and technical capacity of Library of Congress.

The system was adopted by:

1. Australian CIP Programmes (1974-75) with 1919 monograph titles of 83 trade and academic publishers.

Australian CIP Programme provides 4 basic bibliographic products of data printing in book:

(a) Preliminary printed catalogue cards.

(b) Preliminary Australian National Bibliography entry.

(c) Preliminary printed MARC record.

(d) Entries prepared according to AACS.

(e) Ordering of title about 6 months before its actual publications.

2. Germany CIP Programme (Jan. 1976) as a 2-year pilot project with the National Library. York University and British Columbia University were given responsibility for the English language publication programme—one for book and the other for Canadian MARC tap distribution service to libraries.

Communication: The term communication comes from the Latin word 'communis', meaning common. When we communicate someone, we try to establish a certain degree of commonsense with the person communicated.

(a) by sharing some information,

(b) by sharing some ideas, and

(c) by sharing an attitude.

Therefore, communication refers to transmission or exchanging of information, messages etc.

Information and communication are two interlinked terms in the sense that without information communication is not possible and without communication information has no value.

Oxford English Dictionary—Communication is imparting, conveying and exchanging of ideas and knowledge by speech, writing or signs.

Columbia Encyclopedia of Communication—The transfer of thoughts and messages as contrasted with transportation of goods and persons. Verb "To communicate" means—

(a) to exchange thoughts, feeling, information,

(b) to make known,

(c) to make common, and

(d) to have sympathetic relationship.

Noun "Communication" refers—

(a) The exchange of symbols.

(b) The exchange of common message.

(c) The exchange of information.

(d) The process of exchange between two individuals through a common system of symbols.

(e) The art of expressing ideas.

(f) The science of transmitting information.

However, communication is—

(a) Face-to-face conversation between two persons.

(b) Conversation over the phone.

(c) Correspondence between friends.

(d) Transmission of programmes online, television broadcast via communication satellite, i.e. received by millions of persons.

Origin: Communication takes place in many ways and in many forms throughout the history of mankind. Signs language or expressive body language were perhaps the earlier form of communication. Such communication is also used by deaf and dumb persons.

Language—With the evolution of language, spoken words became the common form of communication.

Telephone—With the development of telephone, two or more persons can exchange their information at long or short distance. While in ancient days drumbeats and smoke signals were used to send messages but these messages were effected by winds and was also difficult to verify whether message has been received in correct form.

The invention of writing system, i.e. alphabets by ancient Egyptians made striking impact on the communication process. Written communication enable the records to be stored. In earlier times it was cave paintings, followed by sophisticated technologies such as clay tablets, ink, papurus, movable type and telegraph system.

Communication became more advance with the advance in science and technology like telegraph, telephone, radio, wireless, telephoto device, motion pictures. T.V. has led to institutional and cultural innovations and raised the social power as mass communication. The other forms are books, films, telex messages. The newer technologies are creating a worldwide communication infrastructure, transmitting not just voice but text, data and image as well.

Elements of Communication Process

1. Information source
2. Encoder
3. Message
4. Communication channel
5. Noise
6. Decoder
7. Receiver/Destination

1. Information Source

(a) It is that which originates message or the news.

(b) It may be a person or an institution, author of book, researcher, and specialist.

2. Encoder

(a) It translates the ideas into words, signals and signs.

(b) It translates thought contents of the book.

3. **Message**

(a) Presentation of original thoughts of information source.

(b) Verbalisation of the ideas through language.

(c) Non-verbal messages in the form of signs, symbols, gestures etc.

(d) Information contained in a book and articles of the journals.

4. **Channel**

The medium through which a message is sent is called the channel.

(a) Channels are transmission media through which message travels from the source to destination.

(b) In oral communication it is air surrounding the speaker and the listner.

(c) In written communication pen and paper are the transmission channel.

(d) Electromagnetic transmission channels are:

  (i) Twisted pair of wires,

  (ii) Coaxial cables, and

  (iii) Optical fibres.

(e) Print and non-print media are elements of communication.

5. **Noise**

Noise is a communication process sufers to interferes with the message or information.

6. **Decoder**

The process of translation of the messages or information by the receiver is known as decoding. The function of decoder is:

(a) To interpret the information or message.

(b) A decoder may be anything ranging from human being, telephone receiver to computer.

(c) The message is transformed into signals.

(d) At the receiver end, the signals are transformed into their original form which is done by decoder.

7. **Receiver**

Receiver is the person who receives message or information. Listener is also a receiver in oral communication. In case of electromagnetic communication system, the telephone, radio, teleprinter, television, and computer constitute receiver of information.

Computer: A computer is any device, whether mechanical, electronic, optical or biochemical, is capable of carrying out a predetermined sequence of operations on data, so that data is recorded, stored and analysed automatically. A computer system include input from keyboard, CPU, an arithmetic logic unit and control unit (Memory) and output by monitor or printer and a storage. The computer calculates by using devices called logic gates, which consists of various combinations of switches. There are three basic types of logic gate, namely AND gates, OR gates, and NOT gates, and these enable the computer to perform all types of calculations. The mathematics that explain how these gates work is called Bookean Algebra, after the English mathematician George Boole who developed it in the first part of the 19th century. Unlike Pascal's calculator, and Babbage's analytical engine, modern computers with their switching circuits do not work with decimal numbers. Their operation is based on open binary numbers, i.e. numbers made up of the digits 0 and 1. In computer jargon a^0 and a^1 are called a bit, which is short for Minary digit. Any data that has to be computed or any instructions telling the computer what to do, have to be expressed in bits. Many computers handle data and instructions eight bits at a time. This means that the different parts of the computer are linked by eight parallel paths, so that the bits can travel together, i.e. in parallel or serially, instead of one at a time. A group of eight 'bits' is called a byte. The computer keyboard allows us to enter commands as well as date. Both are converted to ASC II code and travel down the same wire to the computer, but once in the computer they are handled by different circuits. Data on the other hand are handled in another part of the computer called the control unit. When we enter commands, we use English words that find easy to understand, such as PRINT AND TYPE. Each of these generates a number of elementary commands that tell the computer to open and close switches in various circuits, or perform tasks such as sending data to the printer or the screen. To translate command, computers are provided by their manufacturers with system software. By software we mean set of instruction or programmes, telling the computer what to do. System software consists mainly of a group of programmes called an operating system, and two more groups of programmes, called compilers and assemblers, which translate the word processing.

Programme: Although some commands are typed at the keyboard, most are stored in a programme, and are executed when the computer runs the programme. The concept of stored programmes is to control present-day computer. Computer programmes are based on a vocabulary and syntax can be underlooked by the system software and translated in machine code. Every computer only understands machine code, i.e. the language of 0s and 1s that can be fed directly into the control unit. To make life easier, assembly language was developed, which are remand from machine code. New instructions are written in easier form, using commands such as LDA, meaning 'load accumulator'; STA, meaning 'store accumulators contents'; ADC, meaning add with carry and CLC meaning 'clear carry'. The assembly language converts these commands into the strings 1s and 0s the computer understands.

Some languages are good for certain types of tastes, while others are better for other tasks. They are FORTRAN, COBOL, BASIC, DBASE, MICROTECH, PROLOG. There are various types of computers and in different sizes. The longest is the mainframe computer, which houses the central processing unit (CPU). It processes data at higher speed, the disk drive can store more data, and it allows a number of people to use it. The others are minicomputers having small store capacity and many users. There are four types of processing chips used in microcomputers: 6502, Z80, 8086, 80268, 80386, 80486, C, C+, CC*, CCC+, and 68000.

Memory refers to an area within the computer used for holding programme and data that can be directly accessed by the CPU. However, computer data cannot be held as much as data is possible on disk. Disk storage can be extended indefinitely simply by adding more disks. A memory device normally consists of silicon chip made up of thousands of time switches (transistors). Computer memory is of two types: RAM and ROM. Hard disks are of **sturdy**, rigid construction. They are also much heavier than a floppy and a hard disk drive motor can take only a minute to get up speed and therefore constantly spinning, when the computer is not accessing data. The speed of rotation is very high. In IBM PC expansion cards can be fitted to increase the compatibility. An expansion card is printed circuit board, designed to fit into this slot, possibly linked to a part to attach an external peripheral device. These cards greatly extends the capability of the hardware.

Computer is an electronic machine that helps to solve problem. Problems may be wide and varied related to industry, medicine, education, scientific research, law, special sciences and arts—step-by-step procedure to solve the problem.

Special features

1. The instructions given are precise.
2. The number of different types of instructions to be carried out is very few.
3. By a proper permutation and combination of this simple set of instructions, an infinite number of pattern can be created.

Capability of Computers

1. **Automacity:**

A. Electronic Machine

(a) Television
(b) Tape-recorder
(c) Calculator
} Human operation

(i) Start
(ii) Time
(iii) To adjust
} The volumes and stop

B. Automatic Machine

(a) Computer— Needs appropriate instructions
Performs the tasks mail
Ordered stop.

2. **Deligence:** Computer does not suffer from the human traits of tiredness and lack of concentration.
3. **Accuracy:** It works accurately. Mistakes can occur by human error.
4. **Repetitiveness:** Computers can perform the task effectively. Any number of repetition will be done with the same speeds.
5. **Storage capacity:** Computers have storage capacity to store large amount of instructions and data and supply the stored information. It is not possible by human brain.
6. **Versatility:** The powerful machine can store and supply more information by few instructions only.

Limitations of Computers

1. Inability to correct:
   (a) Correct instructions should be given to computer.
   (b) Computer command correct the wrong instructions.
   (c) Computer command use its brain.

2. Dependence on human instructions: The computer cannot generate any instructions of its own.

Set-by-step procedures

1. Tasks should be in sequence: Task-subtasks.
2. Instructions have to be precise.
3. Each step should lead to a meaningful action.
4. Some information (or input) has to be given to enable him to carry out the task.
5. Another important sub-tasks to be performed is the matching of items given in the data.
6. Arithmetic operations such as addition, subtraction, multiply and division are required to solve many problems.
7. During the performance of an action, intermediate results need to be stored.
8. At the conclusion of a task, the result obtained will be recognizably different from the initial information or input with which we started.

Organisation of a computer

1. Reads the instructions.
2. Memorises the instructions.
3. Reads the data.
4. Multiplies the quantity of item.
5. Follows the correct sequence of steps.

I. Computer has an Input Unit

(a) It reads the lists of instructions and data.

(b) It is a memory which stores the instructions and data.

(c) A computer has a central processing unit, that interprets each of the instructions stored in the memory and direct the various units to carry out the tabs assigned to them in the correct sequence.

  (i) Control unit

  (ii) Arithmetic Unit.

(iii) Logic Unit—Arithmetic and logic unit calculates and takes logical decisions.

II. Computer has an Output Unit which—

(a) Writes out the results of the calculations.

General computer has four units:

1. Input Unit
2. Memory
3. Central Processing Unit
4. Output Unit.

1. **Input Unit:** This unit is similar to our eye and ear through which we receive information. Information is obtained through devices:
   (a) Keyboard unit
   (b) Optical reader (video display unit).
2. **Memory:** Information are registered in this unit. The following are stored:
   (a) Instructions
   (b) Data
   (c) Intermediate
   (d) Results of any calculator
   (e) Final output.
3. **Central Processing Unit (CPU):** It is like a brain: It consists of two units—

(a) Control unit—directs the other units of a computer.

(b) Arithmetic and logic unit—It performs the high mental functions like calculators, logical reasoning and the take.

4. **Output Unit:** This unit is like our mouth and our hands. The computer outputs the results using a printer, a television, screen etc.

In view of the above, it may be said that computer is a general device for automatically processing information. There are two types of computers:

1. Digital computers—Generally these are digital computers, operated with binary system of number and operates on digital data.
2. Analog computers—These operates on data presented in the form of continuous variable physical quantities (e.g. voltage, or angular position) by performing physical processing on data.

There are two generations of computers:

1. 1st generation computers—These are characterized by the use of vacuum tubes as active elements.
2. 2nd generation computers—These are characterized by their ability to support multiprogramming and multiprocessors with rather elaborate disc-based operating system.

Computer and Library

Library and computers are now universally recognized as important social institutions charged with the work of information, inspiration and creation. No country can survive without libraries and information centres in the present world. The gradual awareness about democracy, wide extension of education facilities, and intensification of search activities have caused a rapid growth in recorded knowledge. Information service is the need of the day in libraries. Explosion of knowledge has developed the library services to the society. Libraries have become the essential ingredients of a civilized society. Modern technology has changed our lifestyle, nature of the society, economics, political aspects and social values. Accordingly, libraries and documentation centres have also their methods, systems and developed and their services to meet the requirement of the community to improve and adopt to new conditions, in order to fulfill the social role and to carryout its social obligations. The concept of conventional librarianship has altogether changed. Modern libraries have altogether changed from the earlier libraries. Libraries have entered the field of information. There are forced to adopt new technology and change to be an information centre.

Modern libraries have adopted modern tools and machines like computers and other appliances. Computer is an electronic machine that stores and processes numeric and non-numeric information. Computer accept data and process and gives result in the form required by the user. It is a fast electronic media that solve the problems accurately. It performs calculations and comparisons, and store informations which can be retrieved.

Library and information centres are recognized as important social institutions charged with the work of information, inspiration and recreation, storage of knowledge and preserve them in organized manner.

In modern age human society should be—

(a) Fully familiar with intellectual contributions.
(b) In touch with up-to-date information in all aspects.
(c) Aware of the human, social and technological developments.

User service should be:

(a) Economic
(b) Pinpointed
(c) Exhaustive
(d) Up-to-date
(e) Reliable
(f) Informative.

In other words, technology should be:

(a) Capable to retrieve
(b) Efficient at Prompt dissemination
(c) An automation device.

Information technology is capable to provide:

(a) Effective library service
(b) Relevant information
(c) Quick information
(d) Paperless libraries.

Computer Based SDI Services: INSDOC and IIT, Bombay have been offering computerized SDI services since Jan., 1976. The IBM 370/155 computer system is being used as UNESCO provided the initial support as a Pilot project, with the CA CONDEN STATES database. The services have been extended with the INSPEC-A&B database. These programmes are operated in the format phases—conversion of data into the MARC II, compilation of profiles, search, fonting and printing. The computerized data system has record of current information from books, journals, reports, patents and conference proceedings from Chemical Abstract CONDEN STATES tapes. The weekly SDI bulletin is served to scientists. Department of Science and Technology (DST) provides SDI services under the name ALERT services. DESIDOC provides computer based SDI.

Efforts have always been made to increase the potential of computer based information services in India and in developing countries. Computer based information searching is being practiced in India since past several years but at low level. However, it is taking roots to develop the information network by introducing several national data communication networks and government support is also available. SDI services have also been started. Informatics India conducted DIALOG training and searching for the last 10 years initially using telex levels.

Online services (dial-up system) provide a means to receive information by the institutes when they require without maintaining an infrastructure. For questions rarely put, the use of dial-up online service is effective for accessing data. International online services are also available to developing countries.

Prerequisites for starting online services

1. Search large volumes of data.
2. Search timely information.
3. Search several files simultaneously.
4. Search adequate number of abstracting services and merge the search results.

5. More effective database capable of more than 5 million records.
6. Regular updating of news wire services.

Merits of online services

1. Text publications are searchable, such as newspapers, newsletters, journals etc.
2. Images are searchable such as trademark images, chemical structure, patent illustrations.

Computer Network in Indian Libraries: Resources sharing by using the modern technology of computers and communication has given rise to library network. The document that was used to be delivered by post, or inter-library loan is being transferred through 'Electronic Mail'. A network usually consists of formal institutional arrangements, whereby material, information and services are provided by variety of libraries. Library can provide many network facilities like monitoring of vital social-economic projects, online retrieval and update of information, optimum utilization of costly computer resources, sharing latest software tools, dissemination of information, exchange of messages and emergency communication system. There are four characteristics of retrieval network—data, retrieval, access and users. Computer network has five national network—INFLIBNET, NICNET, INDONET, ERNET, INFNET; three regional network—CALIBNET, DELNET, MALIBNET and two local network—LIBSYS (Dialog database) and LIBRATOR.

A network is developed when a group of libraries/information centres decide to exchange information through computer application. In other words, network is a set of interrelated information systems associated with more or less formal agreements in order to jointly implement information handling operations with a view to pooling their resources and to offer better services to the users. Its objectives are to promote sharing of resources by inter-library loan among the participating libraries through computerized networking; facilitate and promote delivery of documents electronically; coordinate efforts and reduce unnecessary duplication of costly books, periodicals, etc.; coordinate efforts for suitable collection development and minimize duplication of costly books and periodicals; facilitate catalogue search and maintain a central online Union Catalogue of books and serials and non-book material, develop bibliographical databases of documents, create database for special institutes and projects, implementation of automation operations and services for fast communication of information, coordinate with networks of regional, state and national level, and evolve standards, uniform guidelines in techniques and methods, hardware, software and services.

Network is what modern communication is all about. Information is useful if it is communicated, transformed and used for knowledge and action taken. Network provides the way to achieve the object of knowledge from every source. In fact the purpose of the network is:

1. to interconnect computers,
2. to apply device to transfer data,
3. to access to remote information systems,
4. to operate the electronic mail, and
5. to provide world telecommunication services.

In India, the importance of network was experienced when we lagged for behind the other countries and the brain drain was fast. The development of Indian economy had a setback. During the Seventh Five-Year Plan, Planning Commission established a working group on modernization of library services and informatics. The report of working group suggested measures to establish network of important libraries in the country to enable effective resource sharing system for the benefit of the communities.

The second effort was made when the Government of India, Ministry of Human Resources Development, accepted the national policy on library and information system for library collection. There were many recommendations that stressed for the national libraries as part of integrated system so that information system may be more practicable, effective and useful to the Indian experts and scientists.

The third effort was made by Association of Indian Universities who prepared a plan for National Policy and prepared a report. A seminar was organized on National Policy on University Libraries on Sept. 29-30, 1986 to discuss various problems and decide a future plan for information system in India. The recommendation was to establish a networking of university libraries, research libraries, and other research libraries, which have no problem of language barrier.

University Grant Commission also considered the programme of information suggested by the Research Group to establish INFLIBNET (Information Library Network) programme to link university libraries, college libraries and also Documentation and Information Centres of India. During the past 10 years many efforts have been made by the Government and non-Government societies/ organizations, institutions and departments for networking by applying computer telecommunications technologies. NISSAT (National Information System for Science and Technology) established under the Department of Scientific and Industrial Research (DSIR), Government of India, has been vigorously promoting an integrated approach to library automation and networking.

There are two types of network:

1. **General Services Network**: Such networks are not related to a specific area of knowledge, specific subject, but the general information of community, for example, NICNET, INDONET, VIKRAM etc.
2. **Specialised Networks**: Such networks cover specific area of knowledge, subject, institution, organizations etc., for example, CALIBNET, DELNET, INFLIBNET, ERNET, VIDYANET, SIRNET, DESINET etc.

D

Decimal Classification-Generally: This is any classification which uses numbers arranged decimally for its notation. One adopts the convention that all numbers follow the decimal point and thus 'O' on the left-hand side of a symbol is significant.

(a) ***Specifica***: In the Decimal Classification of Melvil (Le) (Louis Kossuth) Dewey, a point is introduced after the third numeral to split up the number. Each number has a minimum of 3 numerals using an 'O' on the right-hand side if necessary.

(b) ***History:*** The scheme was developed in 1873 at Amherst College, Mass, USA in the college library. It was influenced by the study of various schemes, the most important of which was one (1870) by W.T. Harris of St. Louis, who many consider was strongly influenced by Bacon's **Chart of Human Learning.** Dewey followed the Harris order closely. He published the 42 page-first edition of his scheme anonymously in 1876, a slim volume, indeed, when compared with the 2,455 pages in two volumes of the 16th ed., 1958.

The Decimal Classification became popular very rapidly and is used extensively in libraries all over the world. Two factors were at work here: the growth of libraries was phenomenal both in number and size as the 20th century came in and a vast new public was attracted to them. Dewey's scheme was easily understood and remembered and allowed for the **relative location** of books instead of fixing places on particular shelves. The progressive subordination shown by the decimal notation and the case of insertion of new topics were revolutionary ideas.

After 1876, editions followed rapidly in 1885, 1888, 1891, 1894, 1898, 1911, 1913, 1915, 1919, 1922, 1927, 1932, 1942, 1951 and 1958. Always expanding and inserting new topics, the editors did not until recently alter the main classes of the scheme, or the classification of many topics, as it was the purpose of Dewey to leave the framework of the scheme unaltered so that libraries need not reclassify—reclassification being an expensive and arduous task.

In April 1930 the Library of Congress began to add Dewey numbers to their printed catalogue cards. It was a logical and eventual step that form the 1951 Standard Edition.

Principles and Outline: The main classes of the D.C. are as follows:

CLASSES

(With a note of division that some readers may expect to find elsewhere).

000 General works (including bibliography, library economy, museums, journalism)

100 Philosophy (including psychology)

200 Religion

300 Social Sciences (including medicine, agriculture, business and industry)

400 Philology

500 Pure Science

600 Useful arts (including medicine, agriculture, business and industry)

700 Fine Arts. Recreations (including architecture, photography and music)

800 Literature

900 History (including Geography and Biography)

Each subject is capable of subdivision into nine subsidiary subjects all of which are theoretically co-equal. Very few subjects divide into nine parts naturally; distortion occurs. Some divisions are overloaded and the last division occurs. The last division '9' is often given over the 'other topics'.

For no apparent reason many allied subjects (e.g. philology and literature) and even parts of a subject (e.g. psychology) are separated.

(c) ***The Relative Index*** is an important feature of the scheme and contains some 63,000 entries in the 16th edition.

(d) ***Auxiliary Tables***: The minutely divided schedules tables are provided, numbers from which may be added to the subject number to define it further.

(i) TABLE 1 – GEOGRAPHICAL DIVISIONS: A list of subjects which may be divided geographically by adding the geographical numbers from class 900, i.e. those numbers from classes 930-999 (committing the initial 9) which indicate locality. Other topics not mentioned may usually be subdivided by place by putting '09' in front of the geographical number.

(ii) TABLE 2 – UNIFORM SUBDIVISIONS: These are a much-extended form of the original nine common subdivisions which are:

01 Theory, philosophy, etc.
02 Outlines, manuals, etc.
03 Dictionaries or cyclopaedias.
04 Essay, etc.
05 Periodicals, etc.
06 Societies, etc.
07 Education, study, teaching, etc.
08 Collected works, etc.
09 History

They may be added to the number for any subject under conditions specified in the introductory paragraph.

Normally, **form divisions** are preceded by a cipher '0', **viewpoints** by '00', and **Miscellaneous aspects** by '000'.

(iii) TABLE 3 – LANGUAGE AND LITERATURE: A list of languages and literature (with notation) which may be subdivided, like 420, English.

(iv) TABLE 4 – PHILOLOGICAL DIVISIONS: A list of philological terms (with notation) which can be added to the languages in Table 3, e.g.

420 is English philology.

525.2 is English syntax.

Table 3 number for French is 44.

Table 4 number for syntax is 52.

French syntax is 445.2

The examples show the mnemonic method of building up numbers in the D.C. Main subject numbers may also be combined as instructed in the schedules from time to time. (Ency. Libnship).

Documents—A 'document' is an object that provides information based on the nature of the subject.

There are two categories—

1. Textual documents
2. Non-textual documents.

1. **Textual Documents**—Textual documents represent their information in the form of books, periodicals, catalogue, statistical compendia, trade publication, patents etc.
2. **Non-textual documents**—Non-textual documents contains some texts but important part is presented in this form, i.e.:

(a) Ionic documents—

(i) Image	(ii) Maps	(iii) Plans
(iv) Graphs	(v) Diagrams	(vi) Posters
(vii) Paintings	(viii) Photographs	(ix) Slides

(b) Sound documents—

(i) Sound records

(ii) Sound tapes

(c) Audio-visual documents—

(i) Combining images

(ii) Combining sound

(iii) Films
(iv) Slide show
(v) Video tapes
(vi) Discs

(d) Documents of a material—
(i) Objects
(ii) Samples
(iii) Artistic works
(iv) Monuments
(v) Books in braille
(vi) Teaching nature games

(e) Mixed documents—
(i) Various textual and non-textual documents together.
(ii) Books, records
(iii) Educational kits

(f) Magnctic documents—
(i) Computer processing—Programmers
(ii) Processing accessories

Periodicals

There are important sources of information used by scientists and technologies through reports, conference proceedings, serials, magazines, transactions, and bulletins.

Various types of journals

(a) Printed full-text journals (Research journals)
(b) Synopsis journals
(c) Miniprint/Newspaper style journals
(d) Microform journals (COM-Computer output Microform)
(e) Online
(f) CD-ROM (Compact Disc Read only Memory)
It is equivalent to 1500 floppy disc

It is undestructive

It can combine text with audio graphic image and moving images.

It is easy to use.

(g) Optical disc:

Optical disc can be

(i) Read-only memory

(ii) Write once

(iii) Erasable with the data/information recorded either in analog or digital formats

Above three Read-only memory discs cannot be changed once produced.

Analog	Digital
Read only digital video-disc	CD-audio CD-ROM (Compact disc read only memory) ORAM (Optical read only memory) CD-ROM/DVI (Digital Video Inteructive)
Write once	WORM (Write once-Read many) DRAW ODDD (Optical digital data disc) CD-PROM (Compact disc Programmable Read only memory) Laser card (Optical card)
Erasable	CD-EPROM (CD-Erasable programmable Read only memory) Data Rom

Data

Websters—Data is something given or admitted; facts or principles granted or presented; that upon which an inference or argument is based or an ideal system of any sort is constructed.

UNESCO—Data are facts, concepts or instruction in a formalized manner suitable for communication interpretation or processing by human or automatic means.

Mc Graw Hill's Encyclopaedia of Science & Technology—Data are quantital values derived from scientific experiments.

CODATA (Committee on Data for Science & Technology): Data is a crystalised presentation of the essence of scientific knowledge in the most accurate form.

Types of data (Science)—

(a) Data with reference to time factor:
  (i) Time independent data
  (ii) Time dependent data.
(b) Data with reference to location factor:
  (i) Location independent data
  (ii) Location dependent data.
(c) Data with reference to mode of generation:
  (i) Primary data
  (ii) Derived data (Refermatted)
  (iii) Theoretical data (Predicted).
(d) Data with reference to nature of quantitative values:
  (i) Determinable data
  (ii) Stackstine data.
(e) Data with reference to terms of expression:
  (i) Quantative data
  (ii) Semi-quantitative data
  (iii) Qualitative data.
(f) Data with reference to mode of representation:
  (i) Numerical data
  (ii) Graphic data
  (iii) Symbolic data.

Types of data (Social Science)

(a) Data with reference to scale of measurement:
  (i) Nominal data
  (ii) Ordinal data
  (iii) Interval data
  (iv) Ratio data.

(b) Data with reference to continuity
  (i) Continuous data
  (ii) Discrete data.

(c) Data with reference to number of characteristics:
  (i) Time series data
  (ii) Cross sectional data.

(d) Data with reference to origin:
  (i) Primary data
  (ii) Secondary data.

(e) Data with reference to characteristics:
  (i) Quantitative data
  (ii) Qualitative data.

Nature of Data

(a) Numerical data
(b) Descriptive data
(c) Enumerative data
(d) Descriptive data.

Properties of data

(a) Amenability to use (Definite conclusion)
(b) Clarity
(c) Aggregations
(d) Accuracy
(e) Compression
(f) Essence
(g) Refinement.

E

Education for Librarianship: The most important problems to be faced in this matter are: (1) relationship between general and professional or vocational education, (2) the purposes of professional education, (3) the instruments for achieving that purpose, and (4) the tangible results or rewards of such an educational programme.

To be really effective kind of vocational training, education must be rooted in a good standard of general education and the relationship between them must be clearly demonstrated. Too low a standard of general education inevitably means lowering of the standard of professional education and a consequent lowering of standards of service. At the same time it acts more directly upon the general aspects in which the profession is held, quite apart from the estimation of its service value.

The basic function of professional education must be sought and realized. It is undoubtedly true that, in its earliest days, it was regarded as a method of reaching basic skills. Gradually, it came to be understood that a comprehension of the principles was of first concern and that adequate skills could readily be developed once the groundwork was well and truly laid. However essentially practical a profession seem to be, it can only be fully effective if it has well developed and well understood theoretical background. The purpose of education is to create in a man a certain attitude towards life. In the case of professional education it is to create in him a certain attitude towards his work without making it a matter of dictation as to what that attitude should be.

Professional education must never be envisaged simply as a mastery of certain facts of skills, however important or good they may be in themselves, but rather as a course of study and instruction at the end of which there should be the 'intellectual breeding' and 'trained judgement'. It implies that, first of all, there must be a very vigorous job analysis so far as librarianship is concerned which will reveal exactly what there is of intellectual content within professional work. It should also reveal the measure of any common ground between the various sections of the library profession: University, Special, Municipal, together with that vague borderland of information officers and documents lists. To some practitioners in certain parts of the world all this may sound somewhat fanciful; yet it is surely only reasonable to try and understand exactly what a man is intended to do in a given employment before an attempt is made to educate him for that post. This has not yet been fully done for the profession of librarian. Whatever may be the differences between the various kinds of library, they resemble each other in that they provide services to some particular kind of community. The nature of that service must be one which is firmly based on real understanding. The most severe charge in this connection which can be brought against the syllabus of the library association is that it has always emphasized the purely technical part of the work of the librarian and has done nothing of itself, to help inculcate that professional 'wisdom', the possession of which alone creates a competent librarian.

The first school established specifically for the education of librarians was in 1887 when, largely due to the work of Melvil Dewey, the School of Library Economy was founded at Columbia. This was to place an entirely new emphasis on the matter and due to the fact that the United States of America has gone on developing Library Schools ever since that date, they have never felt the need for the other kinds of instruction with which we are so familiar in this country. Also, since Library Schools in the United States have been the only form of education for the profession, it has meant that they have been able to provide a broadly based theoretical approach to librarianship in place of the empirical orientation of our British Semi-apprentice system. This pattern of American library education has brought in its train a far greater cohesion throughout the whole profession. It is hardly surprising that, since the end of World War-II, there has been a noticeable drift towards the American pattern throughout the world while British librarianship is becoming more and more isolated.

Some members of the profession thought that even this much educational latitude was mistake with the result that, when the newer Library Schools were established from 1946 onwards they were confined to the syllabus of the Library Association. This is the most effective method known of preventing healthy growth and the Schools have had to struggle hard to maintain the semblance of vitality.

American Library Association was founded in 1876. Its first school of library economy was established at Columbus in 1882 due to the efforts of Melvil Dewey. Upto 1919 many library schools were established. C.C. Williamson of Carnegie Corporation submitted a report in 1823 for restricted admissions in scientific training and schools and universities should come in close relationship for ranking facilities in professional education. In USA the diploma given by library school was final assessment. Various American Universities award B.L.S. or B.S. in Library Science. Since 1929 under revised standards in 1951, the basic training of a librarian starts after the secondary school and comprise five years of collegiate education, two years of general education, two years of subject concentration and one year for professional library education.

The Library Association of UK was founded in 1877 in London. The recognition of librarianship was based on wide experience and standards of service. In UK library school was actually library schools sponsored by the Library Association and Universities. Diploma courses are run by the association or its other units, and degree courses are run by universities and colleges. The syllabus of the

Association's examination was substantially revised in 1961 and 1979. There are part time courses and correspondence courses. Education must always be in advance of general professional practice, leading as it is etymologically bound to do. The educational programme must, therefore, not simply change but it must be the cause of change within the body of the profession (Ency. Libnship).

Expensive Classification of Charles Ammi Cutter: So called because the author compiled seven successive classification scheme, each being an expansion of the one before. The idea was that the basic notation should remain unchanged but that, as the library grew, subjects could be subdivided and the notation expended. In fact the notation of the main classes did differ between expansions. The seventh expansion published in unfound parts was left unfinished owing to author's death in 1903. It is a 'one man scheme with no committee or corporation to perpetuate its growth, and is used a little in America, but hardly at all elsewhere. The Library of Congress Classification was influenced considerably by Cutter's work.

Cutter and Dewey were friends, but the former thought that the notation of Dewey's Decimal Classification would 'not afford that minuteness of classification which experience has taught me to be needed in our library'. Neither did Cutter approve of the order. He worked out a new order which he claimed to be evolutionary within its divisions and used for notation of the letters of the alphabet and numbers one to none. An outline was published in 1879. Eventually appeared the Expansive Classification, Part I; the six classifications, 1891-93, a series of expansions designed for collections of every size, from the village library in its earliest stages to the national library with a million books.

The letters of alphabet provide a wide base for the notation and a fair degree of minuteness is obtained with a short symbol. Large capitals represent main classes and small capital the subdivisions. Relative location (as with D.C.) is a feature and the letters can be used decimally. Initial letters are sometimes mnemonically valuable when they fit in with the scheme; e.g. Main class G is geography; classes BR religion, YF fiction, have mnemonic value. The first classification outline consists of eight main classes, but Cutter recommends ten. By the time the fifth expansion is reached, the main A-Z notation is in full use as follows:

A	General works	B	Philosophy BR Religion
B	Christianity and Judaism	D	Ecclesiastical History
E	Biography	F	History, Universal History
G	Geography and Travels	H	Social Sciences
I	Demotics, Sociology		
J	Civics, Government, Political Science		
K	Legislation	L	Sciences and Arts together
M	Natural History	N	Botany
O	Zoology	P	Zoology, Anthropology
Q	Medicine	R	Useful Arts, Technology
S	Constructive Arts (Engg. & Buil.)	T	Manufacturers and Handicrafts
U	Art of War	X	Language
W	Art	Z	Book Arts
Y	English and American Literature	YF	Fiction.

Class A appears to be lacking in the seventh expansion, which was extensively revised and the notation expanded to four letters. When bound, the parts form a volume as large as the 12th edition of Dewey. There is no general introduction or Index.

Auxiliary tables (common subdivisions) are first given a single-letter notation. These were later changed to single figures on early realization that a change of aspect requires a change of symbol. Superficially, these are similar to the Decimal Classification Common subdivisions, but they are separated from the main number by a point and are as follows:

.1 Theory	.2 Bibliography	.3 Biography
.4 History	.5 Dictionaries	.6 Handbooks
.7 Periodicals	.8 Societies	.9 Collections

They may be applied throughout the scheme.

There is a local list, the table of localities, with two figure numerical notation. They may be used for dividing geography or any other subject (e.g. history, literature) that will subdivide by area. Numbers run from 11-999 and thus cannot be confused with the subdivisions above. These numbers could be further extended and complicated by Cutter numbers for individual names (See also Cutter Author Marks). If one wishes to bring together all materials under country, the local number may come before the subject number.

I

Industrial Libraries: Industrial libraries have grown rapidly in number, scope and efficiency during the past twenty years. This is a sure sign that management are becoming increasingly aware of the volume of technical information available from which the optimum must be taken if their scientific and technical staff are to be kept in touch with current developments. In some cases a library is established only because the engineering staff actually demand it, but the majority are the direct result of management recognition of the fact that such a service is vital if the company is to progress and remain competitive. Budget allocations come direct from management level, and whilst many libraries receive a budget commensurate with their recognized value to the company, others struggle to provide an efficient service in the fact of considerable difficulties, financial and otherwise. These may simply stem from the fact that some managements are still comparatively unaware of the potentialities of a good information service.

Another major problem is that of ensuring that company employees as users of the service are fully conscious of everything that it has to offer. The extent of this problem depends almost entirely on the type and attitude of the potential user. Professional employees, such as graduates, are generally familiar with both the need and the quest for information; the technologist may need to be 'educated' in the use of most information beyond specifications and trade literature.

The librarian who has both enlightened management and user is fortunate indeed, but it would be fair to suggest that the majority do need to make special efforts to achieve this state of affairs.

The most important aspect of industrial librarianship is, possibly, the necessity for extensive knowledge of all aspects of company policy and interests. The librarian must have a good working knowledge of present projects and probable future trends, and must constantly endeavour to keep the library stock close to major and allied fields of subject coverage. The difficulties of this task vary immensely with the size and scope of any given company; in an organization concerned with the development and production of a limited number of product. Subject knowledge once gained enables the librarian to acquire a reasonably comprehensive collection. If the company has diverse interests which are constantly changing or expanding. However, then the librarian must be able to access to what extent the duration of any one project justifies the purchase of books, periodicals, etc. Extensive overlapping in most subject fields now places most librarians into the latter group.

The number of staff employed in industrial libraries usually ranges from one to thirty in this country, and once again this number is often dependent upon the size of the organization in which it exists. Some larger libraries employ their own specialized staff such as translators, economists, etc., and consequently provide superior services. However, the value of smaller libraries should not be underestimated, for they normally give a service adequate for their own organizations.

Facilities in equipment and accommodation differ throughout. Equipment may to some extent be dependent on available space and where the latter is limited, material is often stored on microfilm or microcards. In such cases readers are always provided. Some libraries employ their own photocopy equipment and issue copies of articles, etc., rather than lend out the originals for extensive periods. In exceptional circumstances facilities may even include a binding department. Actual accommodation for libraries and offices ranges from 200 to 10,000 sq. ft.

Services provided should ideally be adapted to companies' interests, and library structure is usually founded on this basis. Scope can be dictated by management, but it is more usual for libraries to evolve and expand fairly freely within the requirements of their users, and of course, the limitations of budget allocations. The function of any industrial library is primarily of dissemination of all information received therein, and various means are employed to achieve this. Current periodical literature is treated seriously, and articles may merely be listed in a weekly news sheet or a detailed, classified and annotated review may be issued at regular intervals. Information regarding recent library accessions is usually included in these bulletins, together with any other pertinent news items, such as forthcoming meetings, conferences, exhibitions, etc. Periodicals are also circulated and library staff are often expected to scan these in order to indicate pages of interest to the recipients. Varying reference facilities are offered; the object being to hold as many bibliographical books as is financially possible, thereby facilitating literature surveys and general bibliographical work.

Techniques employed are usually arranged to suit specific company requirements; standard systems may be used but they may also be extensively adapted to suit specialist demand. Libraries covering diverse subject fields superficially, often find the Universal Decimal Classification adequate, but those working within highly specialized fields tend to evolve their own methods of classification. Some of these are unique but most are founded on commonly accepted systems. In view of the widely varying types of materials held, it is often found advantageous, for example, to employ coloured cards in the catalogue, each of which denotes the type of publication, e.g. book, pamphlet, etc. Many libraries are forced to issue material on a permanent loan basis, owing to the existence of outlying stations or company branches. In such instances a special card which records all the usual details plus the date of issue of name of holder is sometimes a useful adjunct to the catalogue.

With regard to book selection, some librarians are able to purchase any items of obvious value and need to only consult specialists when in doubt; alternatively, the management may co-opt a library committee. These are usually comprised of senior company employees delegated to supervise library activities, and frequently they have the last word in book selection and general policy.

Stocks vary proportionately to company size and requirements; it is not, therefore, possible to give any realistic indication of the holdings of an 'average' library. Nevertheless, in general books, periodicals, pamphlets, specifications, reports, and trade literature stocks are held in varying percentage in every industrial library. Companies engaged upon Government work usually hold some classified material. In these circumstances facilities are often made for this material to be stored in suitable secure conditions, within a special section of the library.

The majority of industrial libraries are small in comparison to those of technical colleges, Government establishments and universities, and thus need to supplement their holdings by calling on external sources for peripheral information. In many instances their companies belong to Research Associations, the libraries of which offer excellent services to their members. Over and above this, interlibrary co-operation with other industries, National Central Library, Science Library, Public Libraries, etc., is the rule rather than the exception. (Aslib Survey)

Information: Today a country's development is measured by the size and complexity of information and communication system. No country can efford the isolation and ignore rapid development in information society. The scientific study of the communication of information in a society is an academic discipline called Information Science. Research stimulate new information which is sustained by the continuous flow of information. Scientist not only collect, store, retrieve and use information but also create it through research.

Need

1. Science dominates the human being and its vital elements, i.e. information.
2. All the social progress depends on the transfer of scientific and technical information.
3. People require information in different situations on a subject in different forms on various occasions, depending on his knowledge of subject. This is reason for wanting information.
4. Scientists and technologists need a great range of literature and attend many conferences and seminars and meetings in order to collect information of relevance to their applied problems. Thus they form the link between research and practice.
5. The information is often called 'power', 'vital', 'economic value', a 'commodity', and a 'source'.

Concept

Terms like information, knowledge, data, language, meaning are in common use, used freely without careful attention to precise meanings.

Harrod's *Librarians Glossary and Reference Books* defines information as "An assemblage of data in a comprehensive form capable of communication."

Harlan Cleveland—"Information is a core, the sum total of all the facts and ideas, accessible or not, that are available to be known by somebody at a given moment."

Oxford English Dictionary—Information is knowledge communicated concerning some particular facts, subjects or events.

S.C. Blumenthal—"Information is data recorded, classified, organized, related or interpreted within context to convey meaning."

D. Bell—"Information is a pattern or design that rearranges data for instrumental purposes."

A. Whyte—"Information is the reduction of uncertainity."

Information vs. Data

Information	Data
1. Information is the result of modeling, formatting, organizing, or converting data in a way that increases the level of knowledge for its recipient.	1. Data are language, mathematical or other symbolic knowledge or surrogates which are generally agreed upon to represent people, object, events and concepts.
2. Information is a pattern or design that rearranges data for instrumental purposes.	2. Data are the smallest elements of information.
3. It serves as a means for the purpose in question, e.g. scientific work. Information is data recorded, classified, organized, related or interpreted within the context to convey the meaning.	3. The distillation of data, through its being processed, results in the creation of information.

Disseminating Information:

1. Primary Publishers (a) Print books (b) Print Journal (c) Market and distribute	1. Construct primary data 2. Related to online network
2. Database producer (a) Acquire (b) Access to primary publications (c) Catalogue (d) Index	1. Construct secondary data 2. Publish, print & bibliographies
3. Databank (a) Access to primary publications (b) Extra data	1. Construct data bank 2. Publish & compilation
4. Online processes (a) Acquire databases (b) Acquire data banks	

(c) Provide search system

(d) Publish user aid

5. Network—Provide telecommunication link

6. Local Library-Information service

(a) Acquire (b) Select (c) Primary publications (d) Bibliographies (e) Compilation (f) Catalogue (g) Index	1. Search online system 2. Construct local catalogue file 3. Inter-library loan

7. End Users

(a) Scan publication in library (b) Use local catalogue file	1. Use online search system 2. Photography services

Workers and producers in information chain:

1. Author(s)
2. Editor(s)
3. Primary publishers
4. Secondary publishers
5. Libraries
   (a) National Archives
   (b) National library
   (c) Public libraries
   (d) University (Academic) libraries
   (e) Special libraries
6. Data Banks
7. Information network

Forms of Information: 'Form' is defined as—

(a) Particular condition

(b) Character

(c) Mode

(d) Sense of mass or volume
(e) Physical object
(f) Mental image
(g) Method or procedures

FORM = Information may appear in many forms—

1. Documents
2. References to documents
3. Data, facts, information in the strict sense
4. Directing data—People and institutions

Belkin—Belkin postulates three approaches for the requirement of information:

Methodological	–	Utility concept
Behavioural	–	Phenomenon concept
Definitional	–	Context of concept

There are eight requisites for relevant and developing structure of information science.

(a) Purposeful, meaningful communication
(b) Request and derived for information
(c) Process of information
(d) Relation between generator and recipient
(e) Effect of information on recipient
(f) Effect of message
(g) Generation of information
(h) Prediction of effect of information

Wersig and Neveling stressed the following approaches –

The structural approach, the knowledge approach, the message approach, the meaning approach, the effect approach, the process approach.

Broakes (A Bibliometrician and Information Scientist): He has divided information into entities. The relationship is expressed in a simple equation. It is also called the fundamental equation of information science:

$$K(s) + \Delta 1 = K(s+Ds)$$

K = Knowledge structure

(s+Δs) = Modified knowledge structure

Δ1 to K (s) = Absorption of increment of information.

He believes that the fundamental problem of information science is to interpret this equation and thereby to explain information process.

Bell (Daniel): He suggests information to be data processing in the broadest sense—storage, retrieval and processing of data becomes essential source for economic and social exchanges. They include:

(a) Data processing of records

(b) Databases

(c) Data processing for scheduling

Machlup—Power of plural "s"

He was an eminent economist (Study of information: interdisciplinary approach). He says—Bond is the focus on information. The word information is interpreted differently by various researchers.

Online natural science and social science the information need:

(a) no single paradigm

(b) no overarching scientific research programmes

(c) no fundamental postulates and axioms

(d) no unified conceptual framework.

The word information involves observation and analysis. Information theorist misunderstood the basic lesson of methodology. The appropriate expression to use in the context would be signal transmission or activating impulses.

Types of Information

Shannon/weaver model:

Sources	Recipients
Channel	Information needs
Media	

1. *By Source*—It is made of communicating messages through—

   (a) Signs (b) Symbols

   (c) Texts (d) Graphics

Source is used to group the information—

(a) Signals—message in the form of sizes, symbols, words and numbers.

   Example—Math formulae, statistical and factual data.

(b) Text matter—carrying large amount of messages or information.

   Example—News, research paper, reports.

(c) Graphics of various kinds—

   Example—Photographs, pictures, graphs.

2. *By Channel*

   Channel disseminates information for grouping information.

(a) Literature—Primary, secondary, tertiary channels

   Examples—Primary

   Original facts & ideas—Journal, article, research reports.

   Unorganised/Unrelated—Conf. paper, proceedings, official, public.

   Widely scattered—Thesis, project reports

   Unassimilated—Diaries, memos, personal files, correspondence.

   Secondary Literature

   Information from primary sources—Bibliographies, Bulletins

   Planned, organized and arranged—Indexing journal, Abstracting journal, Reviews.

   Scattered information—Report, progress, advances

Repositories of assimilated and digested knowledge —Ref. books, dictionaries, encyclopedias.

Bibliographical Key—Directories.

Tertiary Literature

Compilation of primary and secondary sources—

Bibliographies of bibliographies year books

Planned, organized and arranged—Directories, list of research in progress, guide to literature

Aids to searching primary and secondary sources – Information sources, organizations, human resources

(b) Information institutions—Libraries, Doc. Centre,

Information centres, IAC

(c) Distribution agencies—Booksellers, publish, clearing houses, Information brokers.

3. *By Media—Physical Media*
   (a) Oral—Person to person, one to one, one to many
   (b) Recorded—Paper print, microform.
4. *By Recipient*
   (a) Individuals (b) Groups
   (c) Organisation (c) Institution
5. *By Information need*
   (a) By standard
      (i) Popular
      (ii) Scientific
      (iii) Technical
   (b) By type
      (i) Know-why-Readily accessible tools
      (ii) Know-how-Technically oriented tools
      (iii) Show-how-operational skills, maintenance and control capacity, seldom recorded in communicable form.

Information Diffusion Process: Diffusion is an "information transfer process of knowledge", know how, products and facilities. Diffusion means—

(a) Information transfer process of knowledge
(b) Know-how
(c) Products
(d) Facilities

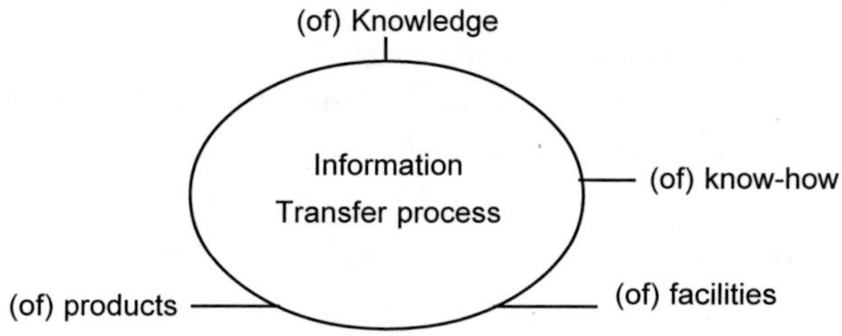

Information transfer process takes place between organizations, communities or firms. Diffusion may be either through the whole organization or between departments.

There are several diffusion model—

1. Epidemic model
2. Stock adjustment model
3. Vintage model

Diffusion process is done through the R & D establishments.

The flow of information commences from the collection of innovative ideas which should reflect social aims and needs. Specialised innovative measures determines the characteristics of information services, service institutions and diffusion activities.

1. **Alerting service includes**
   (a) Current awareness services (CAS)
   (b) Selective Dessimination Information (SDI)
   (c) Retrospective searching
   (d) Document delivery
   (e) Stems from the collection of information. Their processing results in in-house databases.

Interpretation services

Extension services.

2. Gate keeping brings into an organization expert information service at depth. This service is characterized by: (1) wide knowledge of information sources; (2) The ability to use them with great effectiveness, and (3) Offering appropriate services that are highly usable.

Information Diffusion—Meaning: Diffusion is a type of transfer process in technological change of natural environment, societal environment and technological environment.

Knowledge transfer implies a shift of know-how from one population of group of users to another. e.g.

From farming to mining

Farmers, doctors, engineers

It is diffusion.

Example:

Innovation of new harvest of wheat extends the capability of farmers of saving cost, reducing crops loss or damage. It depends on the acceptance of innovation by farmers and their population, the characteristic of innovation and moreover the psychological and social attributes of individuals and groups and their pay-off capacity and support of the new market technology.

In short diffusion is one of the numerous transfer processes within the social economic change.

Variety of diffusion

Information is a property which is spread or diffused from producer to user, from person to person and from system to system. There are many models for diffusion and have different parameters. Such parameters include—

(a) The maximum number of information recipients (receivers) (NM).

(b) The number of recipients to whom a transmitter sends information during the time interval.

Mansfield conceived three-way definition—

1. Inter-Institutional diffusion—Spread of new process from firm to firm within an industry.
2. Intra-Institutional diffusion—Spread of the process within the individual firm.
3. Overall diffusion—Spread throughout the society as a whole.

Diffusion process: Interorganizational diffusion (Information transfer process)—

1. Surveys the adoption and adaptation process of an innovation.
2. Analyses the variance between the firms.
3. Concentrates on individual innovations diffusing through single type of industries.
4. Attempts to explain differences between instructions in time taken to adopt an innovation.

These are two institutional characteristics of diffusion which includes—

1. International approach.
2. An explanation of international differences in the speed of diffusion of innovation.

Epidemic model

There are no specific studies on pacularity of diffusion in economic field. But there are studies in social sciences.

For instance—

The spread of rumours,

The use of new drugs,

New teaching methods,

Steel axe by aboriginal tribes.

There are sociologists, medical sociologists, educationists and anthropologists.

The analogy behind these research is 'Spread of diseases'. It applies mathematical theories as theoretical tool in such cases. The simplest model of Epidemic is working in this area which is developed by Economists:

$m_t + 1 - m_1 = B\ (n - m_t)\ m_t/n$

m – is a member of individuals in a fixed population of n

having contracted the disease between elapse of time epochs + and t + 1.

B – epidemic indicator, depends on a number of factors such as infectiousness of the disease and the frequency of social interaction.

Economic theory Model

The process of innovations has nascent (micro) nature and information imperfect which makes major differences between firms in their expectations how innovations are profitable. It is because—

(a) Firm will differ in their attitude to risk,

(b) Different firms will react quite differently with new innovations,

(c) The difference is significant in some industry also.

The difference occurs because of difference in size of firms within the same industry.

This argument is formalized in "Industrial Engel Curve" which relates to probability of a firm having adopted the new innovation to the firm's size. This model give encouraging results as fitted with data collection and the size of the firm. There is a correlation between—

(a) Nature of innovation

(b) Industrial growth

(c) Cyclic factor

(d) Growth factor

(e) Role of firm's size

(f) Industry concentration

Stock adjustment model

It is used in the analysis of investment behaviour. There are two studies on investment of computers—

(a) Chow's—Technological change and demand of computers (*American Economic Review*, 1963) for USA.

(b) Stoneman's—Technological Diffusion and Computer Evolution, 1976 for UK.

These studies indicates the stock level of computers in any time period. However they study the equilibrium of stock. The increase in the stock level of computers in indicated by the stock position. However, this model is not applied widely.

Vinitage model

This model concerns with decision-making and relate to capital and profit maximization. It is dominated by uncertainty and imperfect information. It embodies technical progress.

This model has been developed by Salter and others. It brings economic theory diffusion. It has following characteristics.

(a) New knowledge is embodied in new product.

(b) Old product is only replaced or scrapped when its operation costs exceed the return it earns.

Thus, each vintage of product embodies the best practice of know-how of its date of production and then remains committed to this nascent knowledge until its date of expiry. The innovations which are cost-saving process within this framework will have the following sequences.

1. Some proportion of existing product for making it profitable.
2. The existing capital stock comprises a number of vintage having old know-how, the never vintage will be slightly more efficient than the old, due to minor improvement in specification.

However, vintage model—

(a) is simple

(b) depends heavily on assumption of cost minimization and perfect information.

Information Diffusion theory

Elfredo A. Chatman identifies three diffusion models—

1. Elements of Diffusion model
2. Attributes of Innovation model
3. Stages of Adoption model.

These three models are studied and applied to—

(a) Awareness

(b) Use

(c) Diffusion of an innovation in a job environment among working poor.

Diffusion of information involves four elements:

1. Innovation
2. Communication
3. Social structure
4. Time

Attributes of innovation represents the characteristics that may make the innovation improved or rejection. The final decision is used to explain the decision-making process of adoption or rejection of an innovation.

The study also analyse the attributes such as—

(a) Relative advantage

(b) Compatibility

(c) Complexity

(d) Trialability of innovations

R & D Information flow: Madhok identifies the following functions of R & D establishment. It is a link in the innovation chain to enable the innovation flow to occur more efficiently. He defined the role of R & D establishment as follows:

1. It should provide an opportunity to bring relevant but different discipline together.
2. It should be in close contact with relevant advances in science and technology.

3. It should apply science and technology at the lowest cost in terms of time and effort.
4. It should be active in technology transfer and therefore preferably located close to the users of its R & D work.
5. It should be able to access objectivity and feasibility of an innovation project.

Information in diffusion of innovation includes:

The listing Post, the interdisciplinary role, Sc. & Tech. application at lowest cost, in time and effort, technology transfer, the feasibility appraisal role.

Gate Keeping of Technical Information: There are still many industries, large and small enterprises, which are paying lip service and establish 'in-house' and procedure to make the best use of external sources of information. But still industries and libraries could not have monopoly in this respect.

There are guidelines which may guide the industries for the maximum use of external sources. They concern to establish:

(a) In-house libraries,
(b) Correspondence information,
(c) Monitoring and business intelligence systems.

There is difference between information need of new industries and existing industries.

Information Sources: Diffusion

1. Library—Books, journals, report, trade, literature, newspaper clippings, patents, standards, manuals.
2. In outgoing correspondence information system—technical subjects.
3. The use of external systems—CAS, SDI.
4. Sharing facilities for scientific, technical and business databases: Bibliographic and Numerical.
5. Information search unit: Study of literature to trigger new ideas.

6. Monitoring or early Alert system: Identification of threats and opportunities.
7. Business intelligence system: Alliances of information and decision support.

There are small firms which needs advice on how to set up in-house libraries or information services mentioned previously. Several documentation centres, information centres and productivity centres are to guide them. There are many manuals containing guidelines.

Use of information and orientation

1. Members of Information Committee of FID
2. ASLIB, London
3. UN Industrial Development Organisation
4. National Documentation Centre
5. National Productivity Centre
6. Literature on "How to set-up an industry library and documentation centre".

Information Network: Development of telecommunication technologies in the late 1960s and the early 1980s has enabled the transmission of digital data over telephone lines paving the way for computer communication networks. It is now possible to transfer information at high speed, cost-effectively and reliably from one or more terminals to another at a distant place.

With the advent of computer communication network, however, a new kind of organization has come into being—the online database vendor. The vendor acquires bibliographic databases from different database producers. The vendor also develops search software to enable interactive search of the databases. Well-known vendors of online services are DIALOG, ORBIT, and BRS (Bibliographical Retrieval Service) of the USA and ESA's (European Space Agency) System near Rome in Italy.

The software developed for these systems enables multi-dimensional access to the information contents of the databases as compared to the limited capabilities in manual or patch processing system. The command language to be used is simple and easy to learn, enabling searchers having no knowledge of computer programming to be able to search the system. The number and kind of database that are now available for online searching have increased from a few in 1970 to over 1000 in 1989. These include bibliographic and non-bibliographic databases.

Information Theory: Shannon's theory of information describes:

"How messages are transmitted and received through electronic systems such as television, radio, telegraph."

It provides mathematical laws to determine the provability of the individual parts of a message which is transmitted without distortion. Telecommunication engineers use these laws to improve the capacity efficiency and clarity of information transmission.

Shannon also refers his theory to electric communication and his model equally applied for application to library and information science.

Weaver extended Shannon's theory. He defines three levels of communication, viz.:

1. The technical problems of physical transmission of messages.
2. The Sementic problem of conveying meaning of the message.
3. The problem of effectiveness influencing the conduct of the receiver.

Shannon in his book *The Mathematical Theory of Communication* concerns with the rate at which information can be produced and transmitted under the wide variety of physical conditions. He emphasized the sender's freedom to choose messages rather than symbols. Shannon is interested in neither discussions nor the mathematical implications. He further remarks that neither the theorem nor the assumptions required for its proof are necessary for development of rest of the theory. Shannon's law key approach is apparent again when he observes that meaning has no relevance to the engineering problem in communication and whenever he uses the term 'information', he treats it as an ordinary cord rather than as a technical term.

Application to Information Science

Shannon's theory has little relevance with information science. The communication mode is simple, clear and so general that its traces are easily disconcerned in works on neutral functioning, person to person communication, spread of rumours, diffusion of innovation, libraries and information centres and others.

The model of communication system is divided into five parts:

(a) Information source
(b) A transmitter
(c) A channel
(d) A receiver
(e) A destination.

The information sources produce—

(a) a message
(b) a transmitter converts the message into a signal
(c) the channel carries a signal across space
(d) the receiver converts the signal back into a message
(e) the destination takes the message.

For example, in a communication system—

(a) A *source* may be a person.
(b) The *speech* the person makes.
(c) Speech organ as a *transmitter*.
(d) Air as *channel* over which sound waves are transmitted.
(e) The auditory system of an other person's body as *receiver*.

(f) The brain of a receiving person as *destination*.

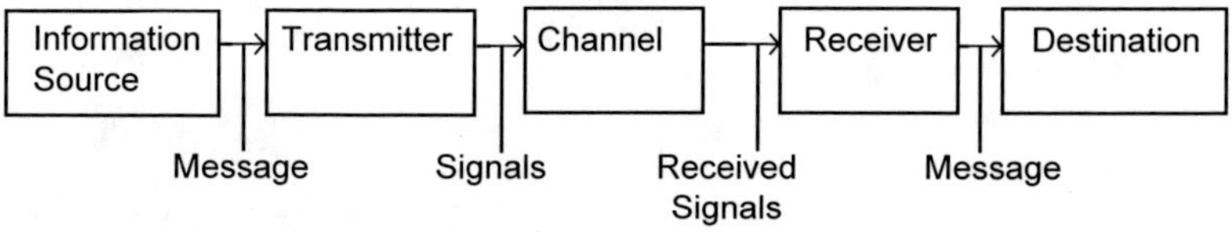

General Communication System

Pi: When the value of an individual is changed because a communication changes the Pi as Pj, it denotes the probabilities of choice associated with available course of action, and the individual is informed accordingly.

Eii: When the value is changed because the communication changes the Eii, which denotes the efficiencies of various courses of action to achieve various possible outcomes, as the individual has been instructed.

Vi: When the communication changes the Vi which denotes the values of the possible outcomes and individual has undergone a change in motivation.

In this way Ackoff derives some equation that carry to quantify the amount of—(a) Information, (b) Instruction, and (c) Motivation communicated by a message. This is more mathematical garnishing. There are more ways of communication.

The message acts and thus it has to be studied as a dynamic force. The person has to be considered as a manifold responder to the message rather than as a simple receiver of it.

L

Library Education: Proper library education not only increases the self-confidence and improves the moral of the worker but also increases services, reduces initial errors and improve the quality of the employees work. Library education is a pragmatic approach. Librarian has no real meaning if he is known with the library techniques. Library education should be directed of providing right book to the right reader at the right time. Library education is based on the fundamental principles of individual development, ideal personality traits, universal approach, decision-making education, development of moral and spiritual values.

Melvil Dewcy for the first time started apprentice course for librarians in USA in 1879. On Jan. 5, 1887 Dewey started training course and arranged furniture from his house and invited reputed librarians to deliver lectures, Amherst Summer School started course in 1891, Bhiladelphia School in 1892, Amount Institute, Chicago in 1893. Henry Rechard Tedder (UK) introduced library education in 1880 under library association. First library school in India was started at Baroda by W.C. Borden in 1911; by Dickenson in Panjab University in 1915; by S.R. Ranganathan in 1929 and in Madras Library Association in 1937. Presently there are hundreds of library schools being run by library associations, universities, colleges, and institutions throughout the country.

Library Education in India: After America and Britain, India was the third country which came a step further in the field of library education. Maharaja Jiwaji Rao Gaikwad invited W.A. Borden, Director of the State Library Department in 1910. Borden prepared a plan for the development of libraries in the state and realised the need of skilled library professionals. Borden was a pupil of Melvil Dewey. He started library school at Baroda in 1911.

Panjab University invited A.D. Dickinson, an American Librarian, to prepare a project for the development of University Library. Dickinson started a training class in 1915 and published a book *Panjab Library Primer*. This school closed at the time of Partition of India.

In 1935 the Government of India started the first L.T.C. Summer course at the then Imperial Library of Calcutta under the late National Librarian, K.M. Asuddaula.

Ranganathan took himself charge of the Madras University Library and started training class of librarianship in 1931 under the sponsorship of Madras Library Association.

In 1937 Kumar Munindradeo Rai Mahari, President of Bengal Library Association, arranged a training camp at Bomasheria in 1937. It was started for working librarians specifically.

Since the demand of the libraries increased by leaps and bounds, other universities also started training courses:

Banaras Hindu University	–	1941
Bombay University	–	1944
Calcutta University	–	1946
Delhi University	–	1947
Baroda University	–	1955
Aligarh University	–	1956
Nagpur University	–	1957
Vikram University	–	1959
Osmania University	–	1960
Rajasthan University	–	1961
Punjab University	–	1963
Kerala University	–	1965
Sangar University	–	1962
Lucknow University	–	1966

Before 1964 all universities started Diploma and Certificate courses. UGC committee recommended the derecognition of Diploma courses and suggested to discounting all diploma courses and rather B.Lib. Sc. Courses were started.

Recommendation of Committee: The advisory committee for libraries in its report submitted on 12.11.58 considered the problems of Lib. Sc. teachers. UGC appointed the committee in 1957 under the chairmanship of Dr. S.R. Ranganathan to advice UGC about the development of libraries. Committee considered the problem of teaching of Lib. Sc. and submitted the report in 1959.

Indian Association of Special Libraries and Information Centres (IASLIC) also held two seminars on "Education for Librarianship" and "Training of Special Librarianship".

UGC appointed a Review Committee for this purpose in 1961 under the chairmanship of Dr. S.R. Ranganathan to review the standard of teaching and research in library science in the universities. The committee emphasized the need for setting up separate full-fledged department of syllabus for the courses to serve as guidelines for various library science schools in India.

Delhi University conducted a seminar in his Department of Library Science on 02.09.1966. Nineteen papers were presented.

Professor Morrisk A. Gelfend (USA) conducted a survey of the University of Delhi in the Department of Library Science and served as visiting professor and consultant in the same Department.

Dr. Ranganathan also presented his paper and gave more weightage to the following points:

(a) Historical background of the development of library education in India.

(b) Need of degree of graduation and postgraduation in Library Science in India.

(c) Immediate professional need.

(d) Provision within the course of true intellectual challenge so as to attract some of the best intellectuals into the profession.

Level of teaching: Library science may be divided in three broad divisions:

1. Lower and Elementary Level, i.e. Certificate Course in Library Science and Diploma Course in Library Science.
2. Middle Level Courses, i.e. P.G. Diploma in Library and Information Science, or Bachelor in Library & Information Science.
3. Higher Level Course, i.e. Master of Library & Information Science.

Specialisation: There are specialisations in library activities, type of libraries, etc., on higher level. Special training is given in documentation and special libraries, information science, classification and cataloguing.

There are hardly one or two specialised courses, like DRTC and INSDOC courses. Rest are courses of general character. There is a need of specialised course to be run by the university departments of Library Science.

Duration of Training: The duration of training courses being run in Indian universities and colleges is as under:

(a) Certificate Course of Library Science:
   (i) 4 Months
   (ii) 6 Months

(b) Diploma Course in Library Course:
   (i) 6 Months
   (ii) 1 year or one session
   (iii) Two years (in polytechniques)

(c) Bachelor of Library & Information Science:
   (i) One year

(d) Master of Library & Information Science:
   (i) Two years

Selection of Trainees

(a) **Admission notice with detailed information:**

(i) Full name of the course

(ii) Minimum qualification required for the course

(iii) Duration of course

(iv) Time of course

(v) Last date of receiving the forms

(vi) Last date of submission of forms

(vii) Last fee of submission of forms.

(b) **Selection Procedure:** Training of professional demand the quality of candidature. If selection of trainees will be proper, it will produce better professionals. The selection procedures may be many:

(i) **By Merit:** The applications of the candidates are scrutinized and arranged according to merit. Merit includes many factors— Educational qualifications, personality traits, I.Q. and background of the candidates.

(ii) **By Admission:** The candidates undergo admission test of I.Q., Aptitude test, current contents etc. On the basis of the test a merit is accounted and admission is given.

(iii) **Counselling:** In addition to admission test and the merit, counselling is arranged to see the worth of the candidate and given admission after evaluating his aptitude and choice of centre.

Such selection procedures help in:

(a) Limiting the seat

(b) Filtering the candidature

(c) Assessment of the candidate

(d) Avoiding the criticism and approaches.

Seminars, Internship and Educational Tour

Each student is to assign on a individual basis to work for some weeks in various section of the library. In this way he is given proper training of library working and thus such internship is useful to the trainees.

Seminars are organized. Students are given a topic on a problem related to library. The trainee prepares the synopsis and a seminar paper, which is presented before other trainees for discussions.

A few weeks of 'Travel and Observation' to various places are to be provided to visit the libraries and institutes and agencies which will have some relevance to his own library problems and needs.

Final evaluation is to share individual experiences and to clarify questions arising from their observations.

Objectives:

1. To assume the society for best services by a trained librarian.
2. To increase the grasping power of subject matters by librarians so as to enable him to engage more intelligently in the activities of librarianship.
3. To make the librarian acquaint with modern techniques and tools of library.
4. To make aware of rapid expansion of knowledge and its record.
5. To enable the trainee to give competence in his particular discipline.
6. To prepare the trainees to engage himself more intelligently in library activities.

S

S.R. Ranganathan: Dr. Shiyali Ramamrita Ranganathan (1892-1972) was one of the greatest librarians of his time. He was the acknowledged father of library science and master architect of library movement in India. Born on Aug. 9, 1892 at Shiyali town in Tanaveer District of Madras state, he was the eldest child in family. His father was a villager and religious minded man; while he was 6, his father died in Jan., 1898. Ranganathan passed Matric in 1909, intermediate in 1911 and B.A. in 1913, all with first division. He passed M.A. in Mathematics in 1916 and L.T. degree in 1917. He was appointed Assistant Professor of Mathematics in 1917 in the subordinate educational service in Madras. He served Govt. College, Mangalore and Coimbatore and Presidency College, Madras till Jan. 4, 1924. University sent him to England to study modern library methods. He attended London School of Librarianship where W.C. Berwick Sayers, an authority on classifications, was lecturer. He returned on July 1925 with an Honours Diploma in Librarianship. Dr. Ranganathan worked hard on the principles of what, why and how in library activities. His approach to library problem was scientific through a 'spiral of scientific method'. He proved library science as science. He enunciated 'Five Laws of Library Science'. These laws were universally accepted. During his studies in England and discussions with Sayers and fieldwork made at England, Ranganathan prepared sample schedules for different subjects and discussed with his teacher W.C. Berwick Sayers. He made experiments in Madras University Library—organized books, classified and catalogued the books, discussed with readers, enunciated new scheme and publicly declared in 1932. It was published by Madras Library Association in 1933 under the title *Colon Classification* and was later further reviewed and revised. The faceted scheme was published under the title *Prolegomena to Library Classification*. In 1947 he was invited by F.I.D. to deliver lectures. He introduced classified catalogue and published classified catalogue code in 1934. He founded school of library science in 1929 by Madras Library Association and was taken over by Madras University in 1931.

After preparation of the classified catalogue code, Ranganathan published, *Theory of Library Catalogue* in 1938. It contained district normatic principles to form the foundation of cataloguing work. He explained the procedure for the derivation of subject headings from class number, known as "Chain Procedure". Ranganathan drafted rules for dictionary catalogue in classified catalogue and published as *Dictionary Catalogue Code* in 1945. Practical examples were discussed in *Library Catalogue: Fundamentals and Procedures* in 1950. The canons of cataloguing is one of the outstanding contributions of Ranganathan in the field of cataloguing which was published in *Headings and Canons*.

It brought fame and honour to Ranganathan when his chain procedure was followed by British National Bibliography, British Technology Index and Indian National Bibliography.

Dr. Ranganathan was a successful organizer and administrative also. Being a librarian he decentralized the library work by organizing divisions based on works. He introduced sectional councils. His theory of organization and administration was included in his book *Library Administration*, published by Madras Library Association in 1935. He suggested staff formula in 1948. Being the Chairman of U.G.C. Committee, he suggested modern techniques, job analysis, and management planning. He introduced three card system for periodicals. His library activities started in 1926 when he was nominated General Secretary of All India Public Library Conference. He drafted model public library act and published *Library Development Plan*. He drafted the library bills of States-National System 1946; Post-war construction of libraries in India, 1947; Library Development Plan with Draft Library Bill for U.P., 1949; Library Development Plan with Draft Library Bill for Bombay, 1947; and Library Development Plan with a Draft Library Bill for Kerala, 1959. The work of Ranganathan of promoted library legislation in India and the main objectives behind it was organizing 'All India Services on Public Library System' at Bangalore 1972.

Ranganathan served as Librarian at Madras University and (1924-44) Banaras Hindu University (1945-47). Moreover he was Chairman, U.G.C. Library Committee (1959). He proposed a plan of 'National Documentation Centre' to Government of India which was materialized in 1951 with the help of UNESCO under the control of CSIR, New Delhi. Ranganathan was persuaded on being the Chairman of IASLIC Conference 1962, Documentation Conference (Delhi) 1967, and recommended the establishment of ICSSR in 1969. Ranganathan was a great thinker. He thought it is necessary to establish a Documentation Research Centre. On meeting in Zurich in 1956 with the Chairman of Indian Statistical Institute, Planning Commission evinced interest for training programme in Documentation, which resulted in establishment of "Documentation Research and Training Centre", at Bangalore in 1962.

International Organisation for Standardisation (ISO) was established in 1956 for the coordination of National standards and promotion of International Standards. India established Indian Standards Institution (ISI) in 1947. Dr. Ranganathan prepared standards of documentation, library building, furniture and fittings. Ranganathan was the master architect of library science education in India. Dr. Ranganathan started annual refresher course for librarians under Madras Library Association. In 1931 this course was taken over by Madras University which converted to Diploma of one year duration. Ranganathan taught in this course till retirement in 1944. He taught in

Banaras Hindu University and Delhi University (till 1955). He conducted research in library science in Delhi University. He taught at Vikram University as a Visiting Professor (1957-59). In 1964, the University of Pittsburgh conferred the Honorary degree of Doctor of Letters on Ranganathan. The Government of India appointed Ranganathan as National Research Professor in Library Science in 1965. He was recipient of Margaret Man Citation of the ALA in 1971 and Mark Twain Society of USA awarded him the title "Grand Knight of Peace". Madras University established Sarda Ranganathan Chair in library science in 1957. He was honoured with 'Padmashri' by the President of India.

Dr. Ranganathan died on 27th Seprember 1972. He wrote 65 books, and several hundred lectures.

U

UNESCO: The United Nations Educational Scientific and Cultural Organisation (Place de Fontenoy, Paris 7e) was formed as specialized agency of the United Nations in 1946. By December 31, 1959, 81 states were its members.

The degree to which the promotion of international understanding in the post-war period depended on the restoration of the free exchange of information on world-wide library reconstruction and development was self-evident; and extensive programmes in these fields formed from the outset a prominent feature of the Organisation's work.

In the world of librarianship, UNESCO's work falls into three main divisions: bibliography and documentation, library development, and international exchange of publications. To these must be added the important contribution of UNESCO to international copyright law, the book coupon scheme and the agreement on the import of educational, scientific and cultural materials. While almost all the programme units of the organisation have taken part in these activities, the division of libraries—documentation and archives, has had special responsibilities for both action and coordination.

Bibliography: A thorough survey of current bibliographies prepared the way for an international conference on the improvement of bibliographical services, held in Paris in 1950, which established the present structure of international bibliography, consisting of prominent librarians representing various regions of the world and a number of specialized subject fields. The International Federation of Library Association and the International

Federation of Documentation working closely with UNESCO and are the committee or national bibliographical groups or corresponding members in 70 countries. The committee advices the Director General on the planning and coordination of bibliographical programmes operated or sponsored by UNESCO. It maintains close contact with non-governmental organizations in the field and devotes special attention to such topics as general principles for the preparation of international bibliographies, new methods and techniques for the communication of knowledges and international bibliographical standards. A bi-monthly reneographed Bibliographical newsletter, and an annual report on Bibliographical services throughout the world issued by UNESCO, keeps the committee, the national groups at many libraries, archives, bibliographical and documentation centre, in touch with one another and with the UNESCO Secretariat.

A provisional Liaison Committee of International Organisations for Librarianship and Documentation was set in 1952; one of its most important tasks was planning, with UNESCO cooperation, of the International Congress on Librarianship and Documentation which later held in Brussels in September, 1955.

Since 1949 UNESCO has published the annual *Index Translationum*, of which the column for 1957, published in 1959, listed 27,715 titles of translations published in 65 different countries. The *Index Bibliographies* is the directory of current periodical abstract and bibliographies. Among other important publications are the *Vocabularium Bibliothecarii* by Lemaitre and Thompson, a *Handbook on National Bibliograpical Services* by K. Larsen (1953), *A Directory of References Works* published in Asia by P.K. Farde (1956), *Union Catalogue: Their Problem and Organization* by L. Brummel (1956):

Humanities

UNESCO has concentrated, by means of conventions administered through the International Council for

Philosophy and Humanities Studies, on assisting international learned and professional associations to publish specialized bibliographies.

Natural and Social Sciences

An International Conference on Science Absracting was held in Paris in 1949, after a preliminary study of abstracting services existing at that time. It resulted in the formation of the International Advisory Committee for Documentation and Terminology in Pure and Applied Sciences, a body of science documentalists working on parallel lines to those of the International Advisory Committee on bibliography, and keeping in touch with each other through a monthly bulletin of scientific documentation and terminology. The International Council of Scientific Unions was established in its present form in 1931. However, it came into existence in 1900. It administers conventions granted by UNESCO for publications such as the Bibliographic geographique internaionale, Bibliographic hydrologique international, Astronomischer Jahresbericht, etc. The ICSU Abstracting Board has arranged for about 50 physics journals published in nine countries to send proof sheets in advance to the Board or to Physics abstracts, Bulletin anlytique du C.N.R.S., or Physikalische berichte, so that abstract may appear from six months to a year earlier than would otherwise have been possible. A similar arrangement is in operation in chemistry for Chemical abstracts, and the Russian Institute of Scientific Information. This experiment is being extended to biological sciences.

UNESCO series entitled Documentation in the Social Sciences contains four social science bibliographies prepared by the International Committee for Social Sciences Documentation, and published annually by UNESCO. There are *International Bibliography of Political Science* (1954), *International Bibliography of Sociology*, *International Bibliography of Economics* (1955), and *International Bibliography of Social and Cultural Anthropology* (1958).

Mass Communication: The Department of Mass Communication issues in series reports and papers on mass communication, occasional bibliographies on press, film, radio, and television matters.

Education: The Clearance House of the Department of Education of UNESCO collaborates with national centres, of which a preliminary international survey appeared in 1957. Advisory services were provided for the formation of such centres in Turkey, Yugoslavia and elsewhere. The Clearance House acts as a centre for universities, Bureau in Paris and the International Bureau of Education in Geneva. It published the monthly *Education Abstracts* (Jan. 1949), and in its series educational studies, the documents and a number of occasional bibliographies.

Library Development: In 1948 UNESCO published a manifesto, the publication library, a living force for popular public library purposes and activities. All consequent UNESCO work in public library development has recognized the close association between education and libraries. Five seminars on public libraries have been organized on services to popular education, at Manchester, UK; on libraries and education, at Malmo, Sweden in 1950; on library development in Lain America.

UNESCO and the Indian Government jointly established in 1952 the Delhi Public Library, a pilot project for South Asia on a whole. This was followed by the Medellin Pilot Public Library, Colombo, opened in 1954, and by the National Central Library in Eastern Nigeria, opened in 1959 as pilot projects for Latin America and Africa, respectively. These libraries are designed to serve as a mode for librarians from countries throughout the respective regions. There are other projects of direct benefit to member states 35 in number. Fellowships in library service have been awarded to librarians from various countries.

International exchange of publications

One of the UNESCO's earliest actions was to establish contacts between war damaged libraries and libraries having material for disposal or exchange. The UNESCO bulletin for libraries published a list of errata and material offered, and national exchange centres such as the British National Book Centre and the U.S. Book Exchange co-opted. Thereafter, the immediate needs of reconstruction was met and international communications has improved. UNESCO was able to handover much of this work to national centres and individual libraries. The UNESCO bulletin for libraries while continuing to publish information on exchanges has gradually become a periodical of general information on all matters pertaining to librarianship. In 1956 a mobile microfilm unit started microfiliming documents of national libraries and archives following the Latin American countries.

Copyright: Amid all the work of promoting access to books, the interest of authors and publishers has not been overlooked. The universal copyright conventions drawn up in Geneva in 1952 by an intergovernmental conference was held under the auspices of UNESCO and signed by 40 countries. The convention is based on the general principles of national treatment whereby each country undertakes to extend to works originating in the other states, and give protection to works of its own nationals.

UNESCO Library: The Library of the Organisation performs two main functions: (1) To serve members of the secretariat in their specialized work and in meeting their various needs in the planning and execution of UNESCO's programmes, including loan and information services. (2) The provision of a central acquisitic service to supply publications to documentation centres within the Secretariat, Field Science Cooperation Offices and missions abroad, including these under the technical assistance, Participating Programmes etc. (Ency. Libnship).

SOME IMPORTANT QUESTIONS

1. Describe the role of perception, learning and motivation in shaping human behaviour.
2. Explain the factors applied to organization behaviour.
3. What are the important principles of learning?
4. What are the selection techniques of staff?
5. Write the qualities of a good manager?
6. Describe Library System Analysis?
7. What is work sampling and what are its uses in libraries?
8. What is time and motion studies?
9. Give your understanding of the concept Management by Objectives (MBO).
10. Give various methods of evaluation of collection:

    (a) Printed Index

    OR

    (b) Document delivery system
11. Describe the role of communication in Human Resource Planning.
12. Explain the attributes of quality for an organization.
13. State the four elements of total quality. Explain the value of ISO-9000.
14. What are the sources of finance for different types of libraries?
15. Briefly explain the different types of budgets.
16. Define the cost analysis and its process.
17. Enumerate the characteristics of information as a commodity.
18. What are the major procedures of information?
19. What is store technology? Describe components of storage technology?
20. Write in brief the generations of computer languages.

21. Describe Data Networks.
22. Describe the structure of Local Area Network.
23. What are the steps involved in making of a xerographic copy?
24. Identify the role of automation for stock taking.
25. What are the elements and the area of computer based acquisition control?
26. Write the methods and purpose of Indexing articles.
27. What are the necessary features of an automated serial system?
28. What are access methods of database?
29. Write the details of the objectives and functions of Database Management Systems.
30. Describe the functions of Electronic Document Delivery System in Resource Sharing.
31. Why library network?
32. Write in brief the difference of data, information and knowledge?
33. Give the silent points of the definition of Belkin, Wesig and Brookes.
34. Distinguish the contents of Library Science, Information Science and Computer Science.
35. What is the role of CD-ROMs as a form of information storage and transmission media?
36. What is diffusion of information and its varieties?
37. What is IAC (Information Analysis and Consolidation Centre) and its difference with other centres?
38. What is machine translation? Mention the various steps involved in machine translation?
39. What are the categories of house journals?
40. Describe various types of trade and product bulletins.

41. Define the Trend Report and mention the qualities possessed by a documentalist for preparing a Trend Report.
42. What is the need of Technical Digests? Mention their various categories.
43. Mention briefly some of the uses or types of Databases.
44. Discuss in brief the process of database search system.
45. Explain various databases used in India.
46. Describe the attributes of Intermediaries?
47. Discuss the functions of Intermediaries?
48. What are the basic facilities necessary for using online retrieval system?
49. Describe various international standards?
50. Explain the purpose and functions of Thesaurus?
51. Write short note on Record Format?
52. Define indexing language and identify three indexing language forms.
53. Describe the components of ISAR system.
54. What are the different norms and viewpoints for evaluation of an ISAR system?
55. What are the various information retrieval techniques developed so far?
56. Distinguish between personal and public knowledge?
57. Explain the modes of formation of subjects propounded by Ranganathan.
58. State your understanding of knowledge spectrum.
59. Describe Ranganathan's spiral of scientific method.
60. Explain briefly the relevance of information economics to library and information studies.
61. Examine the effect of the information society or information profession.
62. What are the uses and forms of electronic media?

63. Write a note on National Library of India.
64. Enumerate the major services of DEVINSA (Dev. Inf. Network for South Asia)
65. State the programmes and activities of UNESCO.
66. What is the programme area of FID?
67. Write essay on:
    (a) IFLA
    (b) ILA
    (c) UNESCO
    (d) Global Information System
    (e) Institute of Scientific Information
68. Explain the purpose and use of content analysis.
69. Describe different kinds of user information needs.
70. Enumerate different ways of ranking journals.
71. Describe 'Science Citation Index'.
72. Explain in detail the 'keyword indexing with example of BASIC'.
73. State the functions of mass communication.
74. Describe the role of Academic Library in the development of education.
75. Describe various committees and commissions formed by UGC for improvement of university college libraries in India.
76. What are the major areas of financial assistance being provided by the UGC? Discuss in detail.
77. What is library budget? Discuss various kinds of budget.
78. Explain in brief the reasons for better training effect of the qualified staff?
79. What are the common methods of recruitment and selection?